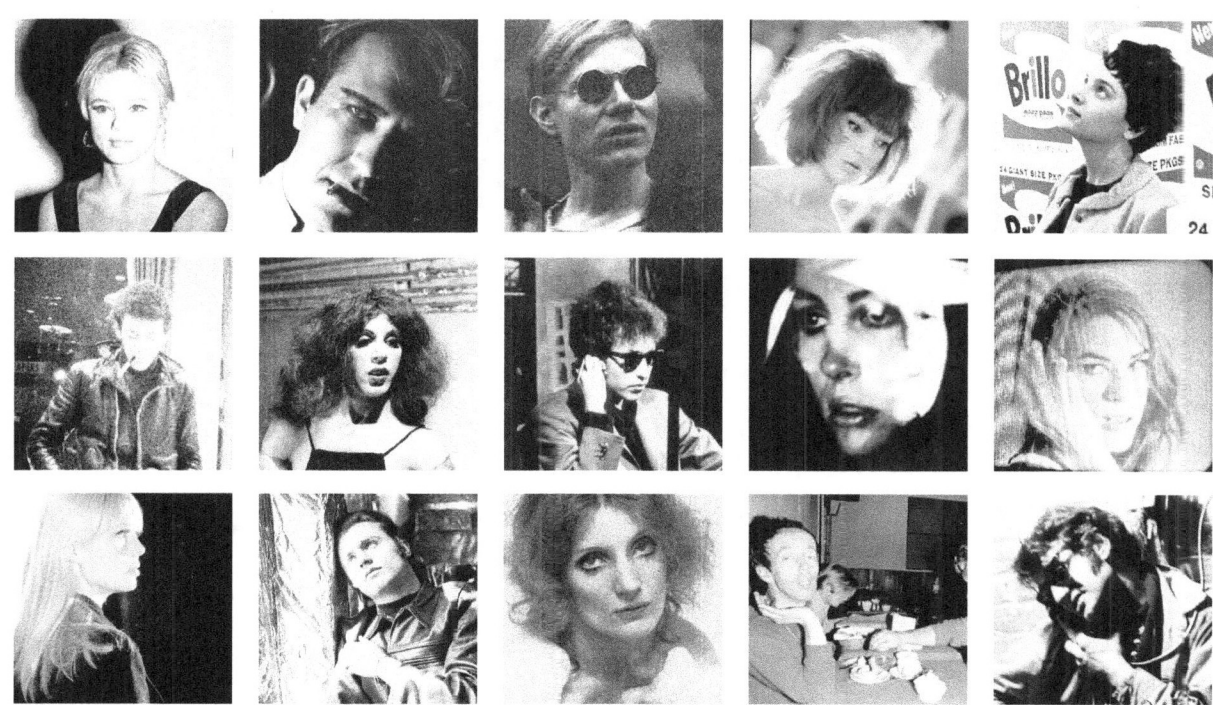

Andy Warhol's Factory People
Inside the 1960's Silver Factory . . . an Oral History

Book I   Welcome To The Silver Factory

Catherine O'Sullivan Shorr

Cover Photo and Portrait Montage on preceding page by Billy Name. L. to R. from top: Edie Sedgwick, Robert Heide, Andy Warhol, Ivy Nicholson, Barbara Rubin, Lou Reed, Mario Montez, Bob Dylan, Ultra Violet, Mary Woronov, Nico, Gerard Malanga, Viva, Taylor Mead, and Ondine

Poster design by Tom & Leo, Paris.

At right: Author attending a 'Paris Photo' reception at the American Ambassador's Residence, Paris, France, 2011.
(iphone photo by Maureen O'Sullivan)

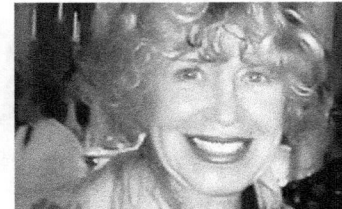

Published by Planet Group Entertainment Ltd.

© 2014 by Catherine O'Sullivan Shorr. The book author retains sole copyright to her contributions to this book.

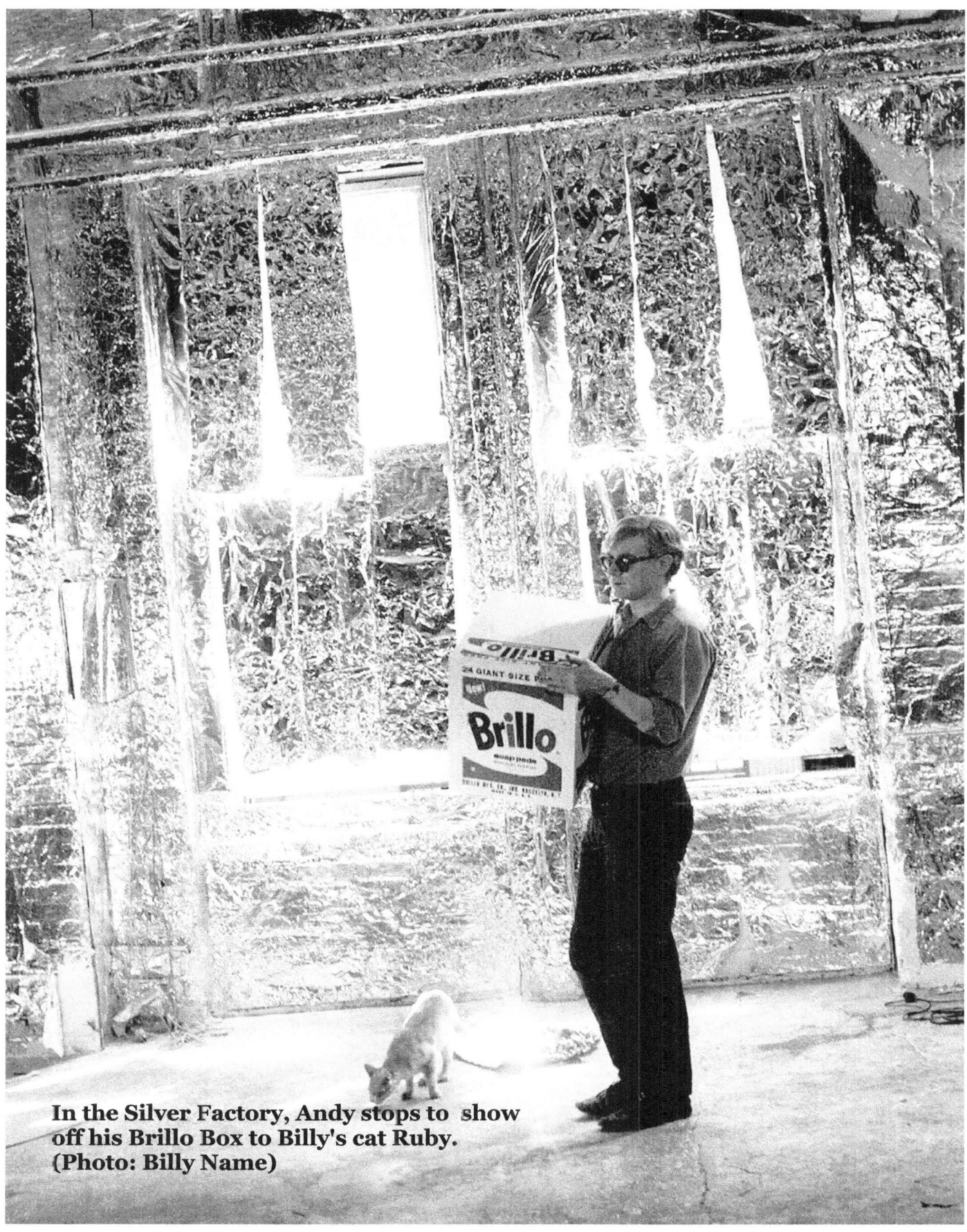

In the Silver Factory, Andy stops to show off his Brillo Box to Billy's cat Ruby.
(Photo: Billy Name)

CONTENTS

INTRODUCTION 6-17

BOOK I: WELCOME TO THE SILVER FACTORY 18

FACTORY FAMILY INTRODUCTIONS 19-27

BEYOND THE BEAT GENERATION 28

IN THE BEGINNING, ANDY CREATED 38

ALL TOMORROW'S PARTIES 62

BACK TO WORK 71

THE TRIANGLE 86

ANDY MAKES MOVIES . . . THE SILENT ERA 98

SILVER FAMILY 120

**For Patrick,
for everything.**

INTRODUCTION

2014 marks the 50th anniversary of Andy Warhol's fabled and infamous Silver Factory, Ever wonder what all the fuss was (and still is) about? So much has been written of this art colossus—his obsession with celebrity, his sloppy silk screens of Marilyn and Liz and Brando, his endless Campbell soup cans and Coca Cola bottles, his mind-numbing movies—that more than a few feel his fifteen minutes of fame should have been up long ago. Instead, he has become a lasting icon of popular taste. As the New Yorker's art critic Peter Schjeldahl wrote in his review of the Metropolitan Museum's huge 2012 show of Warhol and his impact on sixty other artists: "Like it or not, we are all Warholian."

But what about the forgotten Factory people behind Warhol's unprecedented rise to spectacular success, who linked their destinies to his, when, as a frustrated graphic artist, he decided to "start Pop art" because he "hated" Abstract Expressionism...

In a tale reminiscent of 'Lord of the Flies', this book uncovers what is left of the shroud of secrecy and mystique that surrounded this enigmatic personality, and exposes the bizarre, exploitive inside world of the shy, phsically fragile, fanatically self-absorbed man that some say was not just a *creator* of art, but also a destroyer of art—and of people. Only those who survived really knew what lay beneath the pale make-up and fright wig.

For them, it all began in the early sixties. A slight, fey, blotchy-faced character from the Mad Men world of advertising had decided to 'go downtown', where he would encounter and enlist the help of those soon to become his colorful entourage of misfits and muses—culled from the cutting edge of New York's art scene—destined to create his Silver Factory... This wild collection of characters became the first to be dubbed "Famous for Fifteen Minutes."

The 'Andy Warhol's Factory People' book, based on my three-hour documentary series of the same name, is the culmination of shooting fifty hours of their interviews, screening over a hundred hours of Warhol's movies and screen tests, collecting rare archive and news footage, sifting through thousands of candid photographs, and running up copious bar tabs in New York, Los Angeles, Paris, and London.

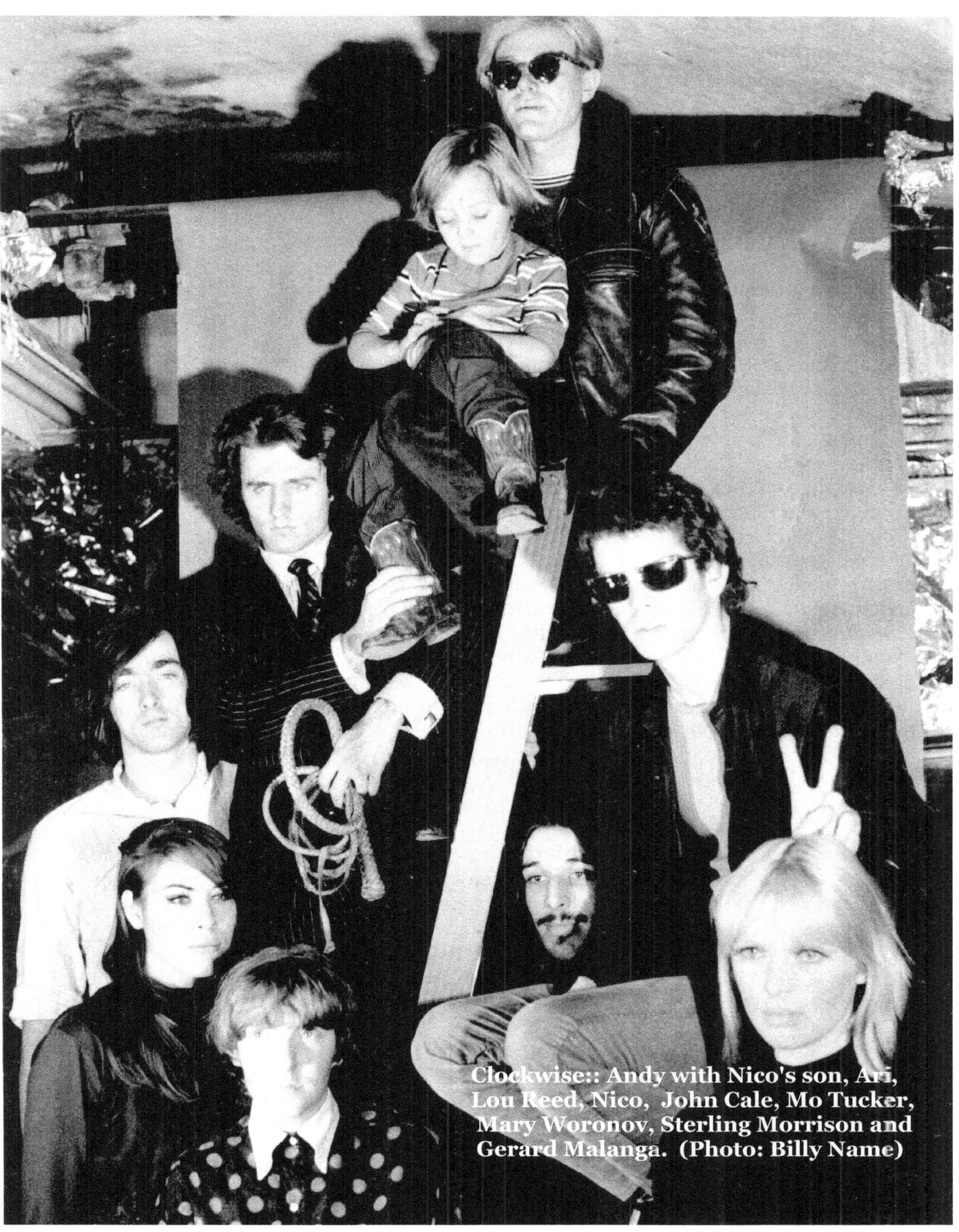

Clockwise:: Andy with Nico's son, Ari, Lou Reed, Nico, John Cale, Mo Tucker, Mary Woronov, Sterling Morrison and Gerard Malanga. (Photo: Billy Name)

Though much of Warhol's life and career may have been already minutely examined by a multitude of worthy and worldly experts, 'Factory People' deals with those essential early dreamers, the amphetamine-fueled avant-gardes who had been at the Silver Factory from the beginning and had followed Warhol's phenomenal trajectory into fame and notoriety. Finding some of them proved to be elusive, since they had rarely reaped any material and social benefits from their proximity to the man considered to be "one of most influential artists of the 20th century."

Perhaps the most important person you'll meet is Billy Name, who created Warhol's cavernous work space, slathered it all in aluminum foil, and became the official in-house photographer, the only one allowed to actually live there. He helped to create the essence of this book, with his cache of candid photographs taken in the throes of around-the-clock work marathons, all-night filming marathons, and, of course, bacchanalian parties. Poet and handsome 'Factory stud' Gerard Malanga, also in thrall to serious speed, worked full-time as Warhol's main assistant, while recruiting future 'Superstars' of all sexes for Warhol's home movies, which often featured Ondine, the wild mad jester of Warhol's royal court, puckish Taylor Mead, reigning underground star, an abundant, ever-changing assortment of accommodating males, and an abundance of heiresses and over-the-top females, among them edgy cult star Mary Woronov, sultry raven-haired Ultra Violet, loopy fashion model Ivy Nicholson, blonde, big-haired Baby Jane Holzer, baby-faced Bibbe Hansen, the charismatic and doomed Edie Sedgwick, ethereal ice queen Nico, chubby, hilarious Brigid 'Polk' Berlin and beautiful clever Viva, all of whom need no introduction (If they do, you may want to stop about now). Their pithy comments on "Life with Andy" made the film possible. As Viva, the vivacious (sometime vicious) 'Lucille Ball of underground movies' would cackle: "Andy? He's the *Queen* of Pop Art!" As six-foot Mary 'Whips' Woronov would snarl: "Oh, this is fabulous, a soup can, ha ha ha! I hate it, now."

The Warhol soup cans—along with the cokes, cows, fatal car crashes, flowers and Brillo boxes—became ubiquitous in our 'Factory People' project, which spanned the years 1964 to 1968, arguably Warhol's busiest and most creative period. Not coincidentally, it also took us four frenzied years to complete our TV show, waaaaay past our network's deadline, having endured a stunning series of mishaps, meltdowns and sheer madness—documented here in gory detail—that felt downright 'Warholian', and made me want to take up drugs again.

Instead, I decided to write about it, and remember my own fifteen minutes in 1966, when Andy, Nico with her toddler son Ari, and the Velvet Underground came to Cape Cod, to Provincetown for a concert (cancelled) and wound up staying with me.

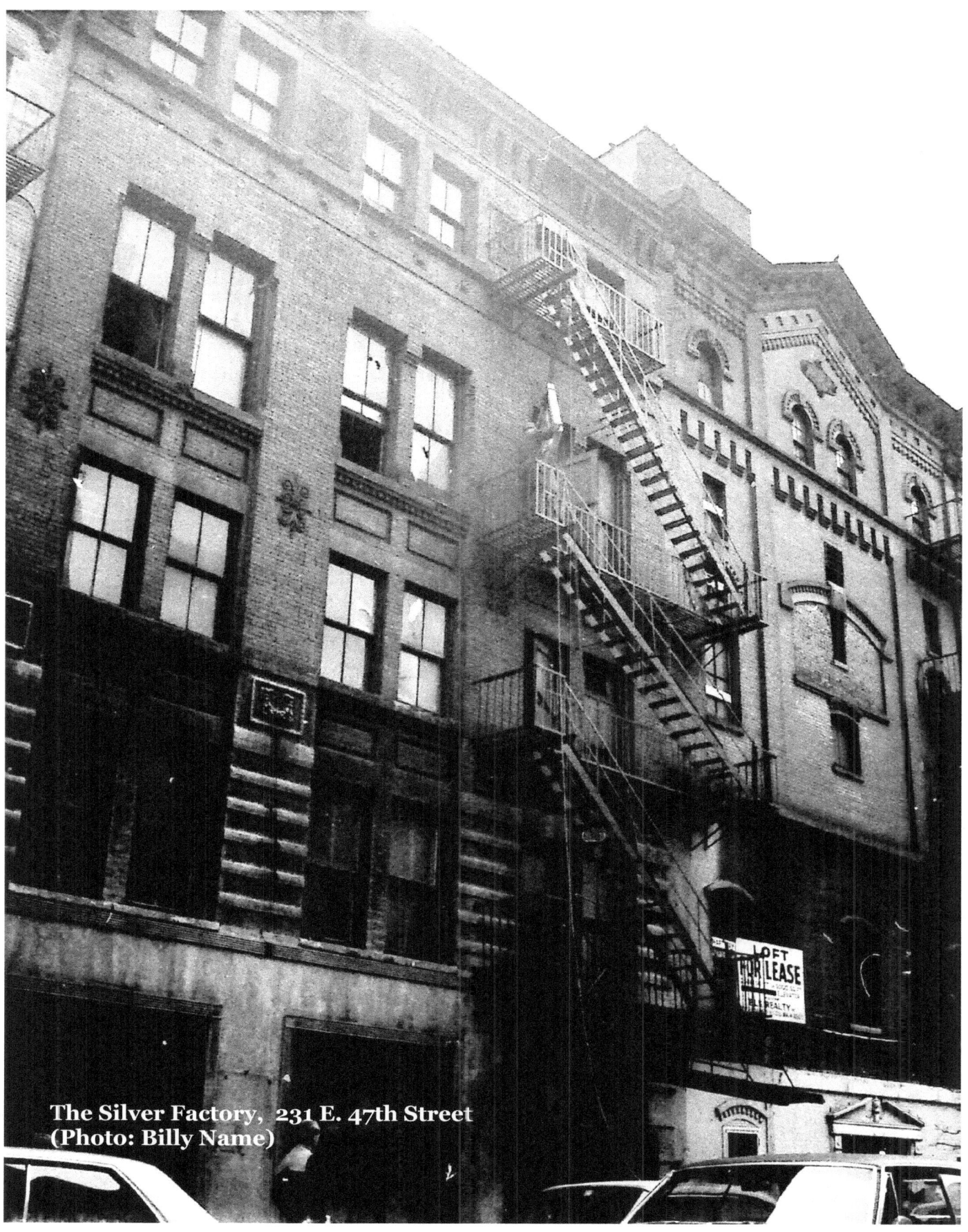

The Silver Factory, 231 E. 47th Street
(Photo: Billy Name)

The different entouragers that dominated the sixties, like Leary's, or Ginsberg's, or Warhols or Dylan's, had to do with drugs and people's attitudes toward drugs.
—Victor Bockris, Biographer, 'Andy Warhol'

In the sixties, I found myself a part, albeit peripheral, of Warhol's Silver Factory 'Family', and an even more obscure remnant of Dylan's entourage. A summer folk-singing stint at the Blues Bag in Provincetown, Mass. gave me the chance to befriend and smoke with Richie Havens, Muddy Waters, Tom Rush, and most everyone who passed through. Mellow, mellow. Then, whoa! Warhol and the Velvet Underground arrived to play at the Chrysler Museum. The police closed the show down, but I was thrilled to have them visit my place, just down the road from mega sculptor John Chamberlain and macho writer Norman Mailer. Well, it turned out that the toilets in their rental house had backed up, and they needed facilities. The Velvets did appear a bit sinister for summer, all dressed in black and "looking like the death crew," as Warhol Superstar Mary Woronov would say. They had nothing but amused disdain for our tie-dyed psychedelica, Buddhist bells and sandals. But that's what was so wonderful and indicative of the time—you could change, at a moment's notice, into someone else, even if you were already famous. Steve McQueen was racing Walter Chrysler's prototype Turbo down the road to Land's End, where Marlon Brando was holed up with his pal Wally Cox. We somehow all wound up there. Warhol was not a fan of hippies, or of a certain Dylan song that had supposedly been directed at him. Our 'Napoleon in Rags' sequestered himself in the bathroom and powdered his blotchy, pockmarked face and blonde wig with talcum, leaving a residue which I mistook for cocaine and snorted off the toilet seat. I didn't realize at the time, and certainly should have, that Warhol considered himself unattractive, and was thus drawn to pale, frail-looking people like himself (Edie Sedgwick), or aloof Teutonic blondes (Baby Jane Holzer, Nico) because he wanted to literally *be* them. Well, we all wanted to be Nico, except, it turned out, Nico herself. Born in Nazi Germany as Christa Paffgen, she'd escaped to Paris and Rome, and appeared in Fellini's 'La Dolce Vita' at fifteen. I worshipped Nico—the Irish tend to get on with Germans for reasons best left to British history—and took her succinct advice about wayward boyfriends and babies. I was happy to babysit Ari, her toddler by French actor Alain Delon, who would toddle off toward the ocean and worry everyone except his nonchalant mother. Nico, like the rest of the Warhol crowd was older, mysterious, impossibly cool. Her flat baritone and surreal beauty seemed in perfect sync with Lou Reed's nihilistic lyrics. We copied her long platinum curtain of hair, peroxiding and ironing our locks into lanky submission until the dank marine layer moved in and undid it all... Warhol had no such problem. He wore his wigs attached to little clips embedded in his skull, and had a bottle of peroxide handy for infection, which everyone used...

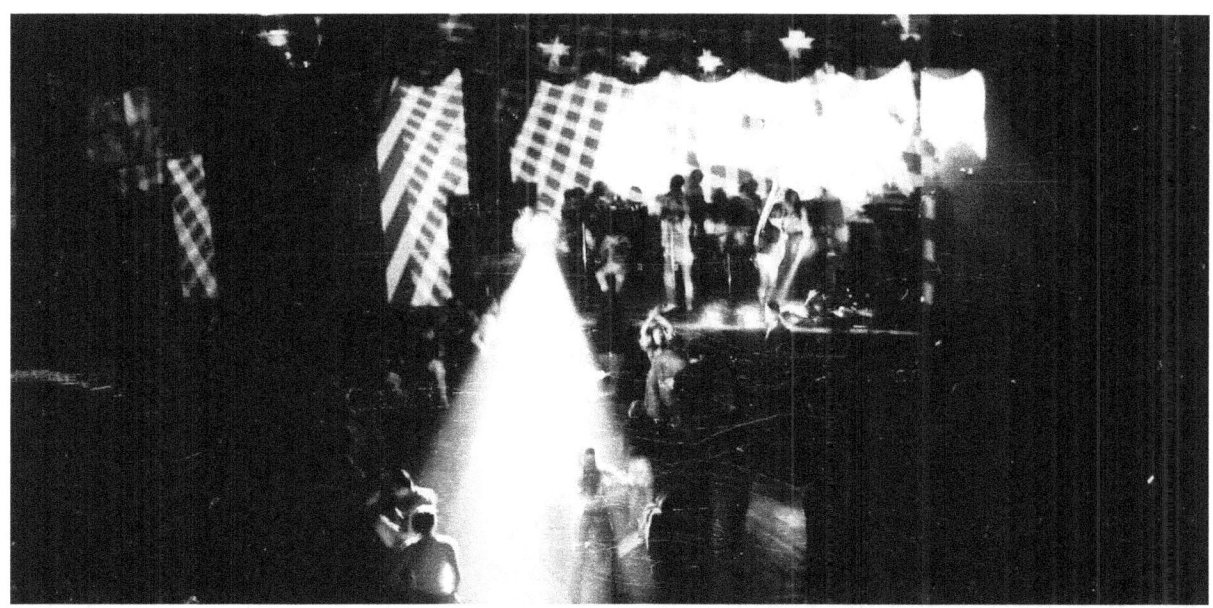

Lights! Cameras! Multimedia! The Velvet Underground as 'The Exploding Plastic Inevitable'.

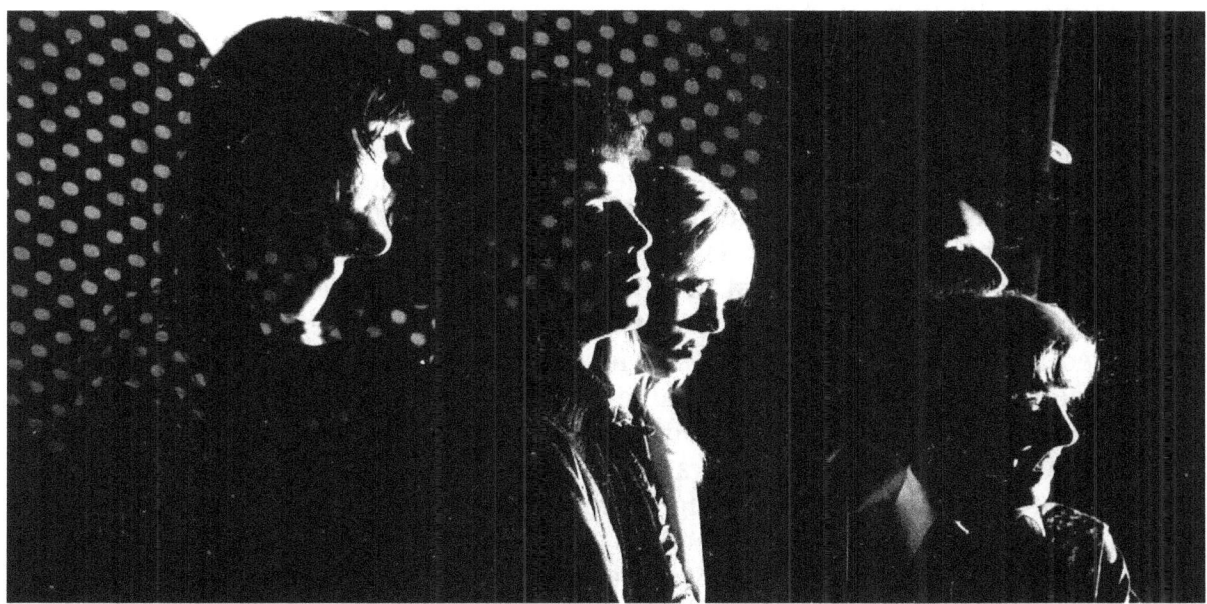

The Velvet Underground at a performance at the Dom on St. Mark's Place in Greenwich Village. (Photos: Billy Name)

. . . Warhol's previous gilded 'Girl of the Year' Edie Sedgwick, with her tiny dresses, boyish hair, and huge chandelier earrings had dropped from favor. According to Warhol, who equated stardom and glamour with its inevitable demise, the annointed 'Girl of the Year' would only last that long in the spotlight before succumbing to exhaustion, drugs, or insanity. He was usually proven right. His women were beautiful and usually from good families, generous free spirits who ran through their trust funds with wild abandon. The men, on the other hand, were for the most part itinerant hustlers, juvenile delinquents and rent boys from poor backgrounds. The exceptions were Warhol's trusted trilogy of Billy Name, Gerard Malanga, and Ondine, who comprised a kind of royal court for their 'King of Pop Art'. I didn't get Warhol's art. A Brillo Box? A silk screen of a soup can? I thought anyone could do it. But no one else did do it, so Marcel Duchamp was right all along about him.

At the end of that eventful summer, I went back to college in sunny Mexico, to Timothy Leary, marijuana and mescaline. Money was scarce, but psychotropics plentiful. Warhol and the Velvets went home, back to the New York underground, amphetamine and heroin. Hop scotching (well, tripping) through a couple of years, I would not see them again until early '68 in Max's Kansas City on Union Square, near Warhol's new 'White Factory'. The back room had become the Factory 'commissary', but Max's served as a second home for the rest of us—a lax one—where we could leave all cares and inhibitions (and sanity) at the door.

But for the Silver Factory coterie, much had changed. Their ranks had been decimated by overdoses, suicide, banishment, or a falling-out over money. Warhol had talked Taylor Mead into coming back from his wilderness years in Paris to star in films with Viva, where he played the perfect foil to her deadpan proclimations on life and love. Though he wasn't paid any better, Taylor got to hang out at Max's with emerging Superstar transvestites Holly Woodlawn, Jackie Curtis and Candy Darling, and charge it all to Andy, who sat nearby with Nico, now estranged from The Velvet Underground. I didn't recognize her at first—the glorious sheaf of golden hair had been dyed a dirty orange mat, her skin looked sallow, her eyes haunted. Nico had considered her spectacular beauty a curse, distracting from her true passion: singing. Now she sat between Warhol and Ondine, chain-smoking, stoned, staring into space. Edie Sedgwick was also gone, also wasted on heroin. As other Factory members met the same fate, the wags were blaming Warhol. His image of 'father figure' to misfits had morphed into something sinister. He was called a vampire, a voyeur, a corrupter of youth. He'd become his own bogeyman, berating himself to confidants over his apparent lack of empathy, but doing little to convince detractors otherwise. According to those close to Warhol, "People had begun to actually hate him."

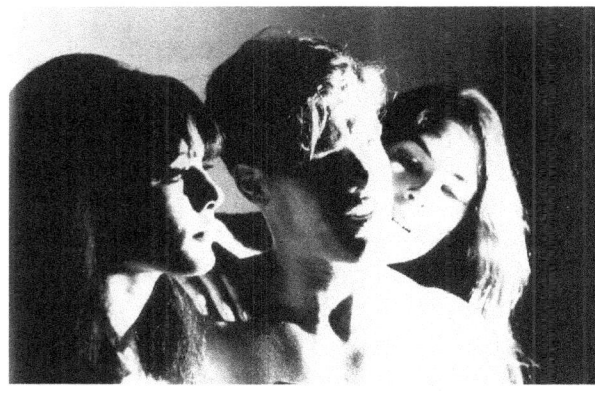

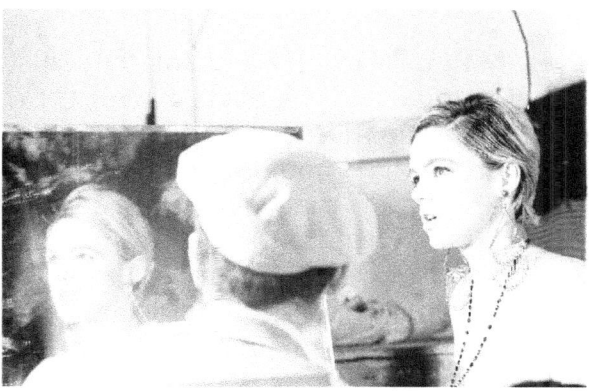

Susan Bottomly (International Velvet) and Mary Woronov, (Hanoi Hannah) toy with their prey in 'Superboy,' circa 1966. The cast also included an unidentified surfer and Ed Hood. Susan and Mary would soon star, but not necessarily get along, in 'Chelsea Girls', 1966. (All Photos: Billy Name)

Edie Sedgwick, the heiress who had it all, films her life in the Silver Factory, 1965. That year she would star in 'Vinyl', 'Bitch', 'Poor Little Rich Girl', 'Face', 'Kitchen', 'Restaurant', 'Afternoon', 'Beauty 1', 'Beauty 2', 'Space', 'Factory Diaries, 'Outer and Inner Space', 'Prison','The Andy Warhol Story', and 'Lupe'.

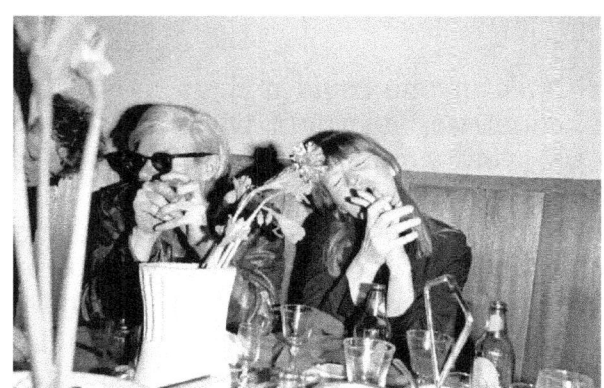

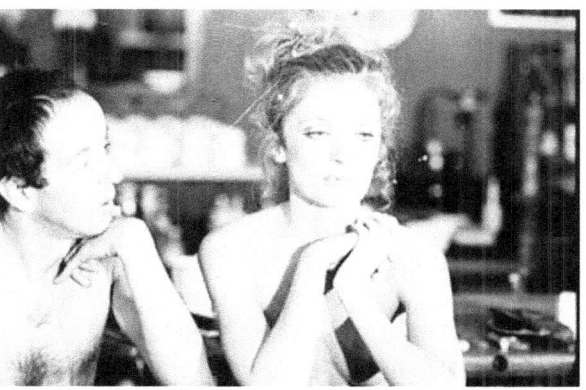

Andy and Nico in the back room of Max's Kansas City, circa 1967. By this time, she had been filmed in the 'Screen Tests', 'The Velvet Underground and Nico: A Symphony of Sound', 'Chelsea Girls', 'I, A Man', '****', aka 'Four Stars' aka 'The 25 hour Movie', and 'Sunset'.

Taylor Mead and Viva converse, sort of, in 'Nude Restaurant' (1967). They also starred in 'Tub Girls', 'Lonesome Cowboys', and 'San Diego Surf". As early as 1963, Taylor was filming with Warhol in 'Tarzan and Jane regained, Sort Of. . .', followed in 1964 by 'Batman Dracula', 'Couch', and 'Taylor Mead's Ass'. Viva's films included: 'The Loves of Ondine' and 'Bike Boy' with Joe Spencer.

Even before Warhol was shot by a disturbed Valerie Solanas in 1968 (effectively bringing to an end the Silver Factory era), we could feel the difference in the air, that uneasy combination of dread and malaise. The 'Summer of Love' slid into something mean and scary, though for a long while we put it down to overactive imagination. But the truth was that soft drugs had gotten hard, and so had a lot of the people.

When 1969 arrived, the hippies among us headed for Woodstock, free love and naked groveling in the mud. Warhol and company, in an attempt to generate income, staged a series of male porno films at a hardcore film house. The expected clientele would come to 'Andy Warhol's Theater: 'Boys to Adore Galore', and leave at the happy ending, but in an effort to go a bit upscale and have cleaner floors, he and Paul Morrissey began work on the aptly named 'Trash' and 'Flesh'. Those hilarious, hearbreaking films, and a retrospective of the art he had done when he "retired" from painting in 1966, would finally bring Warhol his 'overnight' success' as a filmmaker. Jonas Mekas, revered father of underground film, compared Warhol to Godard, Renoir, and Eisenstein, but most people could barely sit through the endless hours of poorly lit, improvised, unedited, and sometimes pornographic footage that comprised a Warhol work. I know the feeling—I watched at least 100 hours of films to find the few minutes used in our documentary. Jonas had a point. No one could make movies like Andy Warhol...

Fast forward forty or so years, and I don't think anyone could make a movie like ours, either. After countless career changes, countries, husbands, wives and lovers blah blah (This book is about Warhol, not us), your filmmakers found themselves together again at last in Paris, home of *Cinéma Vérité*, writing and making movies and documentaries with more freedom—and government money—than one could possibly hope for in the Hollywood studio system to which I'd been tethered for decades. (If you're packing your bags, it does help if you speak the language and have an E.U. Passport). We'd already been working awhile when approached by a TV network to do a series on the arts, and Warhol in particular. So, *voila*! With my fifteen-minute memory of Warhol, I worked up a proposal covering what could be considered the most pivotal period in Warhol's artistic career—The Sixties.

When we first decided to make this documentary, we felt that it would be more interesting (and probably a whole lot more entertaining) to hear, not just from the 'experts', but also from those dreamers and muses who had been part of the Factory from the beginning. We were rarely disappointed. Any preconceptions of Warhol that we may have harbored were jettisoned—along with our initial budget—when we began interviewing those who worked with him, amused him, abused him, loved him, and, indeed, feared him. Our resultant film series disclosed new insights into >

this complex artist's life, and opened a veritable Pandora's Box of contradictory stories remembered by his many muses, his many foes, his few close friends and fewer confidants.

This 'picture-book', unlike an in-depth biography of Warhol—of which there are way too many anyhow—may sometime skimp on technical detail. A drive down memory lane, when dealing with drugs and the sixties, will have more than a few potholes. But this is their story, and it may change your opinion of 'Drella' (Dracula /Cinderella), the nickname bestowed on this enduring enigma of a man, whose deadpan sense of humor and singular personality, or deliberate lack of one, only made him more fascinating to me as a writer.

I've been told it's impossible to unearth the true character of any man, woman or transvestite without talking to them, but I've often felt myself to be in dialogue with the elusive 'Drella', especially at trying moments in this project (the theft of original masters, the disappearance of money, the breakdown of umpteen editing bays, the screaming fits and firings of assorted editors, oh, I could go on). Fortunately, we were saved by Warhol's 'Factory Family' and their formidable collective memories. Because they had, indeed, talked with him, All the Time, we were given an indelible portrait, and quite a complicated one it is. The finished series was not what we expected, but it must work—since we completed and aired 'Factory People', other Warhol 'specials' have cropped up using our format. Is imitation the sincerest form of flattery? Oh, Warhol would probably approve; he loved repetition. . .

At the end of the day, what did we learn from our Factory People? We learned how easy it was to *create* an Andy Warhol work of art, how easy it was to *steal* an Andy Warhol work of art, and how easy it was to literally *become* Warhol himself, and to get away with it. All, it would seem, with his tacit approval and tolerance. As for the odd circumstances behind Warhol's horrific, near-fatal shooting, which appears to be a probable cause of his subsequent decline as an artist (and premature death), those Warholian moments became clear in our interviews, when the most oft repeated words were 'Fame', 'Fifteen', and 'Superstar'.

So, was Warhol a hated demon, as often portrayed, or a beloved savior to his motley group of creative misfits? Both, it seems. In certain families (or cults) it can be a slippery slope from initial attraction to eventual abuse, and those who were part and parcel of Warhol's collective success were, in the end, betrayed. His muses, his knights and princesses and trolls, were summarily ejected from the Factory—not a fairy tale ending for anyone, least of all Warhol.

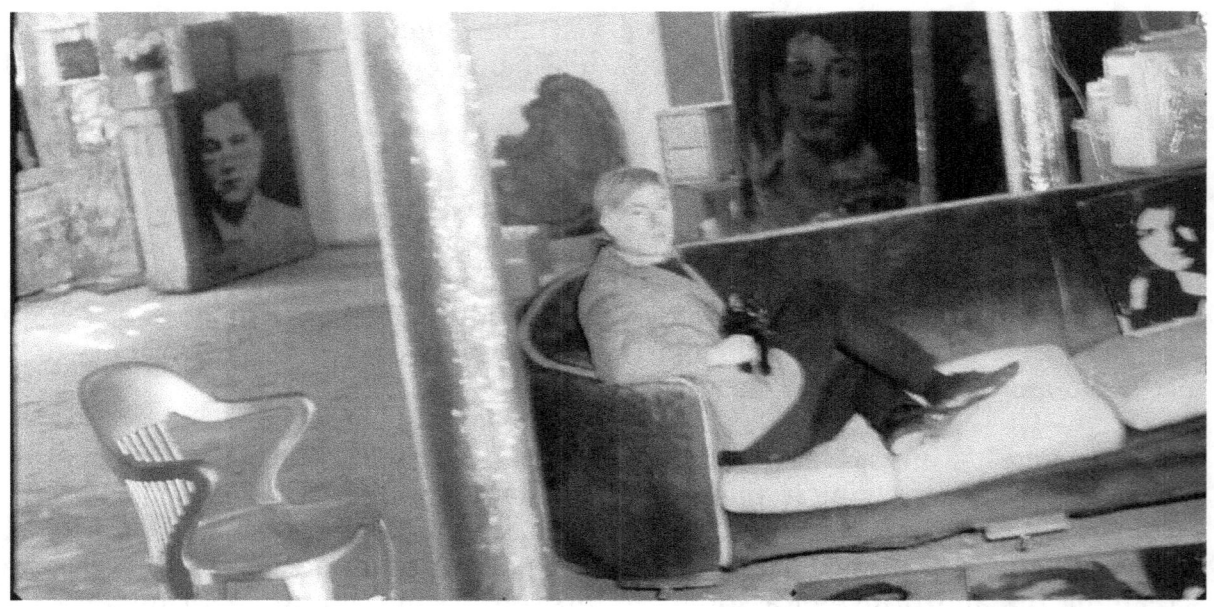

Andy Warhol contemplates the sixties from the safety of his ratty red velvet sofa, found on the street by Billy Name. Star of numerous films, it achieved lasting notoriety in 'Couch' (1964).

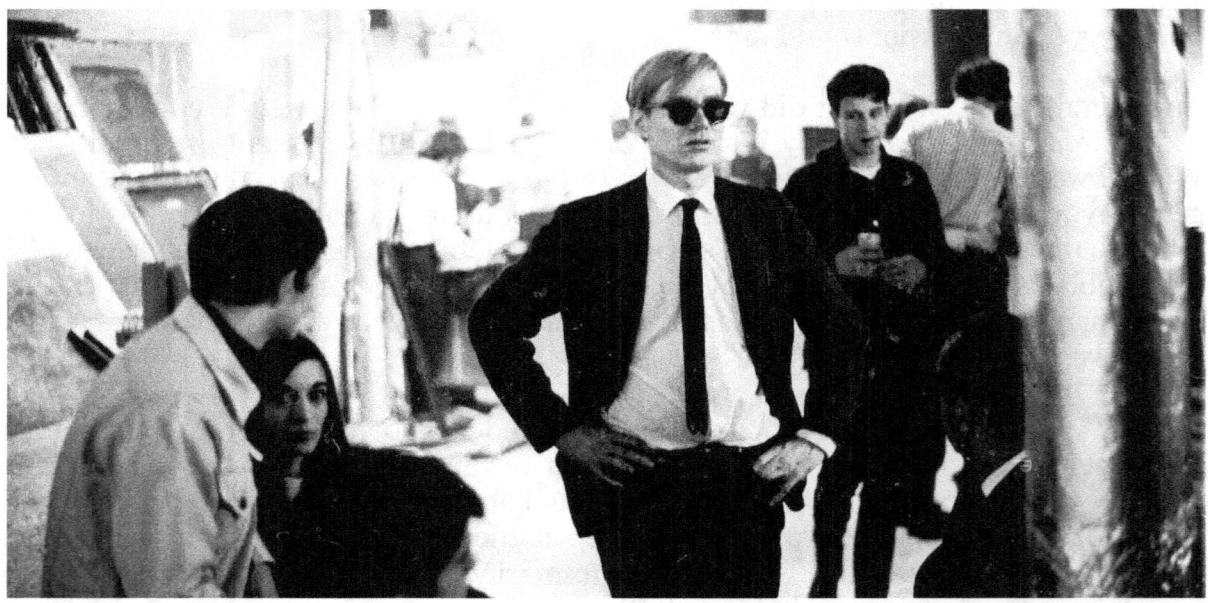

Andy is always the center at a Silver Factory event. Artist/Sculptor Marisol seated at left, Factory screenwriter Ron Tavel standing at right. (Photos: Billy Name)

Some would say—ourselves among them—that Warhol's work after the Silver Factory rarely if ever reached the marvelous heights of madness and brilliance achieved through the collaborative efforts of all those loony drugged geniuses that floated through his grungy freight elevator doors on 47th Street. One by one, they left the fold, under the watchful, if comically inept, surveillance of the F.B.I., who had been busy hounding them for more than a year, trying to pin charges of pornography, rape, and drug abuse on 'Drella' and entourage. The Silver Factory era officially ended with the shooting of Andy Warhol in 1968 by Valerie Solanas, the unstable lesbian feminist writer whom Ultra Violet thought "demented, of course, but with an interesting philosophy." Warhol had tried to supplicate Solanas by putting her to work 'acting' in the film 'I, A Man'. Her strange footage, which we included in our series, is revealing in a most unexpected way. Unfortunately for both, Warhol had forgotten to return (or simply mislaid) a screenplay she'd given him, entitled 'Up Your Ass'. Grounds for murder? Well, as Taylor Mead put it, "Andy did make promises. I wrote a critique of the movie 'I Shot Andy Warhol', and I titled it 'I *Would* Have Shot Andy Warhol'." Taylor was half-joking, but in Warhol's over-the-top world of bisexual, bipolar fantasies, the fabulous craziness had finally spilled over into pathology. Hence the arrival of the suits to the new 'White Factory' on Union Square, nice people, hip and efficient, and certainly more practical, and since they upon occassion suffered the same 'palace' intrigues as the old court, it would be churlish to resent their astounding success with packaging and selling Warhol. But hey, this isn't their story—that would be a bit predictable.

A grateful "*Merci*" to the Warhol Museum, to the wonderful, weird archival footage folk who dug up buried treasures from the 'Happening Sixties', especially when Warhol and his Silver Factory made the news, and to Vincent Fremont, founding director of The Andy Warhol Foundation For The Visual Arts, for his expertise and help with the Warhol Foundation. . . Most of all, a "*Merci bien"* to Billy Name and the Factory Family, who gave to Andy so much of their productive lives, and who graciously gave to me so much of their time. I feel I have become a part of that family, celebrating their late-in-life accomplishments, and, for some, attending their funerals. Their lives were a celebration. At the end of the day, how many of us get a page and photo-op in the obits of the New York Times?

—Catherine O'Sullivan Shorr, Paris, France, 2014

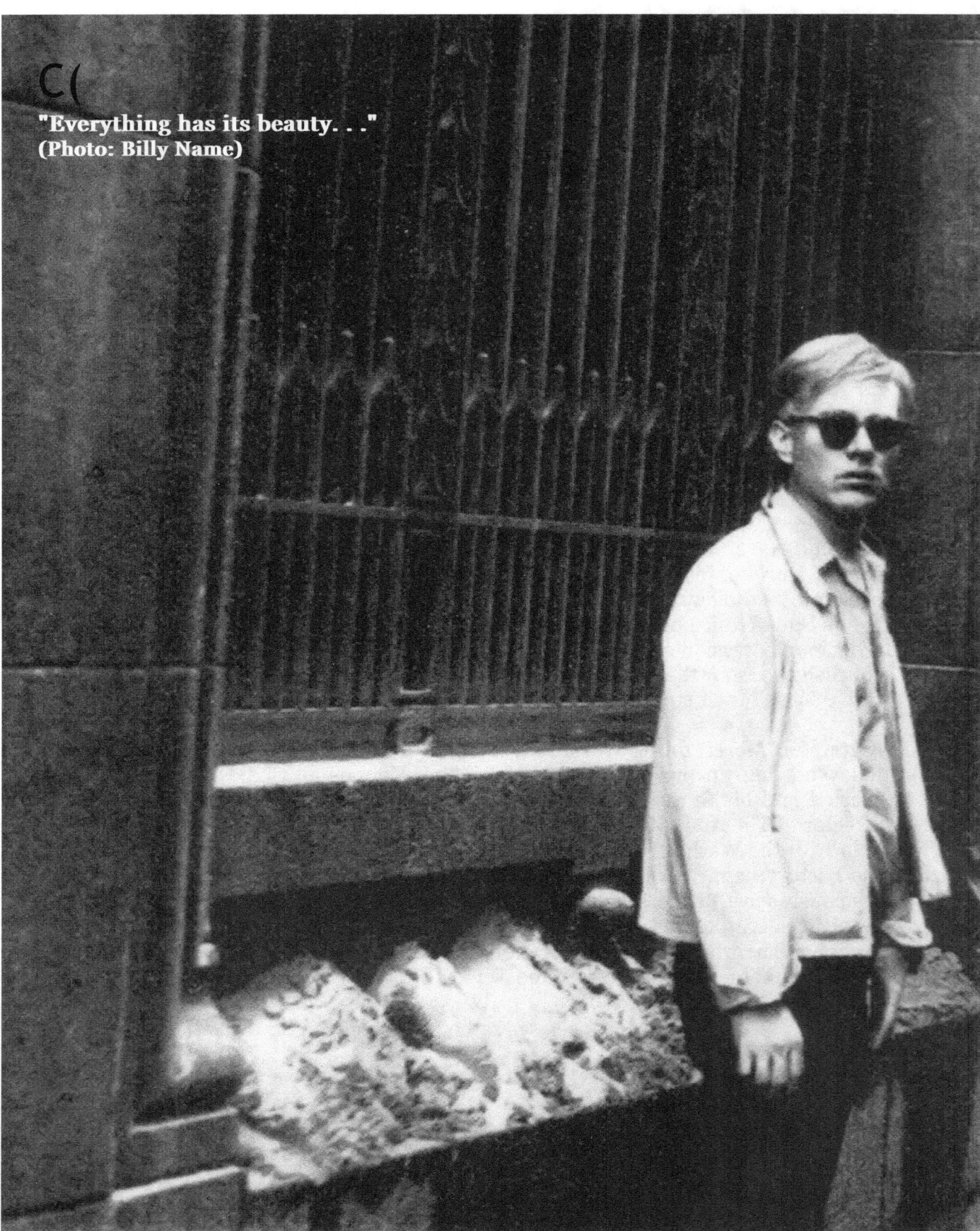

"Everything has its beauty..."
(Photo: Billy Name)

BOOK I

WELCOME TO
THE SILVER FACTORY

*I don't have any favorite color. I decided
. . . silver was the only thing around.*
—Andy Warhol

The Factory... It's something that you can't recreate, as when we were making films there, with the actual people there. As when we were making art, with the actual people there... Imagine living and working in a place like that!
—**Billy Name: Warhol Photographer, Factory Foreman & 'Gatekeeper'**

The Silver Factory was considered the first Factory, which Billy Name decorated with tin foil and where all the notoriety first started. Sure, there was amphetamine, but the craziness also energized everybody.
—**Vincent Fremont: Founding Director, Andy Warhol Foundation for the Visual Arts**

I'm buried alive in museums, cinematheques and foundations. And with the Andy Warhol Foundation, we have wonderful movies with great character, even almost a plot, but the museums show twelve hours of the Empire State Building and no one comes to the other movies.
—**Taylor Mead: Underground Poet, "The First" Underground Star**

I was born Isabelle Collin-Dufresne, and I became Ultra Violet in 1963 when I met Andy Warhol. Then I turned totally violet, from my toes to the tip of my hair. And to this day, what's amazing, I'm aging, but my hair is naturally turning violet. It's all natural... Maybe it's a miracle!
—**Ultra Violet: Artist, Socialite, Warhol Superstar**

I'm a cult star! I'm a cult star, because when I was with Warhol in New York, I was probably the only person there who was also very good, who thought she was going to be an actress, not just a 'star'. I got very, very strange roles because of it.
—**Mary Woronov: Writer, Artist, Actress, Warhol Superstar**

Andy and Serendipity became connected very early. We opened in 1954, down in the basement, and he just stumbled down with a portfolio of rejects. I was waiting for him with open arms.
—**Stephen Bruce: Restaurant Proprietor, Serendipity III**

I just felt the paintings were not interesting. They seemed to be spoofing all kinds of things. You weren't really sure what he was going to do.
—**Leo Castelli: Famed Art Dealer and Gallery Owner, on Warhol's early promise**

Andy would do incredible things when I'd do a film. He'd say "Look at the camera, and don't blink your eyes."
—**Baby Jane Holzer: Warhol Star, Girl of the Year, 1964**

Oh, it's so true to life; it's not even acting! It's just so candid, like the camera isn't there at all, like Andy says.
—**Edie Sedgwick: Warhol Icon, Girl of the Year, 1965**

Andy was Edie's introduction to New York. She became 'Girl of the Year' in about six minutes, and everyone wrote about her style and her leather rhinoceros and her short hair and giant earrings in the midst of all the evil and squalor. She was the princess amongst queens. And so we loved her.
—**Danny Fields: Edie Sedgwick confidant, Music Entrepreneur (The Ramones)**

Andy came and wanted to see the exact spot where Freddie Herko had fallen. He looked up at the window and said, "Gee, if Edie kills herself I hope she lets us know so we can film it."
—**Robert Heide: Playwright, Warhol Confidant**

Andy said, "And what do *you* do?" And my father beamed proudly and said, "I just sprung her from jail." Andy's eyes grew wide. "Really! Tell me all about it."
—**Bibbe Hansen: Youngest member of Warhol Family**

Andy wanted me to join the Factory. They were starting to make movies. No script. Nobody knew what to do. Andy looked like he was lost. I said, "Oh boy, I can't work with these people." But (actor) Allen Midgette said, "Come on! He wants you."
—**Louis Waldon: Actor, Artist, Warhol Star**

The Warhol thing was never who I was. I mean, a lot of people now, because I impersonated Andy and that whole jazz, they actually believe I *looked* like him, and they believe that I *am* just like him probably. Except that I don't have money.
—**Allen Midgette: Actor, Warhol Star**

The Velvet Underground would play the music and I would go through my routines, which I had mapped out for each song. I was very energetic in those days. I loved.
—**Gerard Malanga: Warhol Factory 'Prime Minister', Poet**

They had been thrown out of a place in the Village on 3rd Street, the Café Bizarre, because people couldn't dance to their music.
—**Nico: Singer, Warhol Icon, Velvet Underground Star**

Oh, The Café Bizarre, that's how lame it was. Can you imagine playing at the Café Bizarre? The only bizarre thing about it was that it existed.
—**Lou Reed: Rock legend, Founder of 'The Velvet Underground**

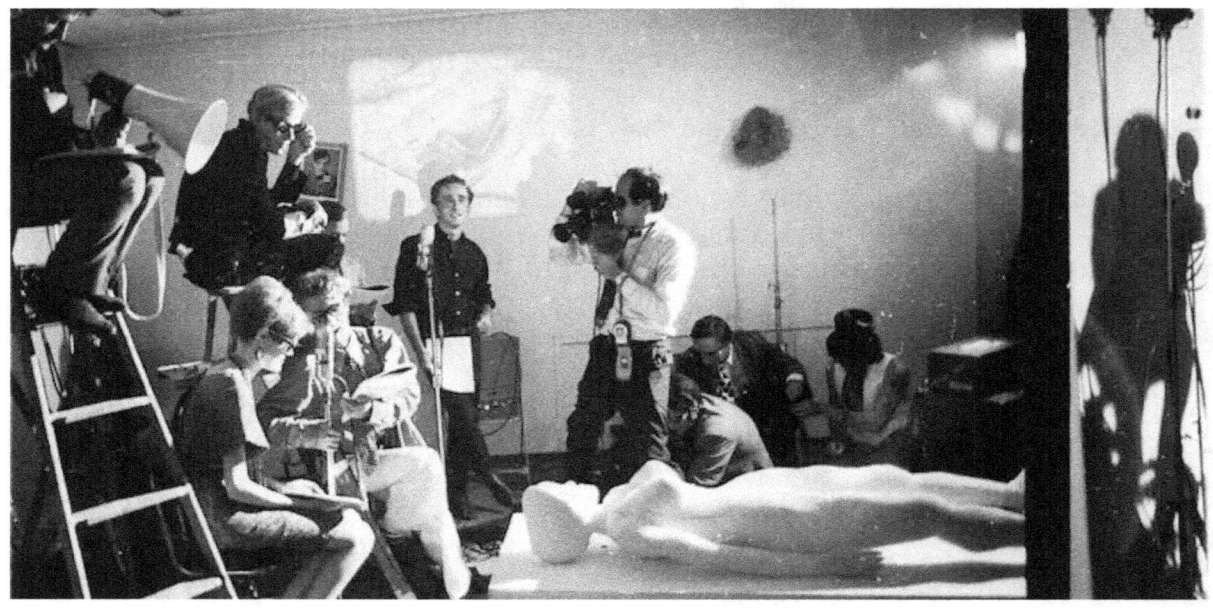

'A Factory 'Happening'... Ingrid Superstar rehearses, Warhol hovers, while the girl on the table waits for her cue.

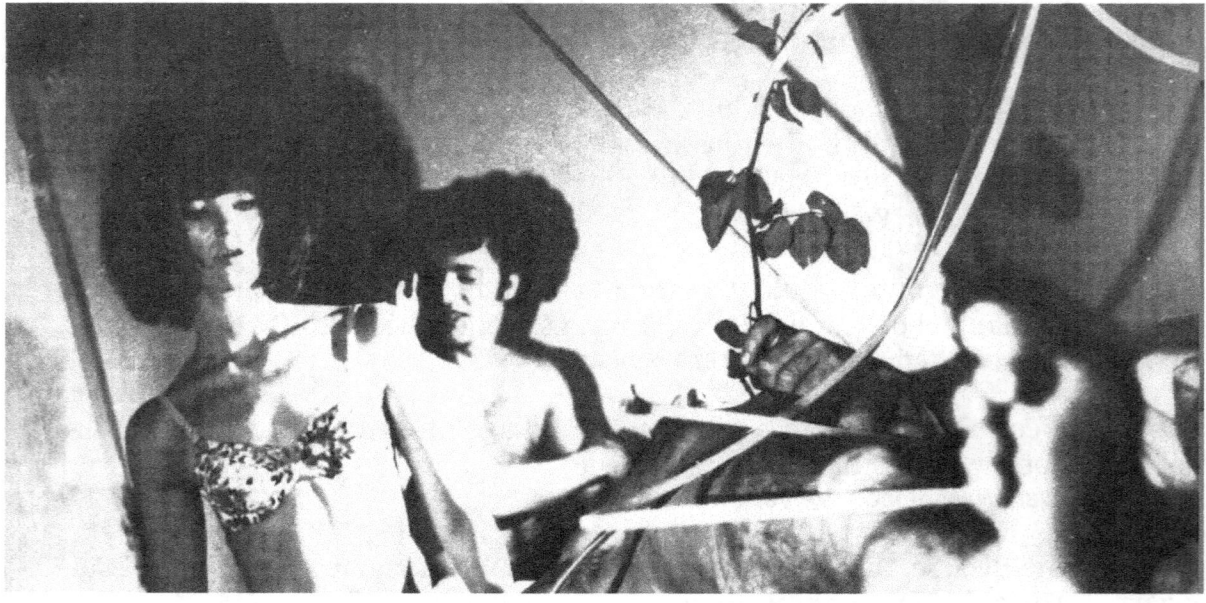

Superstar Ivy Nicholson and co-star Gerard Malanga filming Warhol's 'Batman/Dracula', 1964. (Photos: Billy Name)

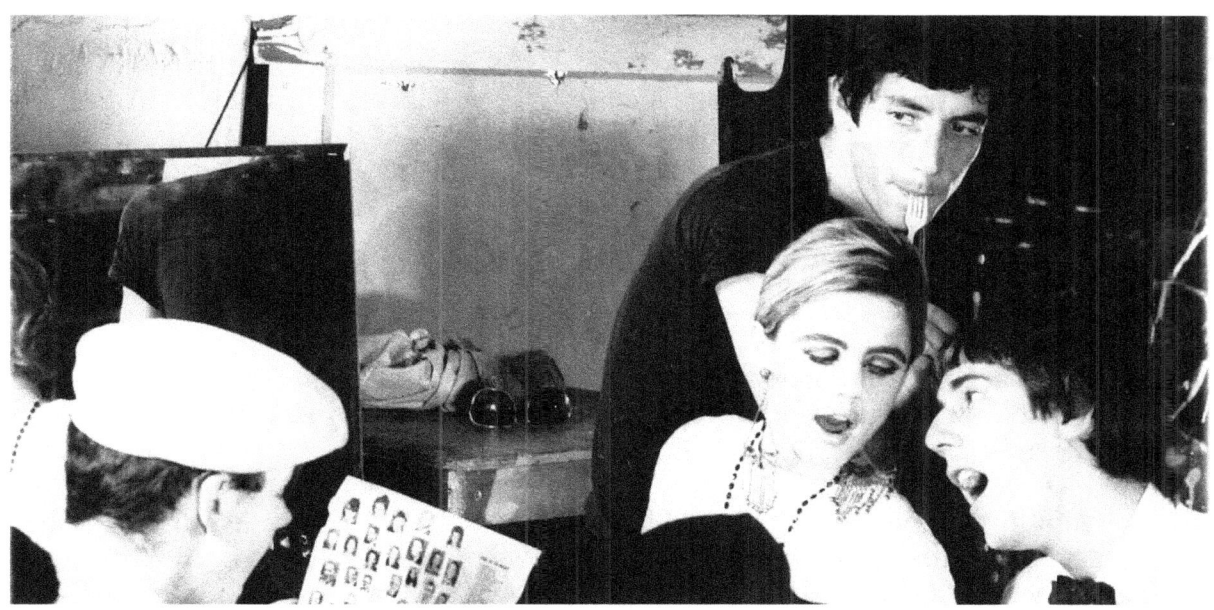

'Girl of the Year' for 1965, Warhol Superstar Edie Sedgwick shows off her chandelier earrings, which started a sixties trend. (Photos: Billy Name)

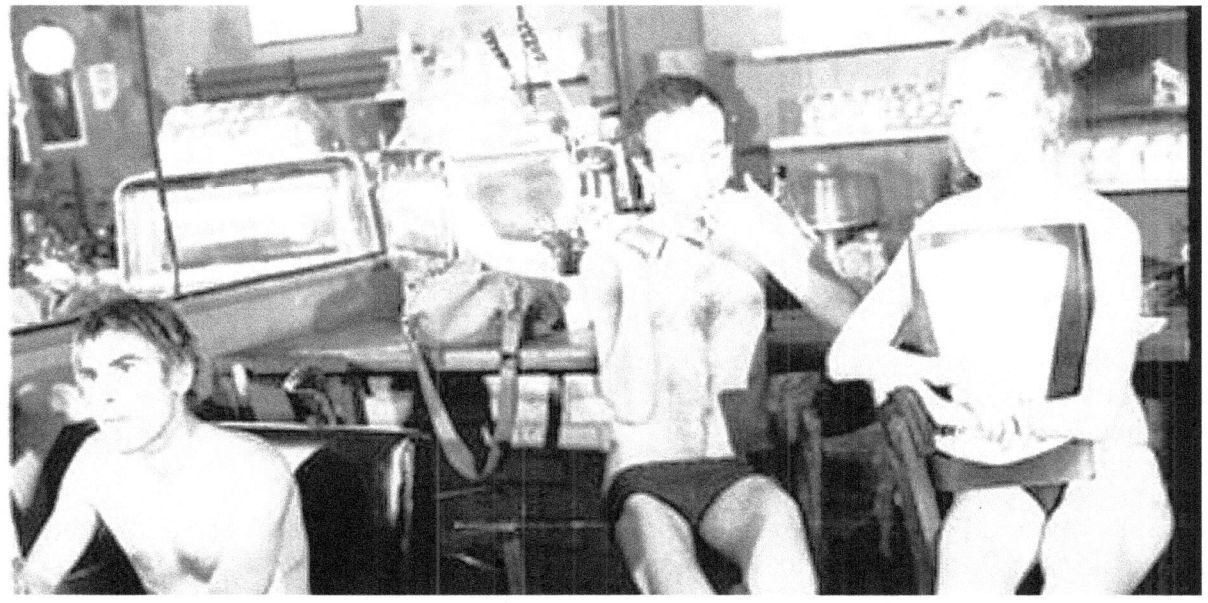

Allen Midgette, left, starred in the first 'Nude Restaurant', with an all-male cast. In this later version (1967), he costars with Taylor Mead and Viva. Warhol "wanted to make an anti-war movie," but decided "to make a nudie so more people would watch."

Andy just said, "No, there are no rules, write about whatever you want." The Velvets did songs about heroin, and bondage and forbidden subjects, brilliant stuff that we weren't hearing at all!
—'Leee' Black Childers: **Factory Acolyte, Photographer, Former Music Mgr. (David Bowie)**

Chelsea Girls was asked to be shown at the Cannes Film Festival. Andy invited me, Susan, Nico, Ultra Violet. . . They didn't show the film—they said it was too dirty!
—David Croland: **Publisher, LID Magazine, young member of Warhol Family**

When 'Chelsea Girls' happened, it would just be outrageous. You see, you'd do anything, thinking that it would never come out, that it would just go in a box.
—Brigid Berlin: **Warhol Muse, Movie Character, and Confidante**

That's when he was permitting people to improvise. It did not come out of thin air, there was already the background—the passion was there for cinema. Andy came in during that very exciting period. And he got the bug.
—Jonas Mekas: **Founder, Film-Makers' Co-operative, Anthology Film Archives**

We were all drama queens. The Silver Factory was the place to throw out tantrums, show our outfits—just blossom. We only got a hundred dollars as salary, but no one noticed that. I mean, to suddenly become a star. You were a star!
—Ivy Nicholson: **Warhol Superstar**

Andy was a user. Andy was a homosexual. He was not a 'woman lover'. He was a woman 'be-friender' and a woman manipulator. Andy had a mother fixation. Andy had a Madonna fixation. But Andy didn't love women.
—Nat Finkelstein: **Photojournalist, Black Star Agency, Warhol Chronicler, 1964-67**

Do you know what my opinion is of Andy? I think he's the *Queen* of Pop art!
—Viva: **Artist, Warhol Superstar**

Andy Warhol tries to say nothing and succeeds. Other filmmakers try to say a great deal, but some uninitiated viewers might find them confusing. Either way, it's a long way fom Hollywood.
—David Dugan: **CBS Newsman**

I spent years in Paris as a poet and a painter. Then I came to New York and went to Max's Kansas City. . . I found a Fellini movie. Because I would be taking so many pictures of the same favorite subjects—Taylor, Viva, Eric, Andrea, Ondine, Candy Darling, Jackie Curtis, Holly Woodlawn—they didn't believe I had film in the camera.
—Anton Perich: **Photographer, Filmmaker, Painter**

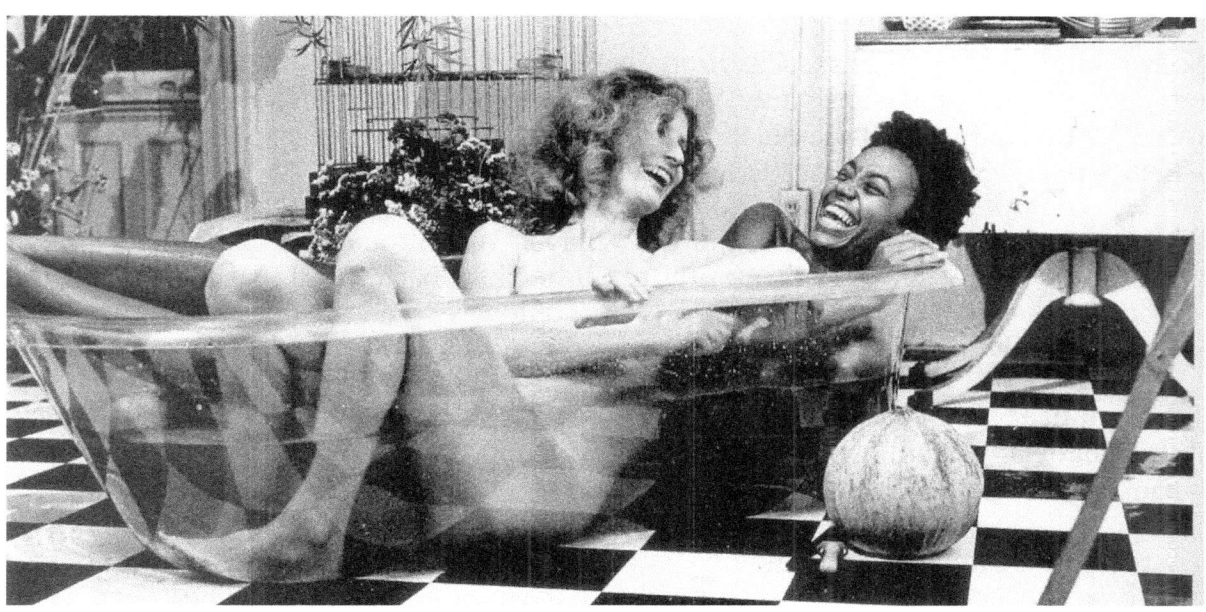

Viva with Abigail Rosen in 'Tub Girls', which also starred a couple of tub boys. Viva's last Warhol film: the infamous 'Blue Movie' with Louis Waldon.

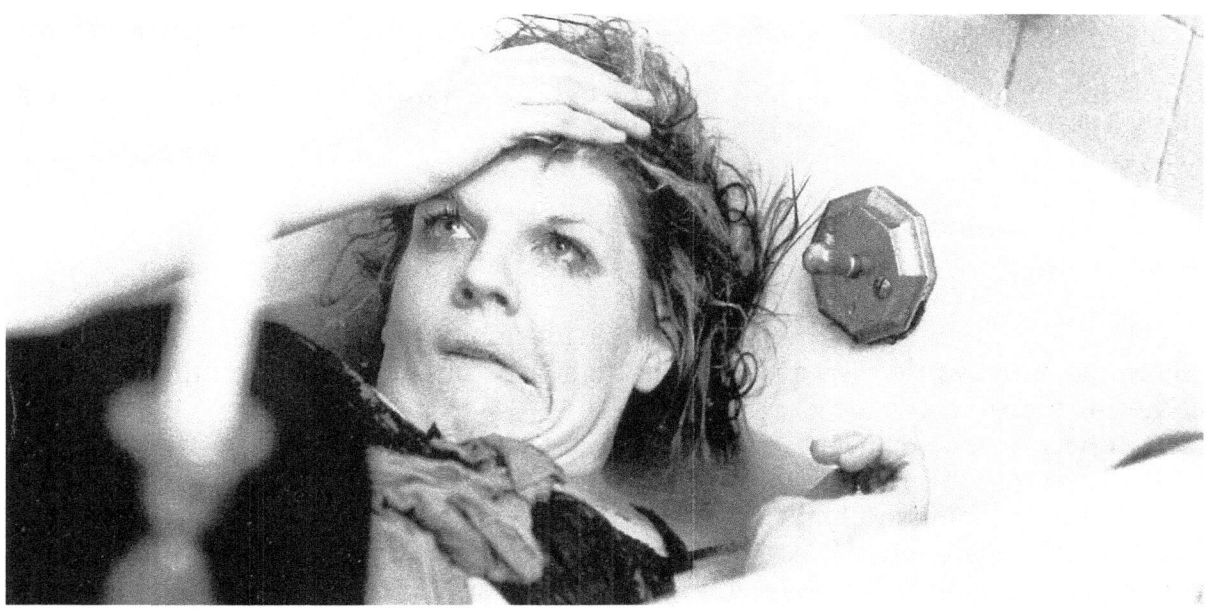

Brigid (Polk) Berlin, a star of 'Chelsea Girls', in her version of 'Tub Girls'. (Photos: Billy Name)

So, we went to Max's Kansas City, and Jackie (Curtis) devised this plan: "Why don't we just go there and sign Andy Warhol's name, and order steak and lobster and wine?" And Andy got all the bills.
—Holly Woodlawn: Drag Queen, Warhol Superstar, 'Flesh', 'Trash

We all went out to this restaurant in the Village. When the check came, nobody had any money. Holly said, "Wait a minute; I'll be right back," and she went down the street and she did a couple of blow jobs. That's how we paid the bill.
—Geraldine Smith: Warhol Star, 'Flesh', 'Trash'

These pioneer female impersonators had such a hard time, making very little money, if they made any at all.
—Paul Morrissey: Filmmaker, Warhol Co-Director

There were strange people moving about his (Warhol's) circles. He himself was mostly an observer of this, not so much a participant as a man who watched them and recorded them.
—Ivan Karp: Former Castelli Assistant, Longtime Warhol Art Dealer

I think Andy Warhol's imagery and consistency has made him one of the leaders in the Pop art field. Whether that's enough, I'm not sure.
—Henry Geldzahler: Curator, Metropolitan Museum of Art, NYC Cultural Affairs Commissioner

Oh, Henry, do you think social imagery is going to come in? You know, like Bob Dylan singing his funny songs?
—Andy Warhol

Warhol is a cultural figure, but not an artist.
—Bob Dylan

The Factory, from the moment it opened its doors, was the most intelligent art commune in the world. It was, on a very high level, a think tank, a communal artistic gathering place.
—Victor Bockris: Biographer, 'Warhol', 'The Velvet Underground'

We were all people who had this divine will driving us, saying, "Art! Art! Art! You just have to create, create, create!" It doesn't matter what you do; if you paint or dance, or make music, use everything! In New York, in the Village, you are free to create.
—Billy Name

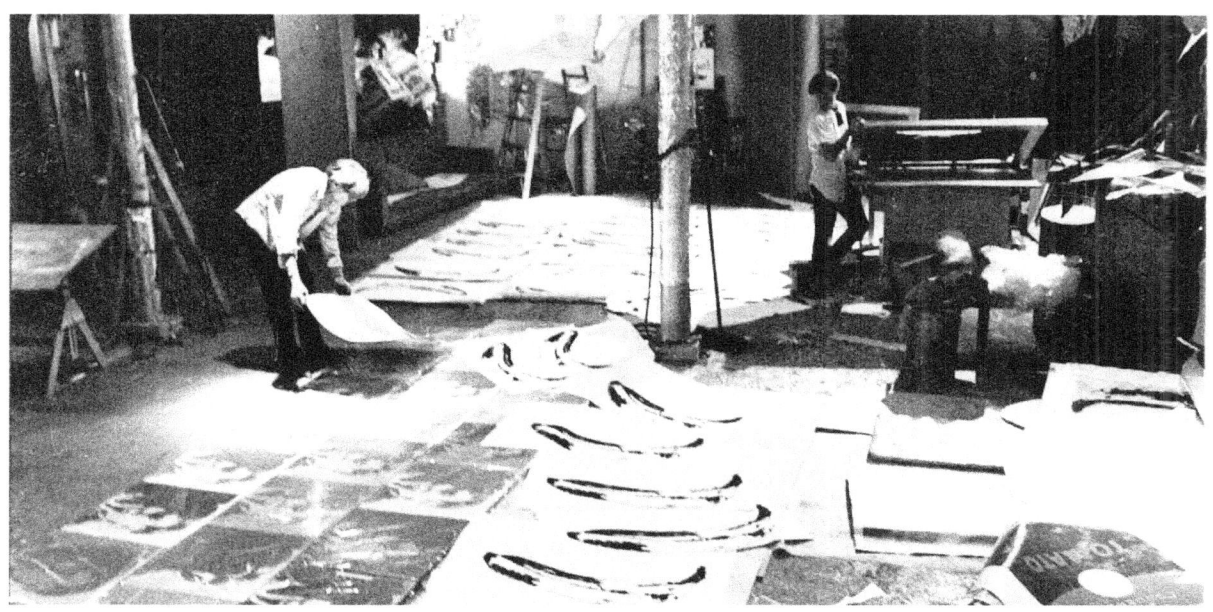

"Create, create, create!" By the mid-sixties Warhol and his bananas would achieve unique fame, due in no small part to his involvement with The Velvet Underground. Assistant Gerard Malanga, at right, helped.

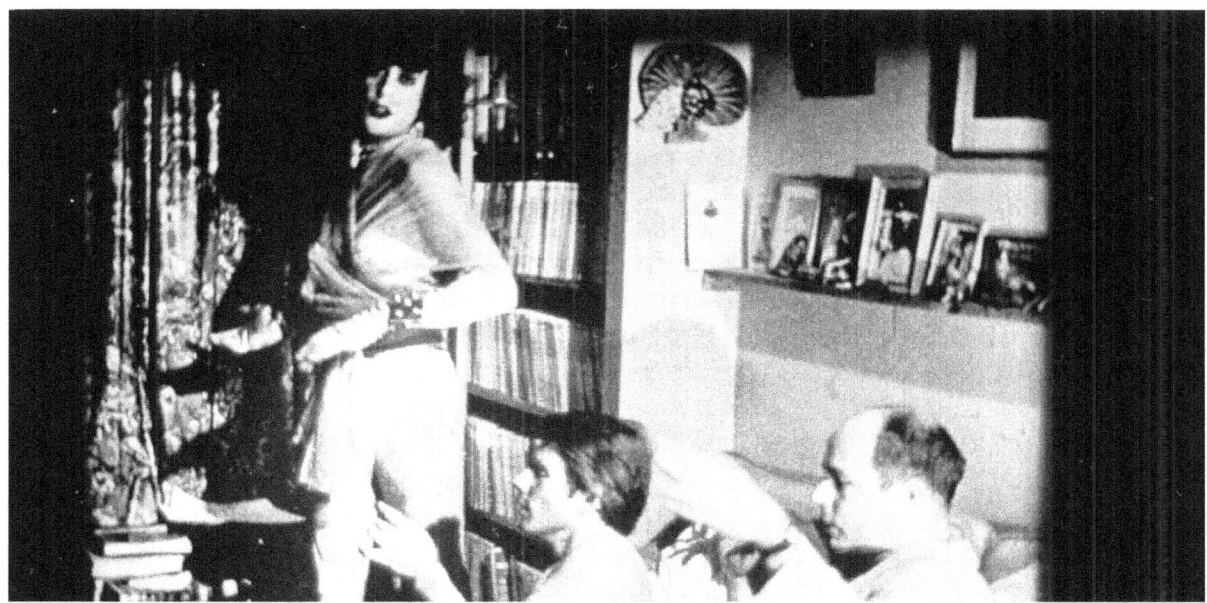

First Factory transvestite Mario Montez, who had his/her own issues with bananas, in a video monitor still from 'Chelsea Girls', with co-stars Patrick Fleming and Ed Hood.
(Photos: Billy Name)

BEYOND THE BEAT GENERATION

I saw the best minds of my generation destroyed by madness...
—From 'Howl', by Allen Ginsberg

Historians would agree that Warhol's Factory and its groundbreaking openness would never have come into existence without those rebels of the late fifties, commonly referred to back then as 'Beatniks—a title they hated, with some justification. According to Warhol biographers, most of whom get their facts and dates straight but have some conflicting views, "Andy Warhol was influenced by the Beats," and he was also "not even remotely interested" in those scruffy poets, writers and irredeemable reprobates that populated downtown New York. Well, as Warhol once proclaimed: "Everybody is right, and everybody is wrong." He was obviously influenced by the manic consumerism of early sixties' Madison Avenue and its 'Mad Men'—he was emphatically one of them. But he also seemed fascinated by the Beat philosophy. As is commonly known, the Beats were rather vociferous in questioning values held dear to America in the fifties. If one discounts those pesky McCarthy years when members of the creative community ('Commies' for short) were burned at the stake, life was still a Norman Rockwell painting. Then, Jack Kerouac's 'On the Road' was published, though with some sexually explicit passages removed, and the Beats became a byword for rebellion. By the time William Burroughs got 'The Naked Lunch' published in Paris, the little run-down Latin Quarter hotel where he wrote it (nicknamed 'The Beat Hotel' by Gregory Corso), had become a magnet for Beat writers, artists, and existential wanderers searching for the same freedom.

The French, naturally, living in Paris, the city of the enlightened, would lay claim to The Beat Generation (*le jazz hot!*), and they still do. So, our producers had suggested we do a series to prove it, and quickly, because *"Merde, there aren't that many left."* Well, I heartily agreed, and wanted to focus a bit on the extraordinary women of the Beat era, like the accomplished Diane di Prima (*'Memoirs of a Beatnik'*, *'Loba'*) Carolyn Casssady, loyal wife of Neal, muse and lover of Kerouac. But sadly, the boys disagreed, and (sorry) Beat a hasty retreat...

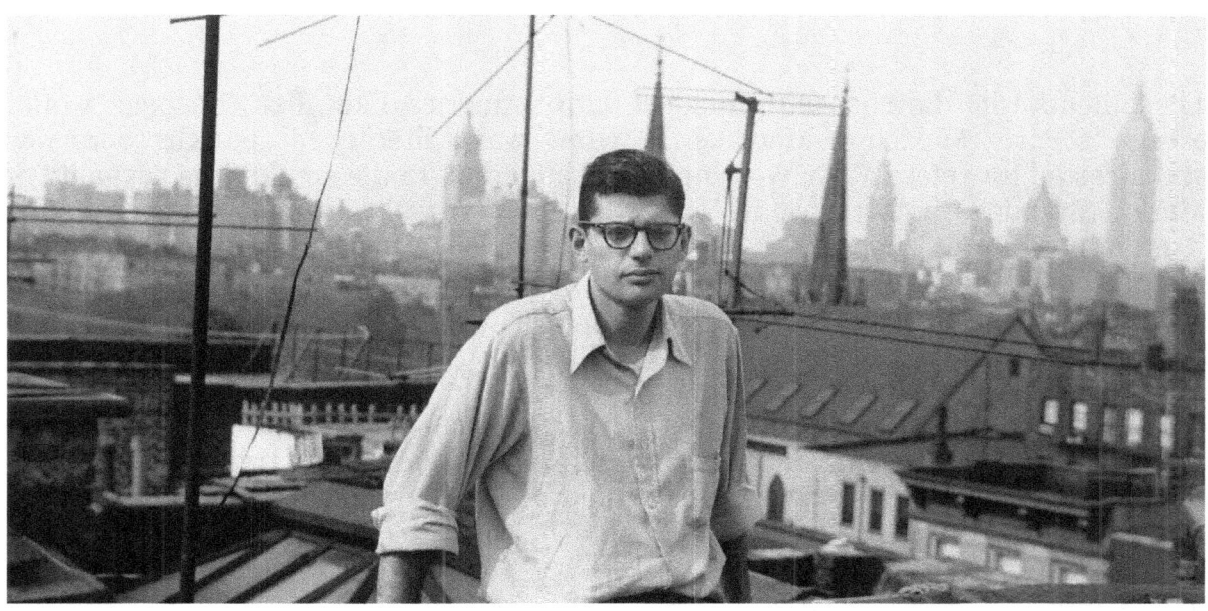

Up on the roof. . . A clean-shaven Allen Ginsberg contemplates his future. (Photo: William Burroughs, from the Ginsberg archives. Corbis)

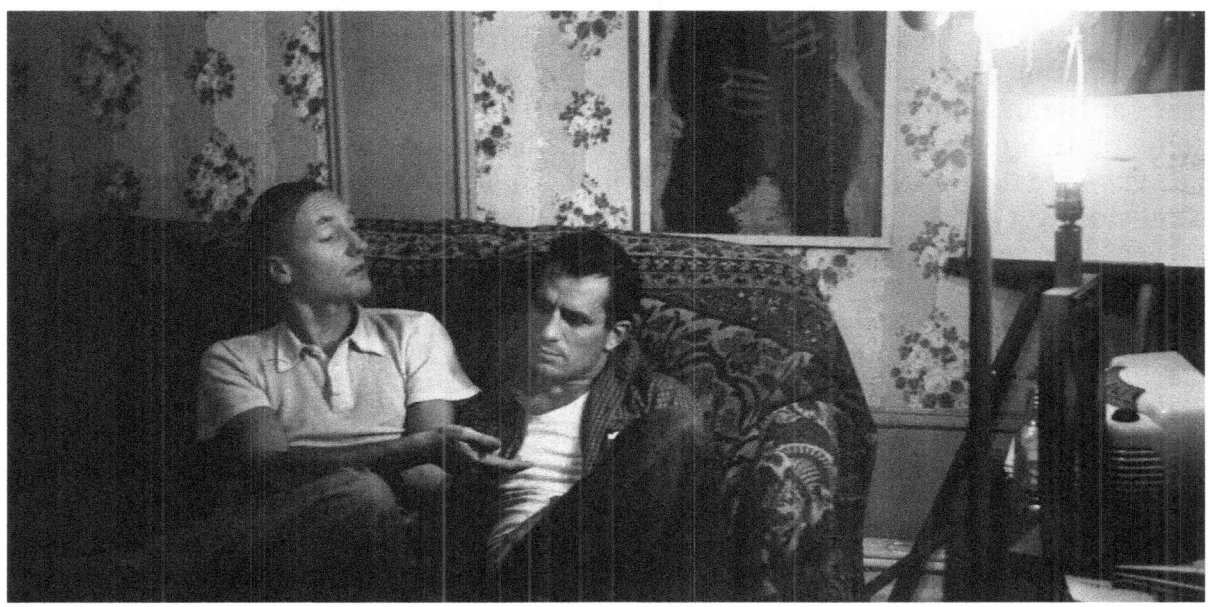

Down in Greenwich Village. . . William Burroughs and Jack Kerouac. (Photo Credit: Corbis)

Those Beats who did choose to tough it out in America, like Allen Ginsberg, would escape to Paris, Mexico or Marrakesh. 'Howl' was a literary hit, but Ginsberg was still arrested for referring, in worshipful gay abandon, to the smoldering sexuality of Marlon Brando's motorcyclist in 'The Wild One' (1953). Ginsberg's vesion of the "best minds" of his generation, "who let themselves be fucked in the ass by saintly motorcyclists and screamed with joy," were less than welcome in fifties America. I was a kid, and intrigued by Ginsberg's poetry, but certainly felt the alienation, reading 'condemned' literature with a flashlight. . . Many creative originals just up and left the country altogether. Others, like Jonas Mekas, arrived from obscure parts of Europe like Lithuania, and fit right in. Warhol, also with roots in Eastern Europe, had much in common with Mekas, but in 1959, while Warhol was trying to break into the rarified art world, Mekas was already an established underground filmmaker. . .

Jonas Mekas: When we came to New York back then , the whole cinema horizon was open; you could see everything! The classics, the past, the present, the experimental. It was so rich that we immersed ourselves completely and immediately into it. There was no way back—we were *in* it! That was the beginning. But later, when I was arrested for showing (Jean) Genet's 'Un Chant d'Amour', and Jack Smith's 'Flaming Creatures', those court cases would affect licensing of *all* films. Then Lenny Bruce, his trial had to do more with freedom of speech. He contributed to eliminating censorship in cinema in America. So I was not just doing the obscenity trial for the underground. No! I did it in the first place for myself. If I want to show some films, why not? They are innocent films. I just did the right thing, no courage needed—to share with people what you like. That is what I did then, and I do the same now. If I see something that I like, I have to share with others.

While we worked on 'Factory People', Jonas Mekas shared with us his extraordinary VHS tapes, a compilation of home movies that he and brother Adolfas began shooting almost from the moment thay landed in New York (He'd borrowed money to buy his first Bolex 16mm two weeks after his arrival in 1949). We studied hours of remarkable footage from the Beat era to the decades beyond, including 'Walden', 'Lost, Lost, Lost', and 'Notes on Andy's Factory'. Jonas and his trusty camera were a major, ubiquitous Village presence, as was grizzly bearded Zen Buddha Billy Name, who still strongly resembles a benign Beat/Biker, wearing his trademark sunglasses, leather, and lots of silver. Billy knew why he and his friends gravitated to Greenwich Village: "It was a miserable period not just for gays, but let's say living people."

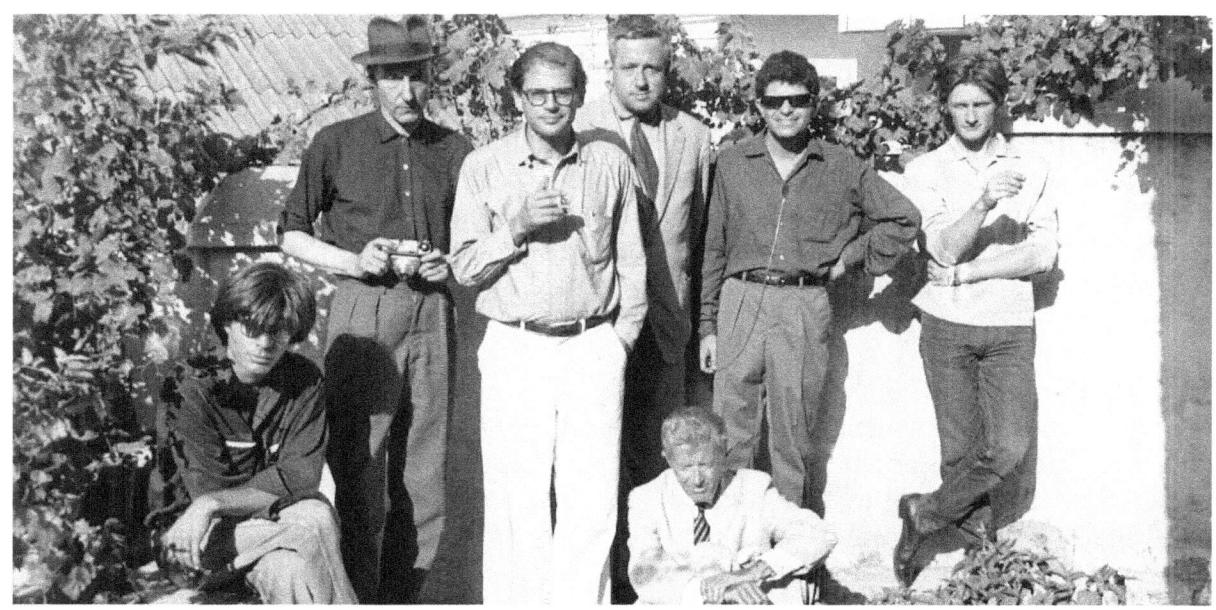

The Beats find a home in Tangiers, '61. From left, Peter Orlofsky, William Burroughs and Allen Ginsberg. Paul Bowles in white suit, with Gregory Corso behind him. (Corbis)

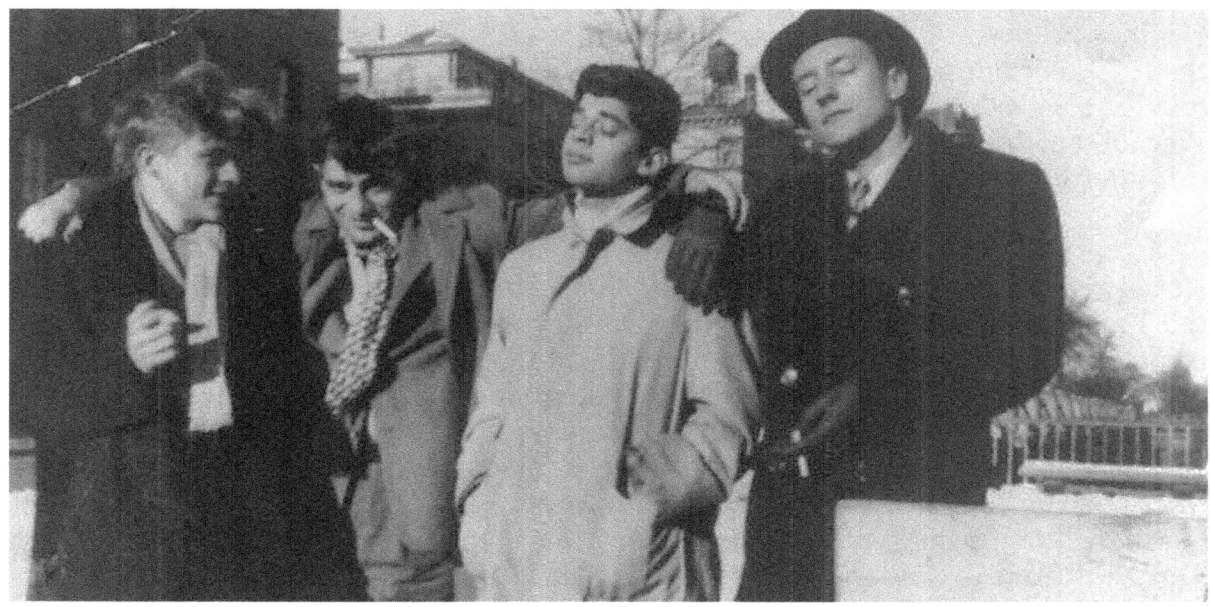

Hal Chase, left, with literary pals Kerouac, Ginsberg and Ferlinghetti, near Columbia University in the mid 1940s. (Corbis)

Billy Name: During the Beat era, the Bohemian Greenwich Village was *The Village*. It was the Café Figaro, which was the coffee shop to hang out in. Washington Square Park was filled with bongo drum players. All of the clubs had jazz musicians who did heroin and smoked marijuana, and you could hang out with these people and just groove. So, Ginsberg and Corso and Burroughs and the whole clique were the equivalent to the art culture what Marlon Brando and James Dean, the rebels, were to the film culture. And in the authentic cultural world, the kings were the poets.

When Billy talked about the fabled Village, he transported me right back to my own feckless, well-spent youth, slumped in smoky jazz clubs drinking cheap wine and wearing black tights, turtleneck and hoop earrings. Uptight upstate New York, ugly poodle skirts and bubble hair had become but a dim miserable memory. History (and history-in-the-making) was an open door on every corner, inviting the lonely misfit to feel at home. I found a rambling railroad flat on Gay (!) Street complete with bathtub in the kitchen and cockroaches with college degrees. My quiet little street connected to Christopher, the Promised Land for pioneer gays from all over the disunited states of America. Here was one of the safest, most exciting places for a girl to live. It was, as Billy would say with a big smile, "The Village." You knew your neighbors, be they artists, musicians or poets, aspiring or famous, who had come there to "Create, create, create!". . . Billy's longtime friend, charming playwright Bob Heide, who lived on Christopher Street and is still there, wrote his own treatise on the foibles of unconventional love, ('The Bed'). At The Kettle of Fish, which seemed to have always been around (since 1950), Heide would hang out with Ginsberg and Warhol, but social convention still decreed that gays be 'invisible in plain sight', and this interdiction persisted into the sixties. . .

Robert Heide: Marlon Brando lived in an apartment in the Village with Wally Cox, the TV actor, comic, intellectual. Anyway, they were painting this apartment a kind of putrid purple, and they got tired and left the cans of paint and the place was a mess. They were reading and speaking existentialism, and this was my idea of living in the Village. This particular night, I wandered into the Gaslight. Allen Ginsberg and Jack Kerouac were reading—they weren't actually reading, they were talking their poetry. Taylor Mead was there, with whom I later became good friends. Allen Ginsberg got up and recited "Jack Kerouac, stop fucking me up the ass, Jack Kerouac." And Taylor read his poem, 'The Statue of Liberty', about a dyke that's been carrying a torch in New York harbor for decades: "Give me your tired, your poor, and let me blow them."

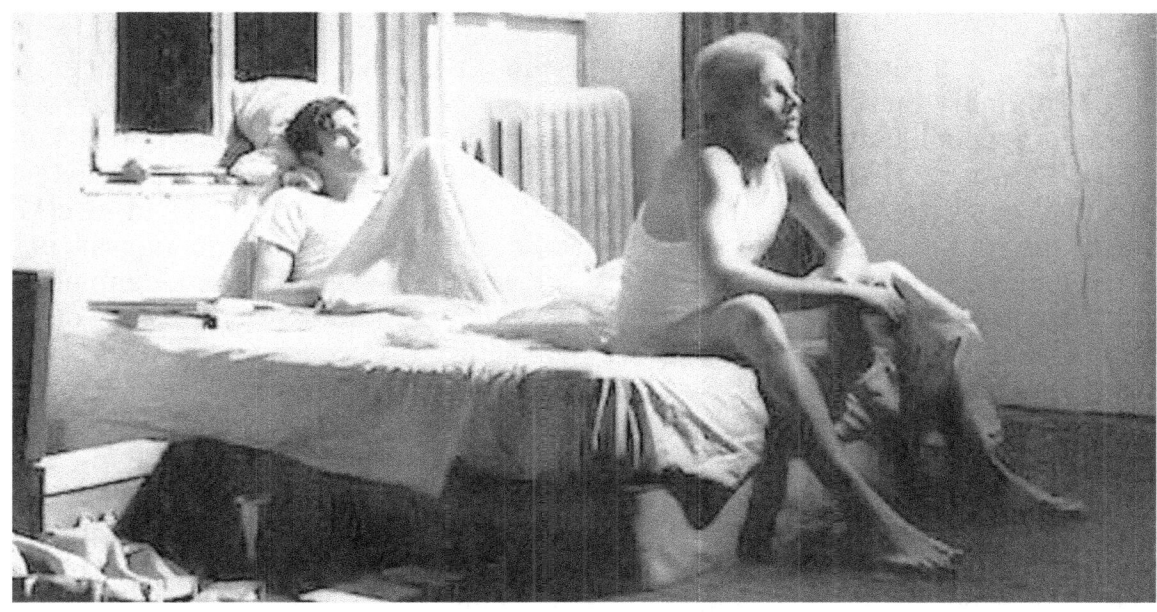

'The Bed', a dark existential play by Bob Heide, was a hit at the Caffe Cino, and later filmed by Warhol (1965) in artist Richard Bernstein's Bowery loft.

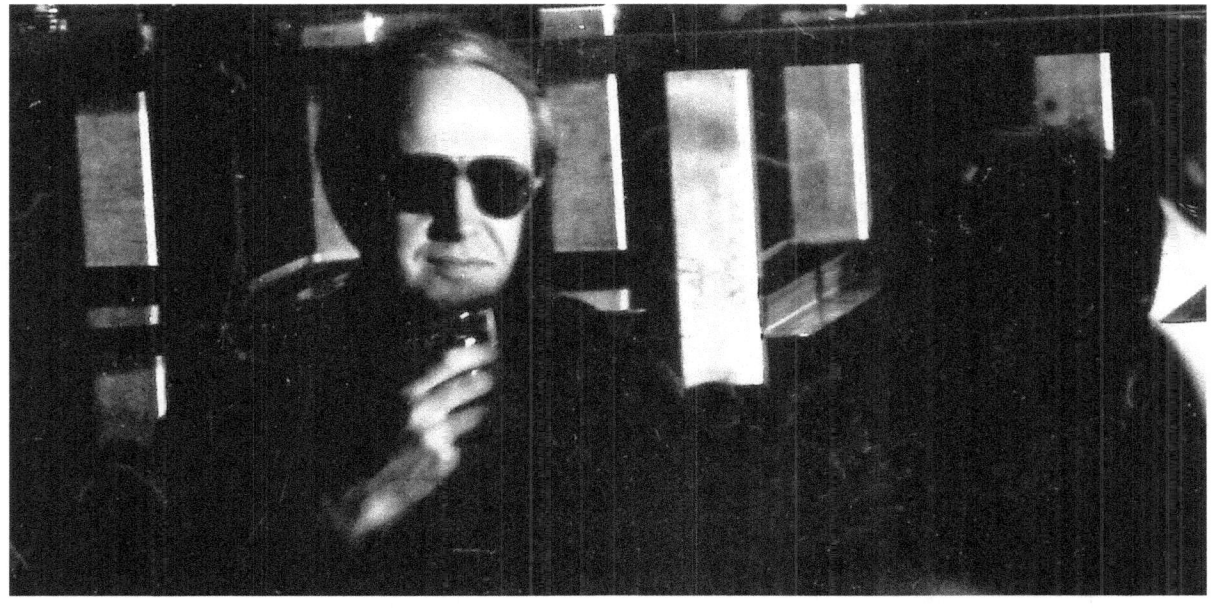

Bob Heide shares a dark existential moment with the camera. (Photos: Billy Name)

Taylor Mead: I got into the poetry scene in the fifties. We were all protesting. It was a revolutionary time. And a great many people from the Midwest and the West, disinherited people like me, came to the New York coffee houses. It was Bob Dylan, and Allen Ginsberg, Gregory Corso. . . We were *outré,* avant-garde, super-duper! Dylan would come in, I would stop reading and bring him up on stage and he'd be playing to the wall. I didn't understand then what being high on marijuana was, but I'd be the only one who could hear his lyrics. He was quite wonderful. He demanded one of my poetry books, and a year later he wanted my next book. I said, "Bob, you're famous now, you can afford to pay for it." He said, "Taylor, I only get paid every quarter; I don't have any money." So he conned me out of it. New York is such a con city anyway, Andy Warhol included. Don't try to get paid by any of these filmmakers.

Jonas Mekas: In 1962 we created the Film-makers Cooperative, and two streets down, we established a little showcase, where we began screening films every weekend. The Cooperative was in my loft, so my home became an office and meeting ground for underground filmmakers. Every evening, they used to bring their films to show to each other. Warhol came, and I did not know who he was. He had to be introduced. But he was there, sitting on the floor. That was one of his film universities, besides 42nd Street.

From the invaluable trove of Jonas Mekas we also unearthed the rare nuggets you will find scattered throughout our documentry series. Please support the Anthology Film Archives, on 2nd Avenue and East 2nd Street. Ironically, the building used to be the jail and courthouse where underground filmmakers were once tried and incarcerated on obscenity charges. Now all their films are shown there. . . Another downtown Warholite, photographer 'Leee' Black Childers, who passed away April 6 at the age of 68, remembered being a baby Beat. "Get us before we're gone," he said.

Leee Black Childers: We're on East 6th Street, which they're trying hard to improve by jacking up the rents. But there's nothing they can do about the history. If you look out this window, there's the loud and cantankerous McSorley's Ale House, which didn't even allow women in until fifteen years ago. Look it up in the Village Voice; they get everything wrong anyhow. It's got sawdust on the floor, and all the old Beatniks, jazz musicians, ne'er-do-wells like myself, and the very underground actors like Taylor Mead. We used to hang out there, because it was the place where you could do as you please, and go to sleep at the bar.

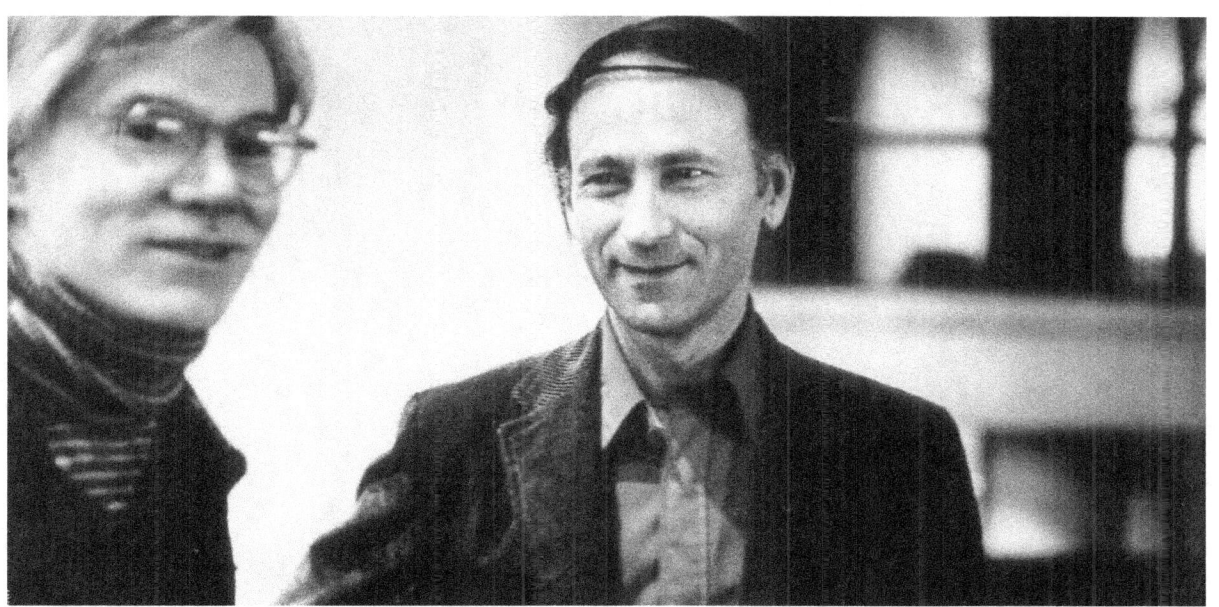

Andy with Jonas Mekas, "patron saint of underground movies." (Photo: Stephen Shore)

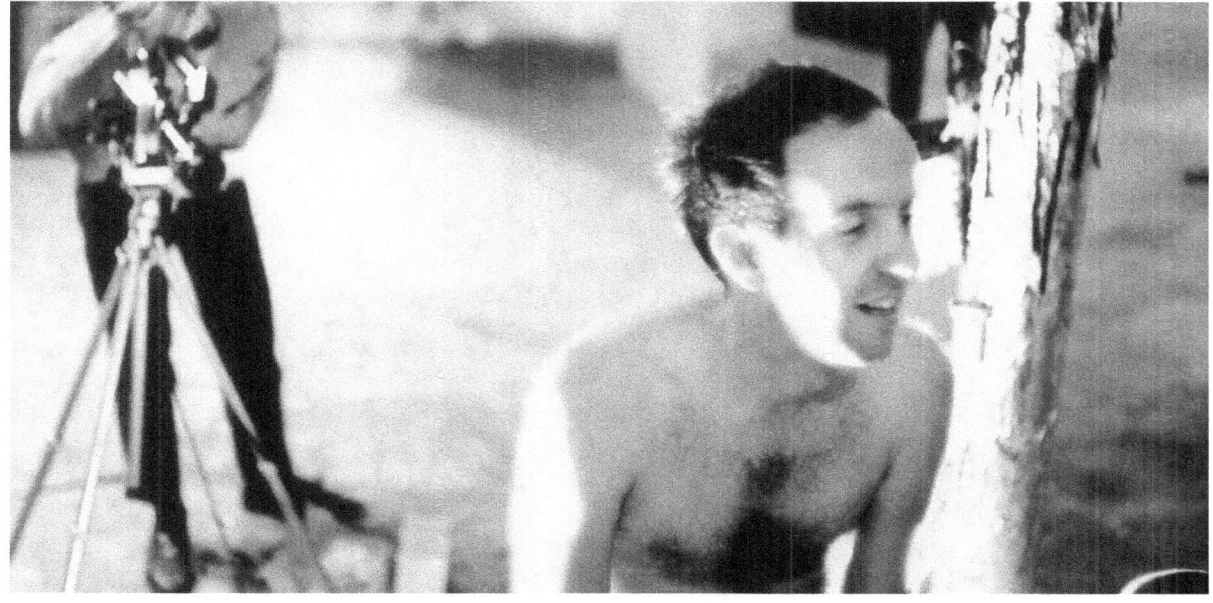

Andy films 'Taylor Mead's Ass' in 1964. (Photo: Billy Name)

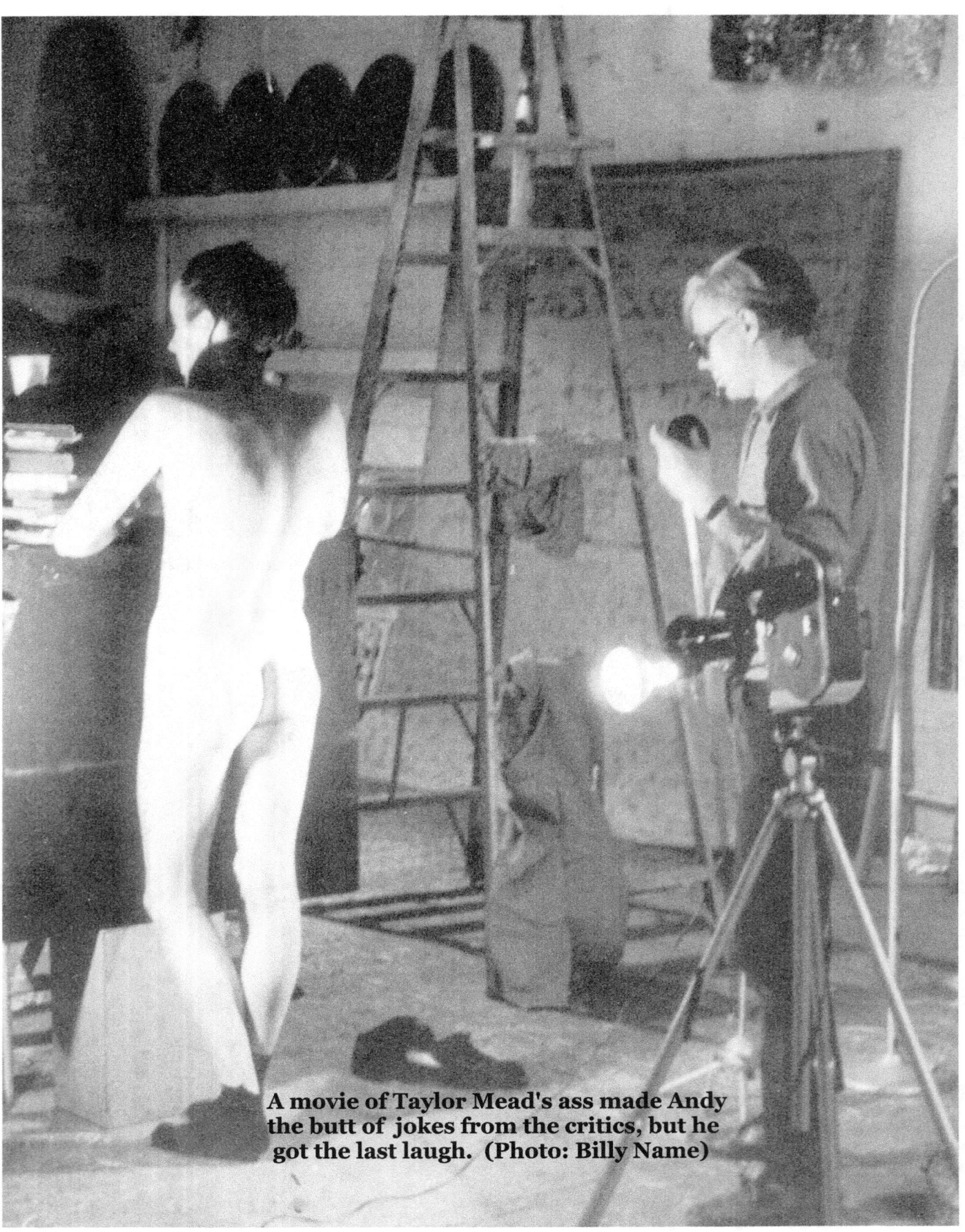

A movie of Taylor Mead's ass made Andy the butt of jokes from the critics, but he got the last laugh. (Photo: Billy Name)

Taylor Mead: I'm an aristocrat, I'm a *ruiné*. I'm drifting away. . . Catherine, *vous parlez Français; que'est que c'est in Paris? Je suis un ruiné, un aristocrat*, a disinherited *ruiné*, but my rent is paid, I hope.

We hope, dear Taylor, that our small contribution helped. In April of 2013, Taylor was evicted from his home of 30 years on Ludlow Street. A month later, at the age of 88, he was dead, a victim of landlord greed and gentrification. Born into wealth, the exuberantly outrageous lad had been cast out by his industrialist dad for—in the fifties—obvious reasons. Taylor Mead, like many of Warhol's aged stars, had to scrabble to keep financially above water. They were difficult to keep track of due to frequent rent-skipping changes of address. In Europe, the puckish Taylor would have been treated like the national treasure he was, and been made a regular on corny talk shows. I had hoped to make a documentary of Taylor's life before he left it, narrated by Johnny Depp. (According to Taylor: "I told Johnny that I'm the most famous actor in the world. Of course Johnny thinks he is, although he's a very sweet guy.") Now it was getting late and I was already drunk trying to keep up with a man in his eighties. After hours of Taylor's wry mutterings, and with chortles still echoing from the elfin 'Leee' Black Childers (that spelling is correct), we decided it was time to take leave of Middle Earth and make a break for reality. . .

News Break, New York, 1963-1965

In 1963, The Beatles appear on the Ed Sullivan Show, John F. Kennedy begins what becomes the National Endowment for the Arts, Martin Luther King "Has a Dream", Burroughs' 'Naked Lunch' is banned in Boston, and he's put on trial. Playboy Magazine is published, but when Hefner features Jane Mansfield on the cover, he gets 'busted' for obscenity. This tasty archival footage, much of it squirreled away in long forgotten family trees, at last saw the light of day in our premier episode. In other news, Bob Dylan records 'The Times They Are A-Changin', and New York's New Bowery Theatre is raided, while Jonas Mekas is arrested for screening Jack Smith's 'Flaming Creatures' and 'Normal Love'. Timothy Leary gets fired from Harvard for testing LSD on students, President Kennedy is assassinated, and Martin Luther King receives the Nobel Peace Prize. President Lyndon Johnson pursues with new vigor the war in Vietnam, and the New York World's Fair opens. New York City is "like living inside a light bulb," according to novelist Truman Capote, and Pop art is featured in all the national magazines. Andy Warhol has his first show of paintings at the Stable Gallery, and critics argue whether "Warhol is realistic" or "turned off to reality. . ."

IN THE BEGINNING, ANDY CREATED...

Everything you do is real, is right.
—Andy Warhol

Victor Bockris: The Factory was born out of the roots of what became the Gay Liberation Movement, which was born out of the Second World War when so many returning soldiers came home with different attitudes toward gay people, because of, ah, some things that had happened in the battlefields. So there was this unusual openness and change, and the gay culture in New York was so creative in the 1950s, so dominated really by gay attitudes or intelligences, that the male groups that came out of the fifties became the trendsetters of the sixties, essentially the amphetamine faggots, the people who Andy drew closest to in the beginning, like Billy Name and Ondine. You knew those people were coming out of a reaction to the fifties... One of the least known periods of the Silver Factory is that early period. Andy is starting to make films but he's still seen as an artist. It's also not known that he did paint, quite a lot in the fifties. He destroyed all the paintings. But he was trying, and he did some works that signaled what was to come.

Victor Bockris wrote the first definitive biography of Warhol in 1989. The two had became close over the years, with Bockris dedicating to Warhol his meticulous>

study of mutual friend William Burroughs. While Warhol moaned that, "Nobody will buy a book about me," his biographer persevered, talking to family, friends, enemies, anyone who had known his taciturn subject from the beginning. Bockris, all proper British disdain and diction, reminded one of a rather dissolute crow. At the time of our interview, he was cohabiting with his demented cat in genteel disarray, well, squalor, at the Chelsea Hotel. We tried to ignore the crimson scribblings covering the walls, as if written in blood. Perhaps he was working on a new book. Bockris had much to say about the Warhol Family, and in the end suffered the same sad fate of many of them—banishment. . . Gerard Malanga, who also lives with a couple of sickly cats, would likewise lose favor with Warhol. But in the beginning, he was the golden wavy-haired boy with the pouting lips, handsome as a Greek god and with a useful talent other than poetry, though neither paid well.

Gerard Malanga: I met Andy in 1962 at a party at the home of Marie Menken* and Willard Maas, who were husband and wife filmmakers. Andy was brought to the party by the poet Charles Henri Ford, who later recommended me to Andy because he needed someone to help him silk screen his paintings. The Pop art movement was still on the runway waiting to take off; they were just starting out, all of them, including Andy. So I had no sense of who Andy was, except when I went back to his house the first day we worked together. Julia, his mom, made lunch for me, and I saw some of his Campbell Soup Can artworks in the living room.

---

*Marie Menken, (1909-1970) the gifted filmmaker often called 'the mother of the avant-garde', took many artists under her ample wing, among them Jonas Mekas and Andy Warhol, whom she would later follow with her camera around the Factory. According to Gerard, when he arrived at the Menken-Maas home on Montague Street in Brooklyn Heights, "Marie was chasing Andy around the kitchen table trying to kiss him." The six-foot-two Menken was hardly a beauty like Ultra Violet or Baby Jane Holzer, but she *was* a Warhol Superstar, making a memorable appearance in one film as a quite effective bull dyke prison guard. Gerard recalled her role in Warhol's 'Blow Job', as the below-camera presence performing fellatio on DeVeren Bookwalter (though some say the chore was done by husband Willard, which would make more sense, since the couple were both considered gay). Gerard also kept for picture posterity the firsts shots of Warhol and him taken together (in a photo booth) which he created as a Christmas card. Written on it, in Gerard's handwriting: 'With love from Andy-Pie and Gerry-Pie'. It was part of his pretending they were a couple.

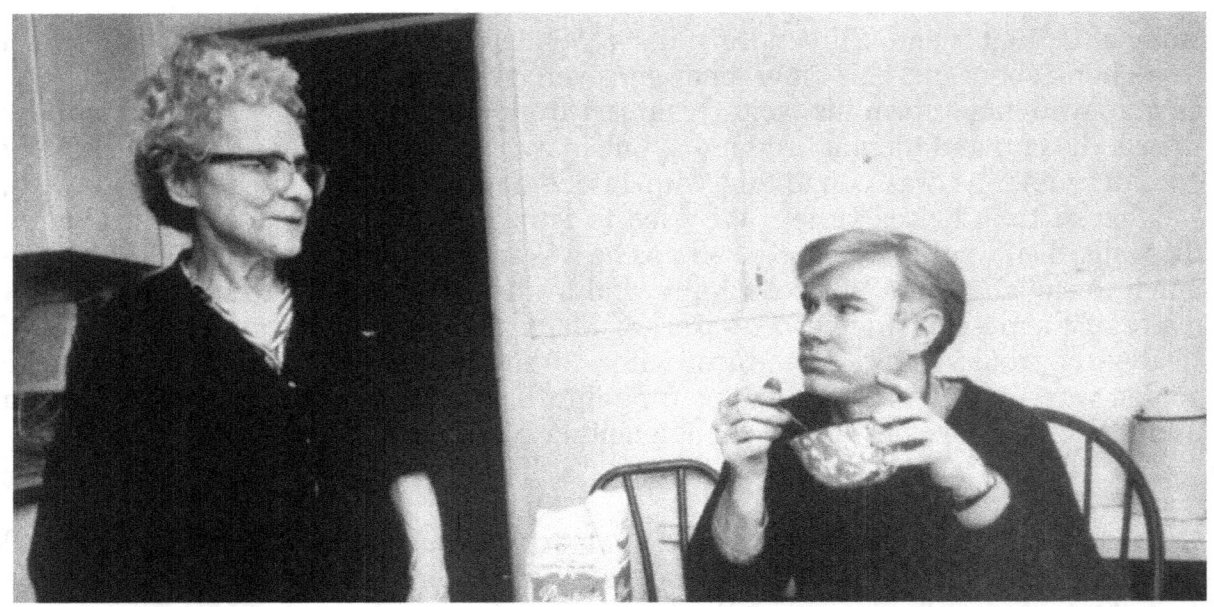

Andy breakfasts with doting mom Julia. The inspiration for much of his early art came from her simple kitchen. (Photo: Ken Hayman/Woodfin Camp, Getty)

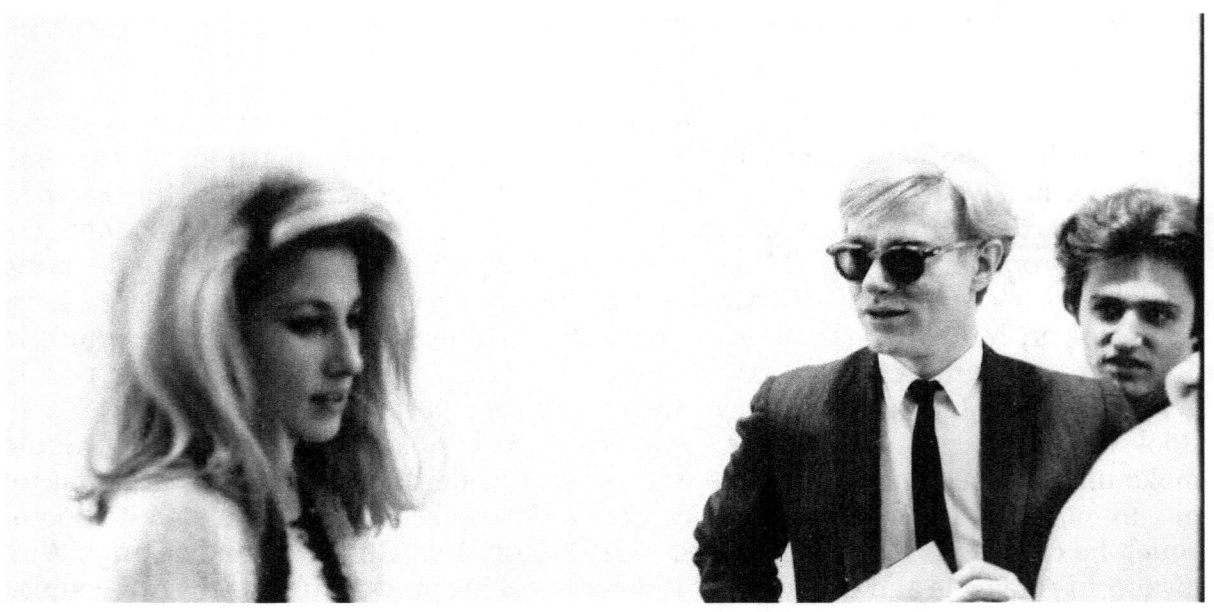

Baby Jane Holzer meets Andy and Gerard at a gallery opening. (Photo: Billy Name)

. . . Everyone we spoke to had vivid memories of the first chance encounter with Warhol, some from waaay back, like Gerard Malanga and Billy Name and Stephen Bruce, whose famous frozen hot chocolate sundae was also unforgettable. . .

Billy Name: When I first met Andy I was just paying my rent by being a waiter in a posh coffee house on the Upper East Side called Serendipity. Andy knew me as one of the waiters, and Stephen Bruce, its founder and I were sort of buddies. . . It's still there, and Stephen is still there. He showed some of Andy's early work in that boutique. Andy would come in all the time; he was Stephen's friend. Stephen would have some of his early collage books and drawings, but Andy was not famous yet.

Stephen Bruce: Andy and Serendipity became connected very early. We opened in 1954, and he discovered us within the next six months. We were in the basement; he just stumbled down with a portfolio of rejects and I was waiting for him with open arms. Andy was very generous. He did about thirty-five portraits of me and dozens of shoe things which I kept in my apartment. I had Andy Warhol work for sale at twenty-five and fifty dollars a shoe drawing. We had a lot of the Factory people working for us, like Billy Name. They were sort of moonlighting at the Factory with Andy Warhol, but they were making frozen hot chocolate and sweeping floors at Serendipity.

'Au recherche du shoe perdu'. . . According to Warhol biographer Victor Bockris, "Serendipity was one of Warhol's first factories. He created works of art right at the table in exchange for meals." However, it was quite obvious that selling drawings in a coffee shop, even one with the clientele that Serendipity attracted (like Jackie Kennedy and kids), was not going to get Andy accepted as an artist.

Stephen Bruce: At first, I never thought Andy changed his shirt. I said, "I see you every day in the same shirt." He said, "Oh no, I bought a hundred of them. I wear a new one every day."

Billy Name: "Gay" wasn't the word then. It was mostly *faggots*—anybody who was successful. There is no really kind term to express the homosexual world before the gay revolution happened. But it was a sub-culture, because everyone was so terrified and paranoid all the time of losing their jobs. . . So the Warhol Factory was very instrumental in allowing those revolutions to happen and become known.

Gerard Malanga: I'd started working for Andy in June of '63, in a building that used to be a firehouse on East 87th Street, two blocks from where Andy lived with his mother. Andy was renting from the city for a hundred dollars, but in October he'd received a notice saying that they were putting the building up for auction. In February, Andy signed the lease on what would become the Silver Factory. When we moved in, all business shifted to the Factory. The townhouse now became off limits to the media, or to even Andy's friends for that matter. In hindsight, he realized that it was a good idea, to keep his situation private. Nobody ever went back up to 89th and Lexington Avenue. The only person there was Julia, his mom.

We'd heard so many stories about Warhol's beloved mother that we put some into the series. Warhol looked so much like Julia that he could have been her clone, and she would seem to be the culmination of every hoary chiché explaining "why good boys go gay." While Julia may have brought Warhol comfort in those early New York years, she could also be cruel to her fragile son, making him feel ugly and unloved. And her constant presence was a reminder of his poverty-stricken childhood. "Ma" kept to her immigrant Slavonic roots, making little effort to master English, and could seem quite crone-like to the uninitiated, especially when she drank. She roamed the cluttered townhouse with her yowling collection of quasi-feral cats, a scene from the pages of a grim European folk tale. By the advent of the sixties, Warhol wisely decided to banish Mom to the basement.

Billy Name: At the time I was a lighting designer for the Judson Dance Company. At my apartment on East 5th Street, I had covered the interior with aluminium foil, the telephone, the toilet, everything. Ray Johnson brought Andy to my silver apartment one night, and Andy said, "Billy I just got this great loft uptown and would you do to my loft what you've done to your apartment?" I went up to look at it, a decrepit old hat factory. The floor was concrete; the walls were crumbling concrete. Andy had set up a painting area in the front of the loft where windows were. He could only paint in the daytime because there were no electrical outlets. So he needed someone with skills for electrical installations, and I had all that from my theatrical experience. The first thing I did was to install overhead lights, spot lights, and the sound system, and make special places for Andy to work. Then I did, as an installation, an event, and a happening, the silvering of the Factory. Everything was painted silver; even the column were wrapped in foil. The floor was silver, the walls, the furniture, the toilet, the phone *(laugh)*. The guy would come to collect the coins and then replace the silver box with a new black one, which I would silver all over again.

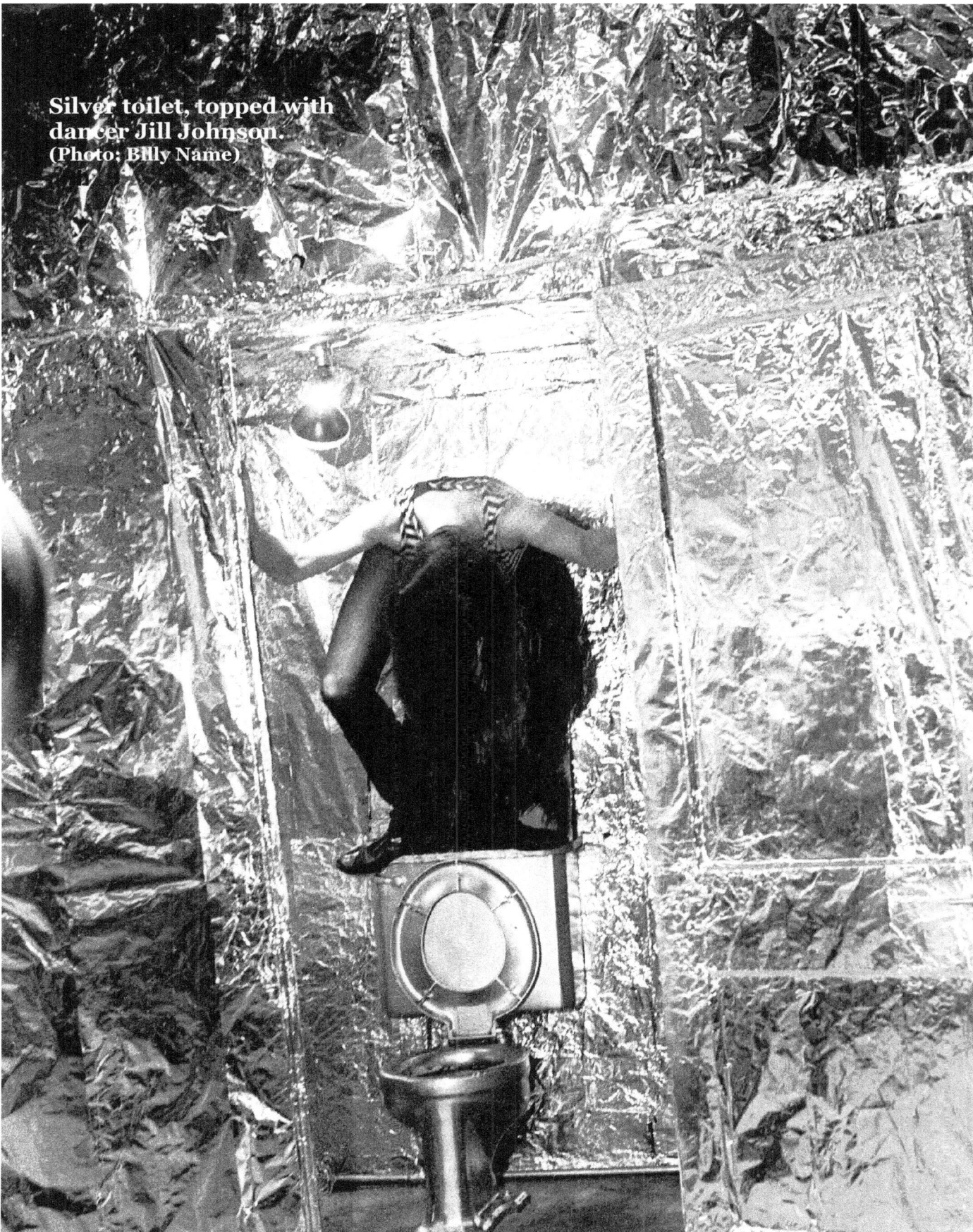

Silver toilet, topped with dancer Jill Johnson. (Photo: Billy Name)

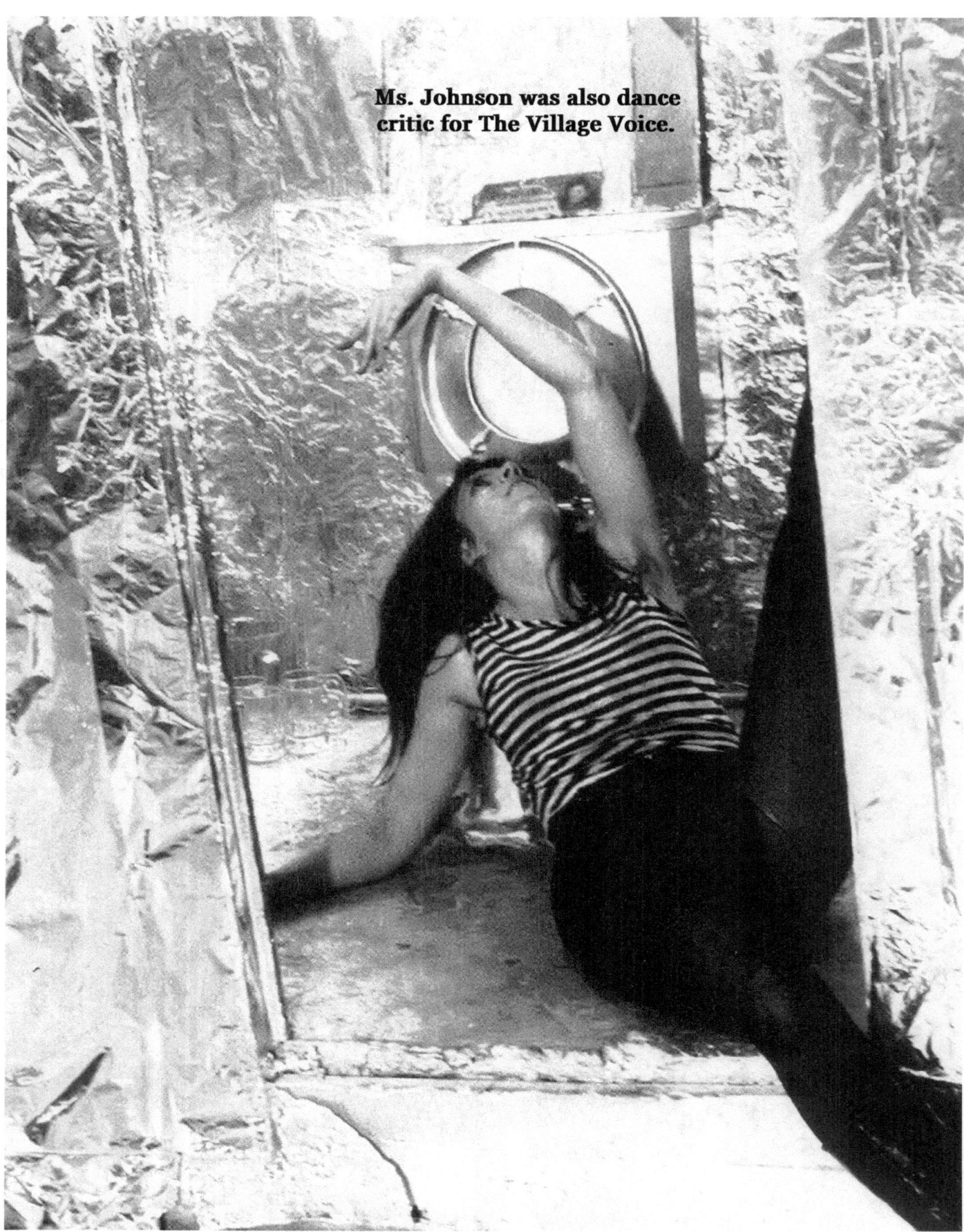

Ms. Johnson was also dance critic for The Village Voice.

Mary Woronov: The first time I came to the Factory, I was an art student, and Cornell University had this program where everybody had to go and live at an artist's studio. Rauchenberg's studio was all white. Then we saw Warhol's studio, which was black and silver. I could not see any art anywhere. Then Gerard (Malanga) came out of the mist. Earlier that year, Gerard had picked me up at Cornell. He'd come up to read poetry, because he was a poet, you know. I couldn't care less about poetry.

Gerard Malanga: Andy was working towards a show at the Ferus Gallery in Los Angeles. We were silk-screening a lot of Elvis Presley paintings that were for the show, as well as Elizabeth Taylor's portraits. We were storing them in the back of the fire house. One night, there was a huge leak in the ceiling. The next day, we discovered that all these canvases were damaged. We made a new screen and re-did that image that was slightly different, and I was instructed to shred those paintings. I did shred some of them, but I got distracted because we were doing so many different things that I neglected to finish that job.

According to Gerard, who should know, those rejected paintings that did not get shredded have been "popping out everywhere, being sold as authentic Andy Warhol." (With all the other 'unauthenticated' Warhols crawling out of the woodwork these days, The Warhol Foundation for the Arts must have its hands full). Warhol's output from that period, roughly 1962-1964, has been the most popular, literally flying off the auction shelves. First they crawl, and then they fly. . . A celebrity death helps. Elizabeth Taylor had not been cold 24 hours before a Warhol portrait from 1963, 'Liz#5, Early Colored Liz' was put on the market by Phillips de Pury & Company. The buyer paid $26.9 million for one of thirteen. That same week, a bidding war broke out at Christie's for a 1963-64 self-portrait, which showed the artist in four photo-booth poses. The 'winner' paid $38.4 million. Also in recent news: Warhol's 1966 print of surly, side-burned, leather-jacketed outlaw biker Brando in 'The Wild One' sold for $23.7 million. In the film, someone asks, "What are you rebelling against?" Brando responds, "What'd ya got?" The budget was $2 million.

Andy Warhol: Making money is art.

Leo Castelli: It's difficult to talk about Andy as a person because he's terribly spare in his emotional manifestations. He almost created a culture, but it was based on material that was handy. . . He had a genius of putting all those things together, and making a work of art of the whole climate here in New York.

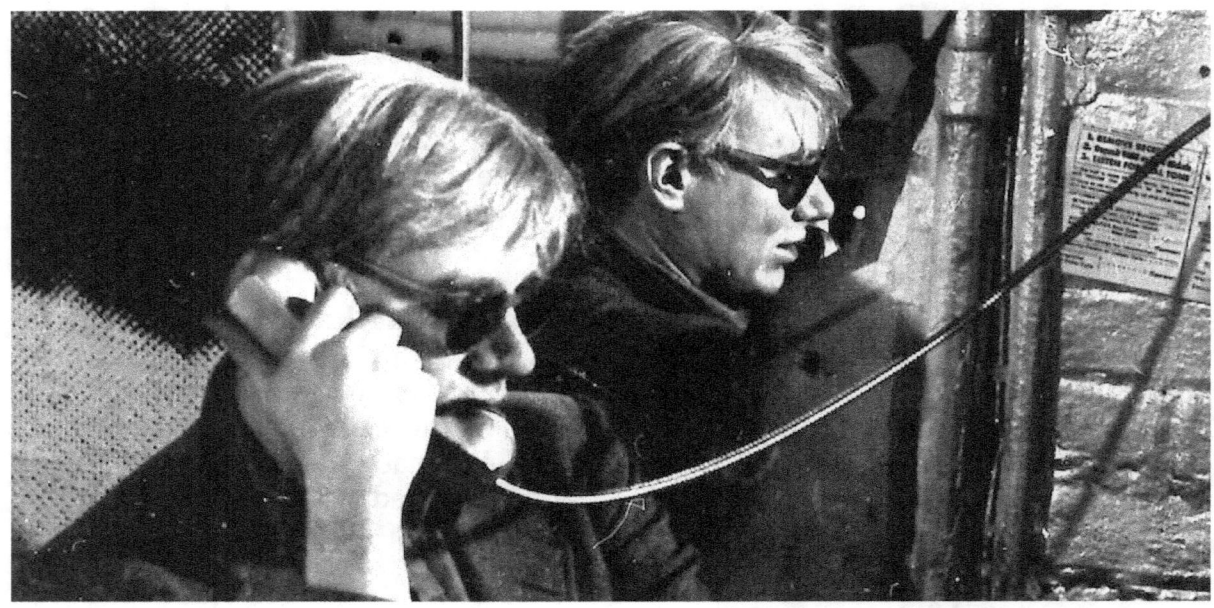
"Operator, I lost my dime. again." Andy tries to phone home from the silver-painted pay phone.

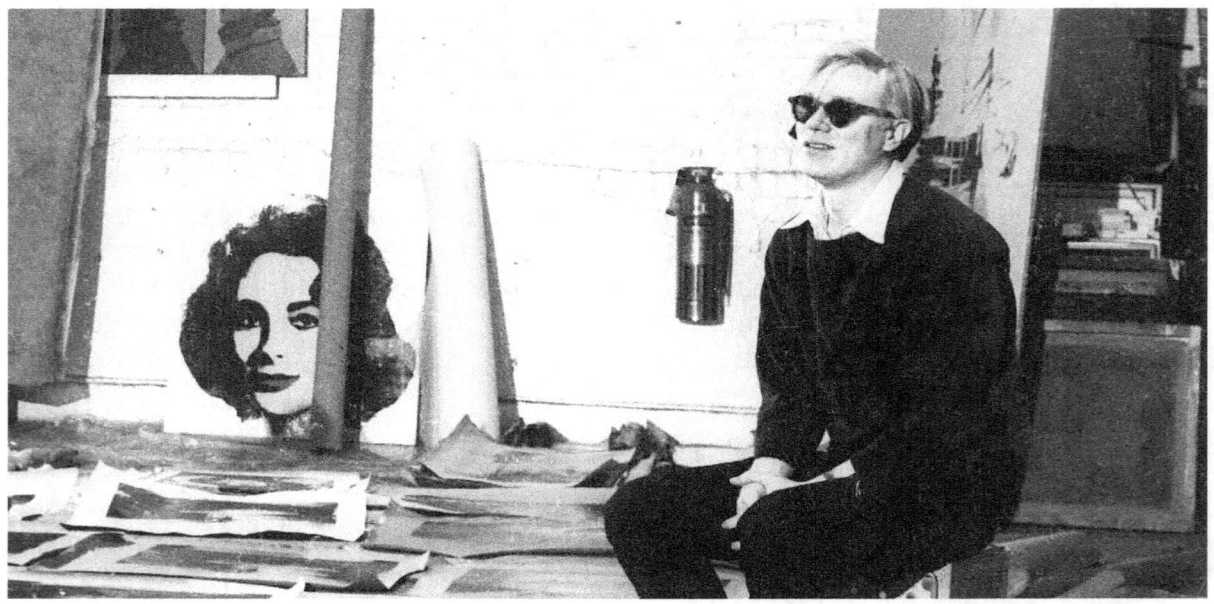
Andy with fellow icons Elizabeth and Elvis, who had been inspired to emulate, in 'Jailhouse Rock', Brando's legendary rebel in 'The Wild One'. (Photos: Billy Name)

Considered to be at the peak of his career by 1964, Warhol defected from Elinor Ward's gallery for the long-pined after Castelli, who, with the help of Ivan Karp and Henry Geldzahler, was taking over the art world. Billy Name—then Linich—handled the tense negotiations with the warring dealers. Castelli would soon have his own frustrations with the quixotic artist, who had his share of detractors. His messy silk-screening methods and sloppy reproductions seemed a clever mockery of mass production, a psychic slap in the face to those who still thought of him as merely a commercial illustrator, or perhaps a message about chaos and the randomness of existence. The art world eagerly awaited the answer in his next 'statement', which was not exactly reassuring: "My work won't last. I was using cheap paint." . . . Warhol had more important things on his mind than dissolving paintings. He had just been to Hollywood! He and Taylor Mead had even made a movie out there! Well, sort of—the hilarious 'Tarzan and Jane revisited, Sort Of' would never be released.

Andy Warhol: Vacant, vacuous California was everything I wanted to mould my life into—plastic, white on white. I wanted Tab Hunter to play me in the story of my life.

Gerard Malanga: A friend of Andy's, a painter named Wynn Chamberlain, took an interest in driving cross-country to Los Angeles for the Ferus Gallery show, and neither Andy nor I drive. Then Taylor Mead took an interest, so Andy invited Taylor and Wynn, and they did the driving in Wynn's station wagon. Andy and I sat in the back seat, luxuriating across country. . .

One wonders about the wisdom of putting Taylor, in thrall to heroic quantities of Quaaludes, cannabis, and assorted alcoholic refreshments, in charge of a moving vehicle. Warhol, ever budget conscious, wondered about the frequent 'pit stops' at gas stations along the route. Were they driving a guzzler? No, they were harboring one. Taylor admitted he'd been giving blow jobs to the young station attendants.

Taylor Mead: We drove across the country, because Andy didn't want to fly. Later he said he just wanted to see the country. So, we drove across the United States with Gerard and Wynn Chamberlain, and as we approached the West Coast, the motel signs were all . . . Pop art! Andy had done the Campbell Soup Cans a few months before, and it was like Pop art was meeting the great *King* of Pop art from the East!

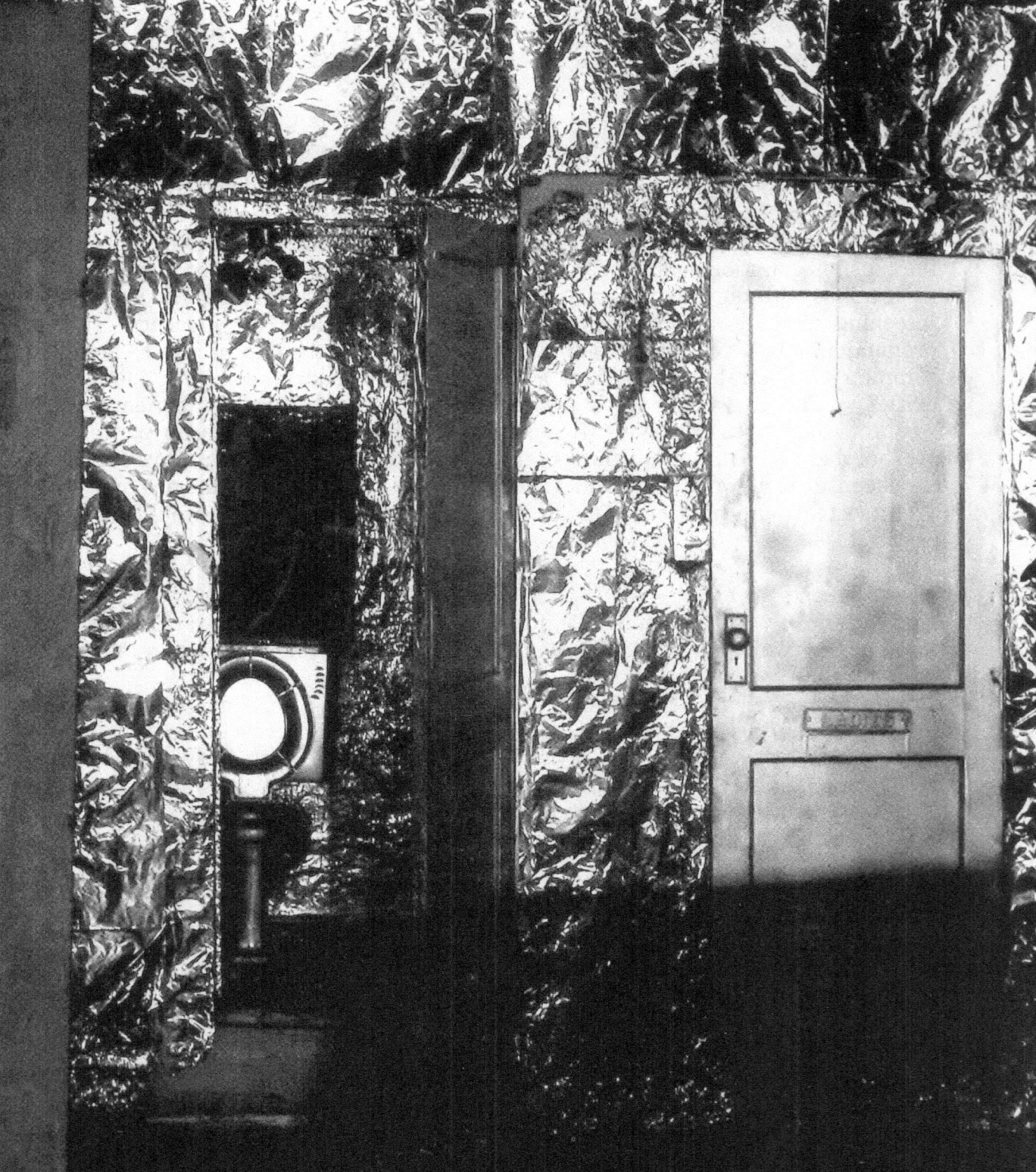

Everyone is 'On The Road'. . . except photographer Billy Name

. . . Pop-realist painter Wynn Chamberlain happened to be more than simply another zany traveling companion. Art curator Henry Geldzahler had told Warhol it was enough already with soup cans and coke bottles, that "Maybe everything isn't so fabulous in America." Chamberlain suggested to Warhol that he create a series of silk screens depicting violence. Newspaper headlines and AP photos of suicides and car crashes would eventually litter the Factory floor. Warhol's Death Series was divided into two parts, the first on famous deaths, the second on people no one had heard of, because he "thought it would be nice for these unknown people to be remembered." So Warhol hadn't invited Wynn on the road trip just because he had a handy car and a driver's licence. Why Taylor went along for the ride is quite another story. . .

Taylor Mead: In Kansas, I picked this sort of pseudo-modern truck stop full of truck drivers and young locals, and when we walked in it was like we were from another planet. People all came over. "Who are you? What are you doing here?" in a kind of American open way, but it was a little scary, like we were too freakish for them. So I let Andy pick the rest of the places, like this motel we were staying in. . . Andy said, "Oh, Taylor that bellhop really likes you, but he wanted ten bucks." Andy had this fucking Carte Blanche account, but he wasn't about to spend any money. The next morning Andy was like, *(mimicking)* "Taaaylor, the bellhop came into my room and wanted ten bucks, so I said, "The rich guy is down the hall." I told Andy I didn't have the ten bucks. And there's Andy, soooo disappointed that I didn't have a good story to tell him . . . Finally we got to L.A., and Brooke Hayward, Dennis Hopper's wife at the time, called her father, Broadway producer Leland Hayward. He had a suite at the Beverly Hills Hotel, so we moved in, and Irving Blum gave us a phone number for "anything we needed." We would have had the best hustlers in L.A., but Andy would go, "Oh Taylor, you call. My mom brought me up to never push yourself forward."

According to biographer Victor Bockris, Warhol's mom had probably also been responsible for her son's reluctance to fly. Although he'd already flown around the world in the fifties with a former boyfriend, Julia harped about the death of Elizabeth Taylor's husband Mike Todd in a small plane, instilling in Warhol from then on a lifetime fear of flying. Taylor Mead was having lunch with Julia, listening to her say, "Andy no fly. Too many big shots die in planes." His version of the famous road trip may have been recounted to other biographers, bartenders, and anyone else who would buy him a drink, but it still had us on the floor when we shot the interview in his local "watering hole." I mentioned that I hadn't heard that term in a long time, and he suggested another scotch. Revived, Taylor continued. And continued. . .

Taylor Mead: But the trip to California was amazing! Andy was already a sensation, and we were with Marcel Duchamp. But at an opening at the Pasadena Art Museum, a cameraman from Time pushed me away to take a picture of Marcel. I said, "I'm Taylor Mead, who the hell do you think you are?" Then we made a huge party with all the wealthy of L.A. and I couldn't get in! Marcel came out and took me to his table. Later in New York, he invited Ultra Violet and me to his house. I saw a painting on the wall, and said, "My God, that's the most beautiful Matisse I've ever seen!" I did not know he was married to the daughter of Matisse.

Vincent Fremont: All artists are visual beings. They should be allowed to do anything they want in the visual realm. Andy took the heat, coming out of history and Marcel Duchamp and that era. He took it a huge step forward. The Campbell's Soup Cans—they said, "But that's not art!" I still see this at retrospectives. There will be two old ladies in front of the canvas clucking, "*This* isn't art." But that's what distinguishes any artist who's talented and has a vision. They see the world differently.

I'm sure those old ladies had their own vision of Campbell's soup, since the company has been around forever. We found old cartoons of the cherubic soup kids slurping, a fifties commercial of a perfect housewife scanning rows of soup cans, threw in pictures of Warhol in the market filling his cart with his 'models', seasoned them with a few finished paintings, added a pinch of cheerful music, and stirred it all together. Voila! Art! . . . Henry Geldzahler, arbiter of modern art, might have thought otherwise, but he did compare Warhol to the playful Duchamp, who had also once been fascinated with repetitive imagery.

Henry Geldzahler: The Campbell's Soup Can was the 'Nude Descending a Staircase' of Pop art. Here was an image that became the overnight rallying point of the sympathetic, and bane of the hostile. Warhol captured the imagination of the media and the public as had no other artist. Andy was Pop, and Pop was Andy.

Taylor Mead: As Andy used to say, timing is everything, and pop schmop. But it was the right time to turn the spotlight of commerciality back onto the corporations and say, "This Campbell Soup Can won't cost you 25 cents, it'll cost you 25 hundred dollars." And people bought it! I think the rich like to be slapped in the face a little bit. . . But then again, anyone who bought those earlier cans is a billionaire. We semi-famous people should know better.

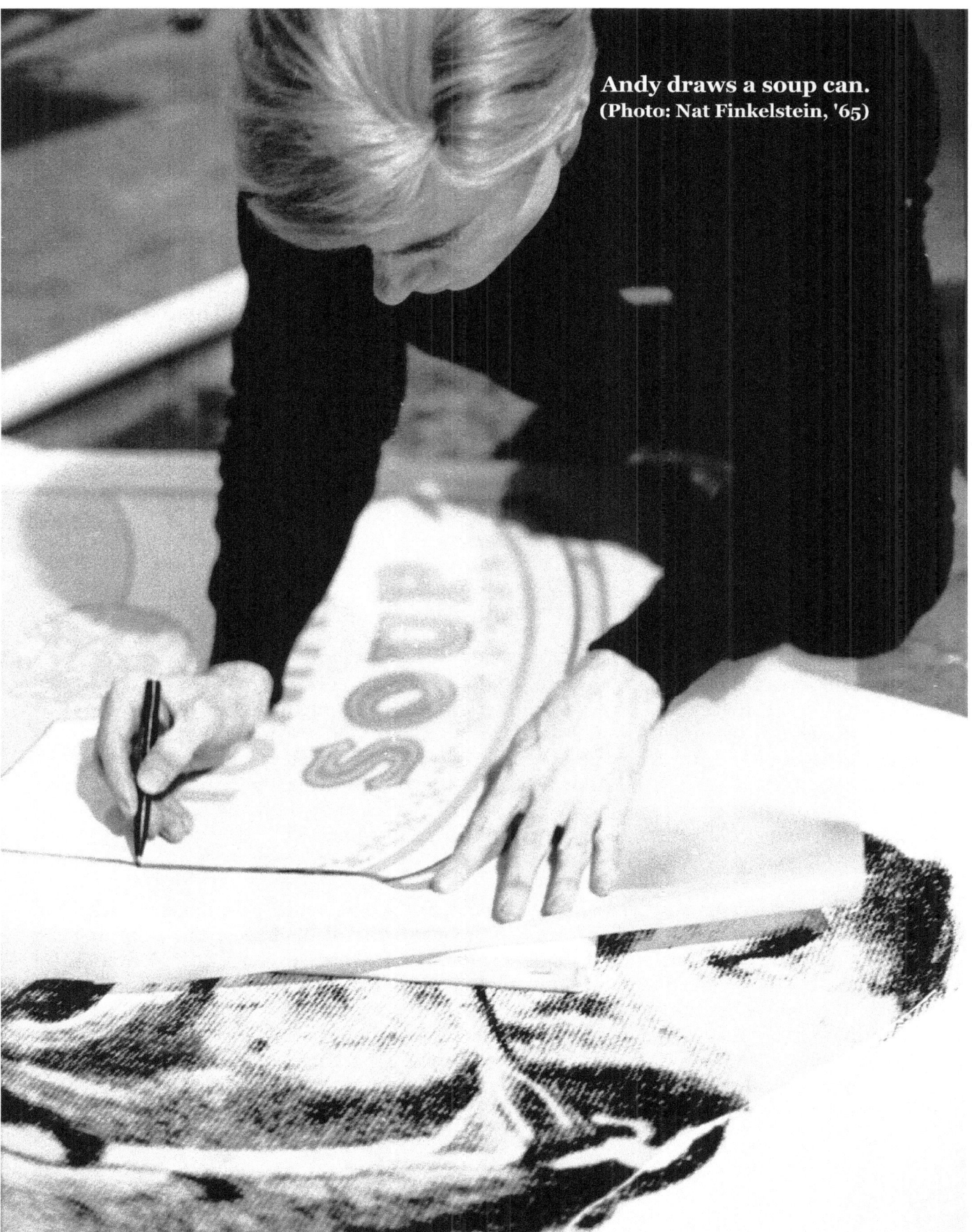

Andy draws a soup can.
(Photo: Nat Finkelstein, '65)

Warhol's Soup Can series of 32 paintings had a less than stellar opening at the Ferus Gallery in Los Angele—only five were sold, for $100 each. The art dealer Irving Blum bought them back to keep the set intact. (In 1996, the Soup Cans sold to the Museum of Modern Art in New York for $15 million). That first exhibition had closed in L.A. on August 4, 1962, the same day Marilyn Monroe died. Warhol had immediately decided to paint a series of Marilyn portraits. "I wouldn't have stopped Monroe from killing herself," he said. "Everyone should do whatever they want to do." Warhol did twenty-three Marilyn portraits, using a publicity photo for the 1953 film, 'Niagara'— after which he did the Marilyn diptych, 100 repetitions of the same face, the colored paint slathered on the canvas made the screens clog, giving each Marilyn a slightly different expression... The speed and endless possibilities of duplication in the silk-screening process suited Warhol's talent as a conceptualist. Though some considered this new art to be a direct descendant of Dada-ism, Duchamp, the pre-eminent Surrealist, did not consider Warhol's work to be remotely connected, saying it "applied to today."

Leo Castelli: The key figure in my gallery is somebody I never showed, and that was Marcel Duchamp. Painters who were not influenced by Duchanp don't belong here.

Louis Waldon: I met Duchamp in a coffee house in New York. He used to show up and play 'Go' all the time. He was a brilliant man, very funny, nice, too. Andy was totally influenced by him. Art was *dead*. Anything can be art, found objects that everybody was picking up. Smashed beer cans off the street; "Hey, look at this! Put it on the wall. Oh, it's art!" And Andy saw that everybody was feeling that way. So he started making all this art. Some of it was really bad. Andy kept them. He said, "That is art, man." Now these things are selling for a fortune.

The familiar images of Marilyns and Elizabeths, Soup Cans and Brillo Boxes, Cows and Flowers, would make Andy Warhol the iconic artist of his time. But back in 1963, Warhol's Soup Cans had been considered a byword for bad art. Marcel Duchamp, by then considered the "spiritual godfather of Pop Art" liked Warhol's work: "If a man takes fifty soup cans and puts them on a canvas, it is not the retinal image that concerns us," he said. "What concerns us is the concept that he *wants* to put fifty soup cans on a canvas." Warhol's favorite dish goes on... Campbell is releasing a special edition of its tomato soup, imbedded with the immortal phrase: "Everyone will be famous for fifteen minutes."

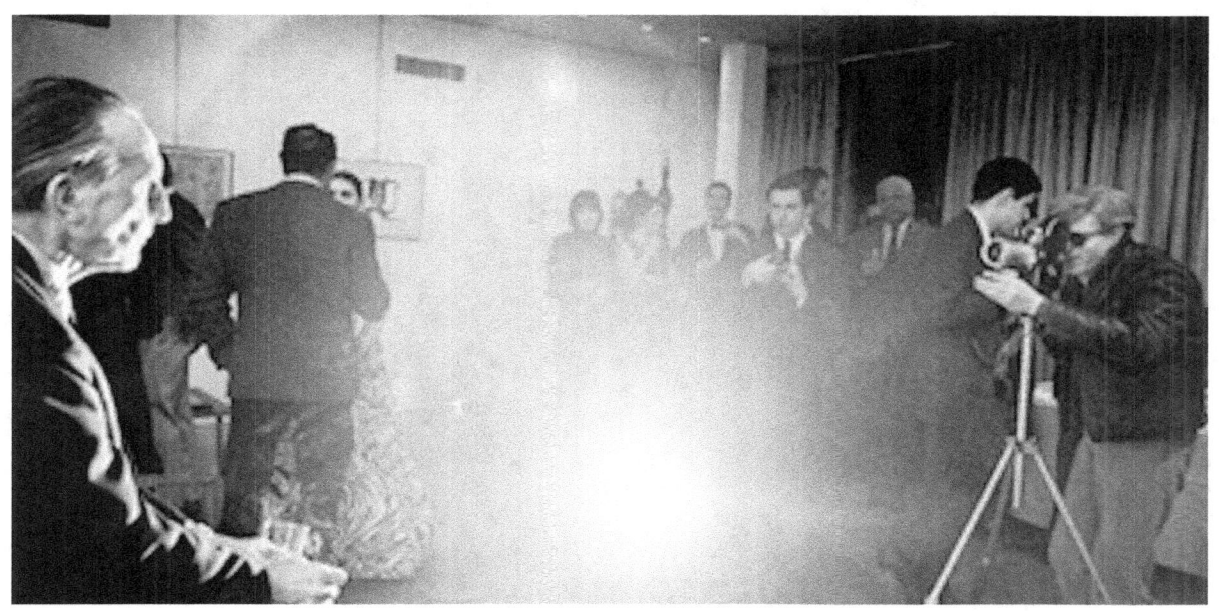

**Marcel Duchamp patiently poses for Andy, whose work he liked despite reservations.
(Photo: Nat Finkelstein)**

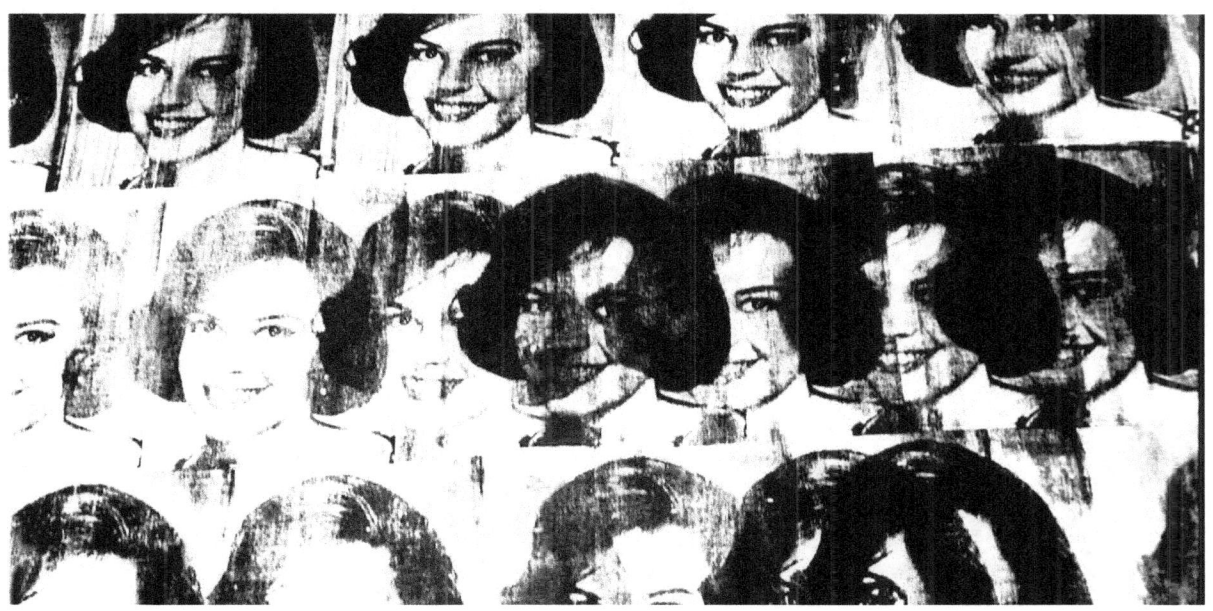

**A familiar image. Publicity still of Natalie Wood, silk-screened and multiplied into art.
(Photo: Billy Name)**

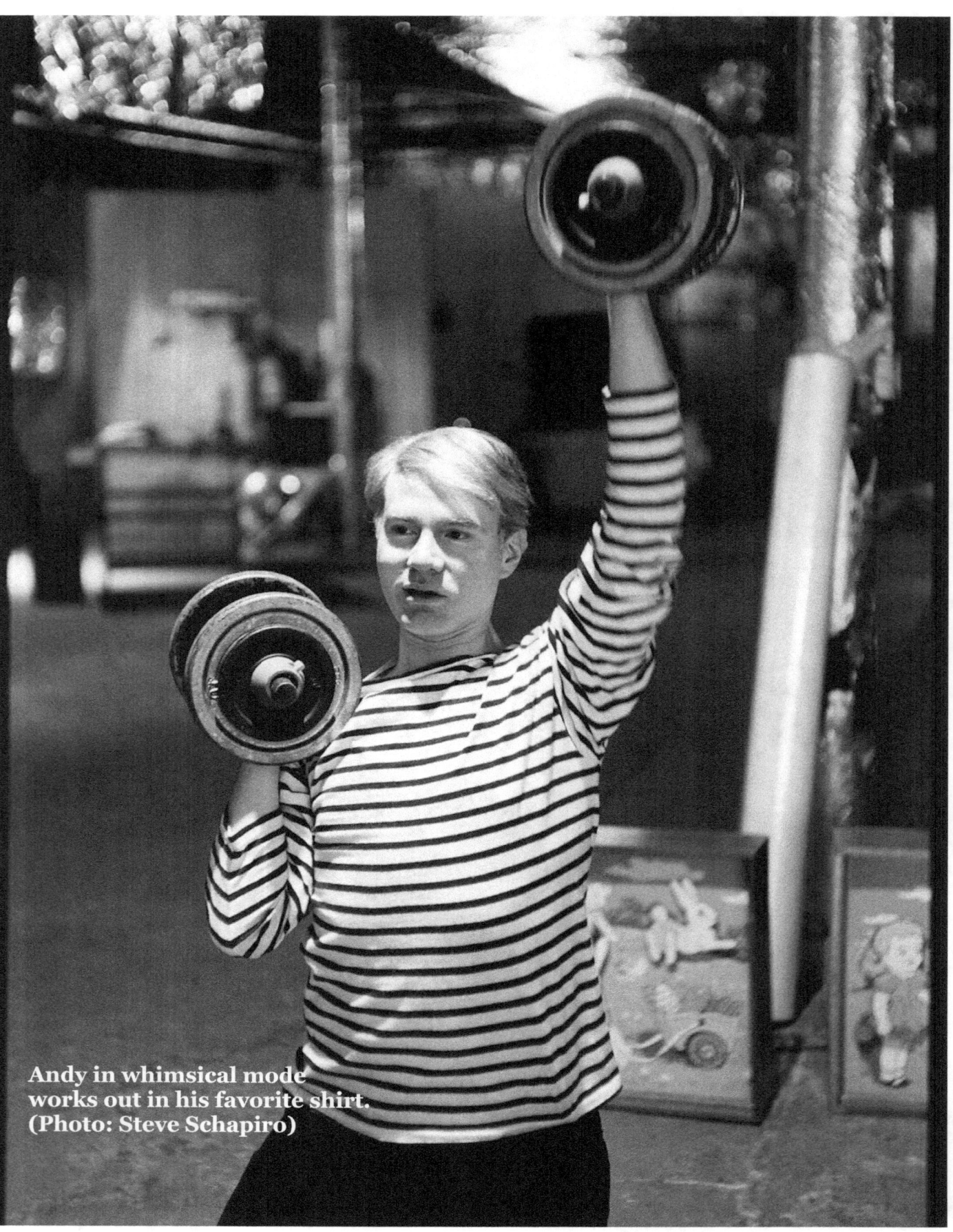

Andy in whimsical mode works out in his favorite shirt. (Photo: Steve Schapiro)

Billy Name: Andy had won awards in New York for his commercial graphics design. He wasn't just a fresh phenomenon, a guy from Pittsburgh who came to New York and then started doing fine art. No, he was integrated into the art community. He knew my friend Ray Johnson, this Zen master of committed collage as real life; he knew the experimental composers John Cage and La Monte Young, the underground filmmaker Jonas Mekas.

Victor Bockris: Billy Linich, who changed his name to Billy Name, was the manager of the Factory. He was somewhat the equivalent of Gerard in many ways. He was very good-looking. He had the 'New Look'. He loved Andy. I think they had a brief *liaison dangereuse* at the beginning. But it wasn't like anyone rejected each other.

Billy Name: Andy and I had been for a time lovers, so we were intimately synchronized. We loved each other, and I'm talking in an altruistic sense. And we loved what we were doing. I had the skills that he needed to free him to make the art. Then I could make my art as the arena. . . That whole thing started to break down somewhat when people from the outside came in to something that had already jelled and were expecting something from it.

Nat Finkelstein: Andy needed an established photojournalist, because of that, uh, group surrounding him, people who were gay, people who were queer, people who were not going to get into a major magazine. I had that entrée. My God, by the time I went to Warhol, I had already shot two popes and a couple of presidents, so I was not awed by these people. The major photography magazine at that time was Pageant. I had essays there. I had stuff in the New York Times Sunday Magazine. Andy saw that. I was covering the anti-war demonstrations in Washington, documenting American society, and it looked to me that Warhol and his Factory were going to be a major part of American cultural society. "This is happening! This is what is going on!" I wanted to do an essay on Andy and the Factory. Andy wanted to break out of the New York culture womb, and go nationwide, so it was kind of a marriage of convenience. Besides, I liked the girls. After a while it was a pleasure. I was the only heterosexual guy with a bunch of beautiful women.

Not quite, Nat. Photographer Steve Schapiro also covered bold faces (the Kennedys, Martin Luther King). His often whimsical portraits of Warhol from 1963 to 1966 ensured him a place in pop cultural history. According to Steve, who I saw in Europe for Paris Photo: "Andy hid behind a posed emotionless mask which allowed him to watch everything happening around him without showing any sign of a reaction."

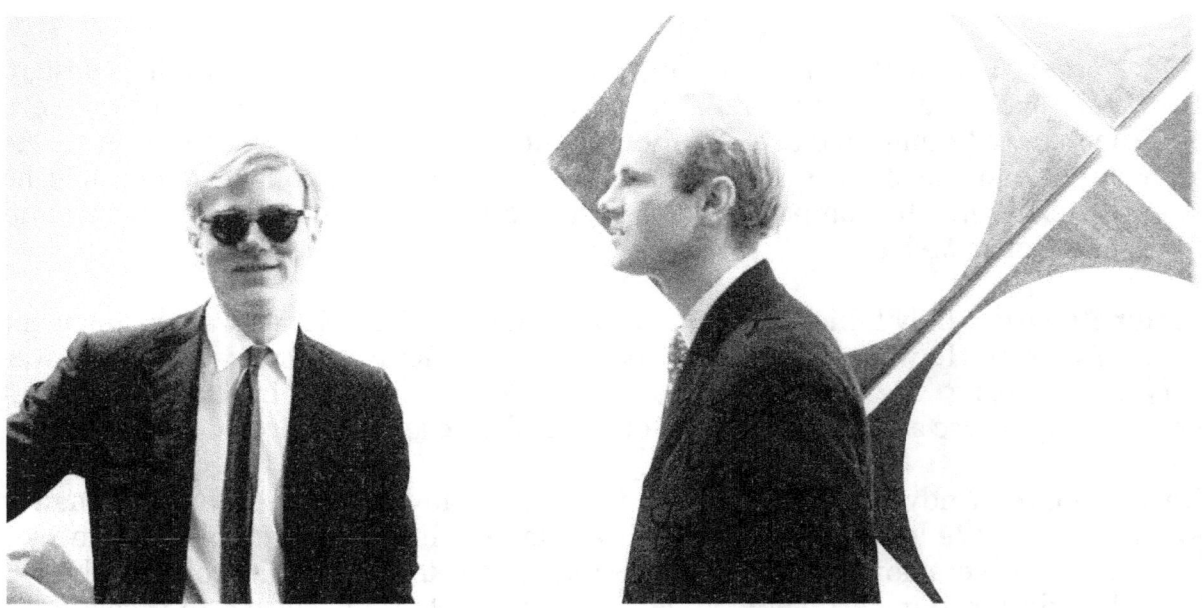

Andy and fellow artist Jim Rosenquist, also with the Leo Castelli Gallery, attend an opening for Robert Indiana, famous for his tilted 'LOVE' letters.

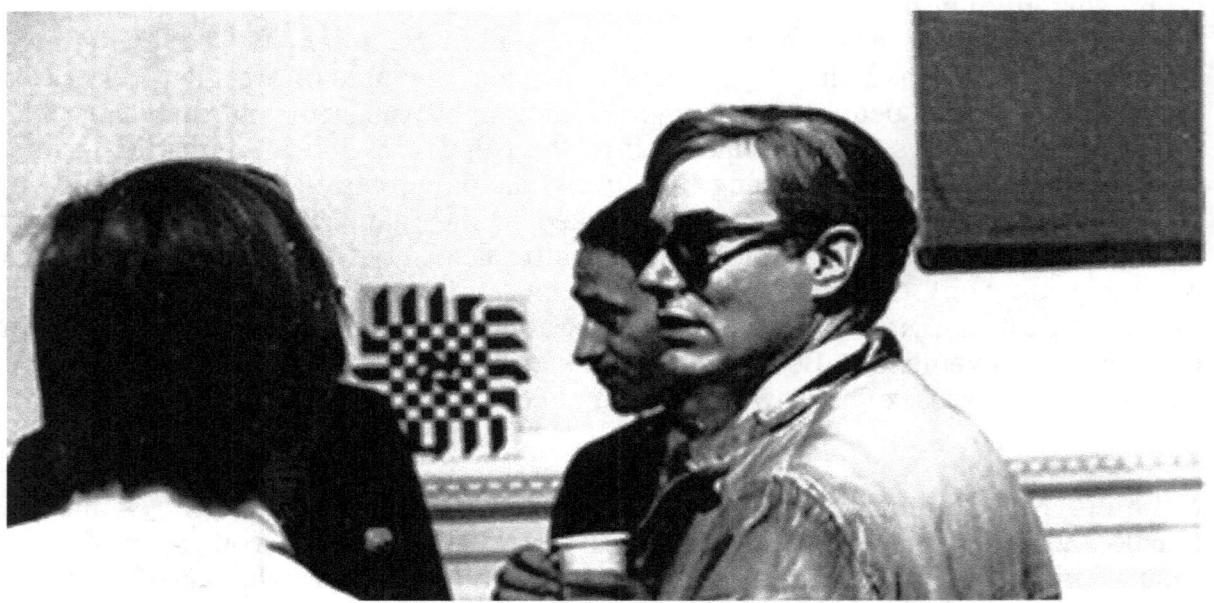

Andy attends a party for Salvador Dali at Henry Geldzahler's chic, art-filled apartment (note small Marcel Duchamp in B.G.), with experimental avant-garde filmmaker Jonas Mekas. (Photos: Billy Name)

... Meanwhile, Nat Finkelstein was so busy taking photos and other liberties that he rareley got a shot of himself. However, the few we saw of him and Edie Sedgwick, with whom he was close, confirm that he was an affable, fairly good-looking guy, and only became trollish and curmudgeonly with age. Interviewed in Paris where he was having a one-man show, he was refreshingly frank, if a tad pugnacious, especially after a few flutes of good French champagne, informing us that he had been "the only photographer who had the guts to give Andy orders when taking his picture." This certainly must have endeared him to the Factory regulars. But Nat did say that he had made a good friend (not in the biblical sense) of the striking Mary Woronov, though she not share his opinions of her pals Billy and Ondine. And she could be opinionated. Warhol was a bit cowed by Mary; she clocked in at six feet, with a mighty intimidating scowl. He wanted to call her 'Mary Might', but she promptly nixed that idea...

Mary Woronov: The guys who hung around Warhol, Ondine, Billy Name—these were really, really intelligent and gay people. They were not allowed to be gay and they were terribly repressed and they ended up being screaming lunatics but really smart and really funny and I was attracted to it... Well, that and drugs.

Ultra Violet: I became Ultra Violet in 1963 when I met Andy Warhol. At the time, I was madly in love and enchanted with Salvador Dali. He used to have a phenomenal five o'clock tea, and one day in walked this personage. I thought it was a woman of a certain age. The hair was uneven, black, white, gray. Her voice was very weird. You felt you had to put a coin in her mouth for her to say something, coming from the other world. Anyway, that person said to me, "Well, you are so beautiful that we should make a movie together." I said, "When, where, how?" He said, "Tomorrow at the Factory." I said, "What is your name?" Andy Warhol. I had vaguely heard of him in the art world. But in '63 that little dwafe, dwaf, dwarf* was totally unknown.

---

*Ultra Violet, being French, had an interesting take on the English language, even after being here lo these many eons, which charmed the pants (almost) off our French camerman. He was old enough to remember her smoldering Hedy Lamarrish beauty, and I could tell he was flirting and going into producer mode to show off. (He's made about 400 documentaries). So after a couple of hours I let him finish the interview, what the hell. Women open up to handsome producers easier than neurotic filmmakers. I had better luck with Jonas, who has an eye for the ladies, even in his eighties...

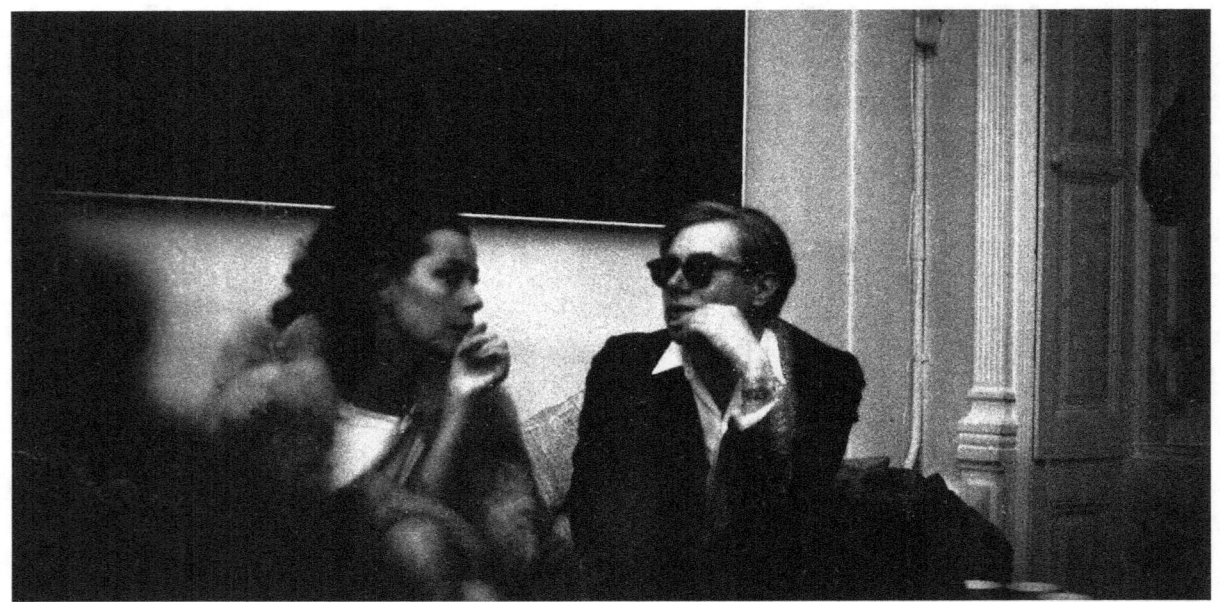
Ultra Violet meets Andy Warhol for the first time at her lover Salvador Dali's cocktail party.

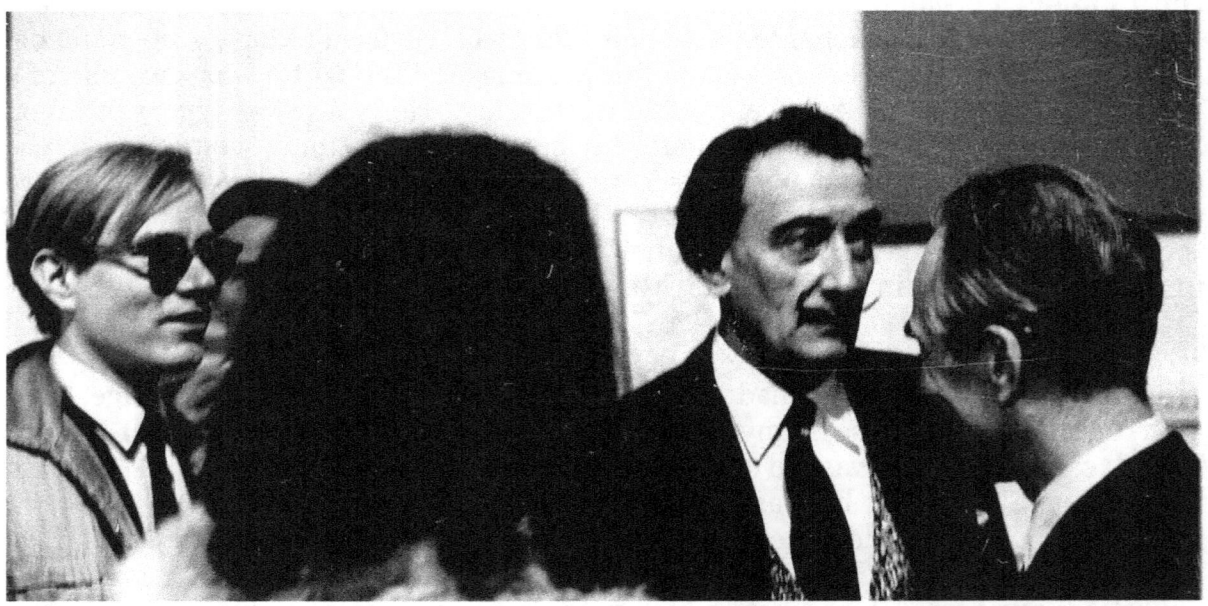
"Leave Dali; Dali's too old." Ultra torn between Warhol and Dali. Art dealer Leo Castelli looks on. (Photos: Billy Name)

Jonas Mekas: In Andy's cinema there were several stages. First, the silents. The camera gazes for a long time. 'Sleep', 'Haircut','Mushroom', 'Eat'. Then he went into sound. I will tell you why Andy went into sound. I filmed 'The Brig', for the Living Theatre, and the theater was closed by the police. We went onstage with the actors one night, to film secretly. I needed a sound camera, so I chose an Auricon, which was used by journalists and news people because they could immediately develop it. The evening after I shot 'The Brig', I invited Andy and the Living Theatre people. Andy was so impressed what you can do with this camera, so easy, one person. By myself, I was a one-man team *(laugh)*. That is when he went into this early sound period.

Victor Bockris: Andy had started to make films, but it wasn't known yet. So he was still seen as an artist. Which means a more limited audience, a more limited press. So, in a sense those were quiet days. There were some beautiful photos of Andy and Gerard making the Brillo Boxes, where you see the whole room full of these old boxes, and there's the two of them crawling around the floor doing bits and pieces.

Along with Billy's iconic photos, we licensed clips from a film by Marie Menken, in her own unique scatter-shot style, of the boys and their boxes, scrambling around like factory workers on overtime, which I suppose one could say they actually were. When we later attached Menken's manic filmmaking to sixties archive footage of the real thing, actual Brillo Boxes being packed and loaded on to a truck, you couldn't tell the difference. One Warhol Brillo Box was put on auction at Christie's in 2010. The estimate was $6-800,000. It sold for $3,050, 500.

Gerard Malanga: Andy was having a show in April at the Stable Gallery, various wooden boxes that we had to line up in an assembly line and silk screen. That was Billy's first photo documentation. He was actually photographing what that was all about, in the terms of the first art project of the Factory.

Billy Name: Gerard and I would paint the base coats on sheets of brown paper, to make them look like cardboard boxes, then Gerard and Andy would silk-screen the designs on the sides. The first show that Andy had at the Stable Gallery was all the Brillo Boxes and the Campbell's boxes, and I designed the layout. At the gallery, it was the day of the show and the boxes were just being delivered. Andy had to go home and get dressed for the opening, and he said, "Billy go over and set up the show!" *(laugh)* So I said, "I'll just do it like a warehouse."

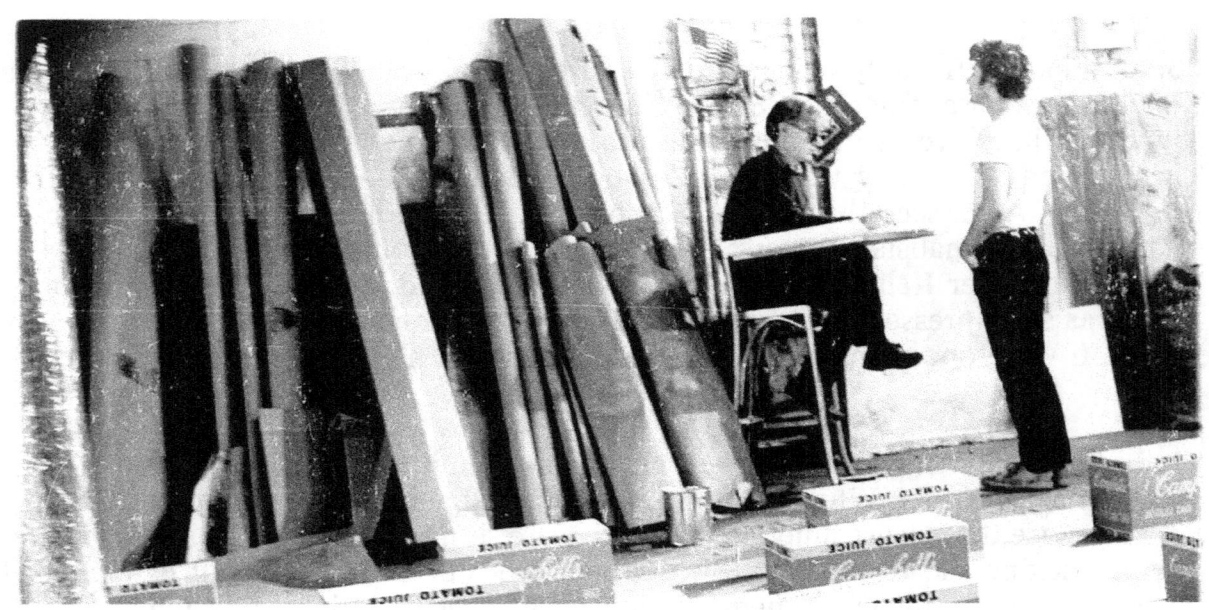

Andy, Gerard, and Billy work overtime for the Stable Gallery opening. (Photos: Billy Name)

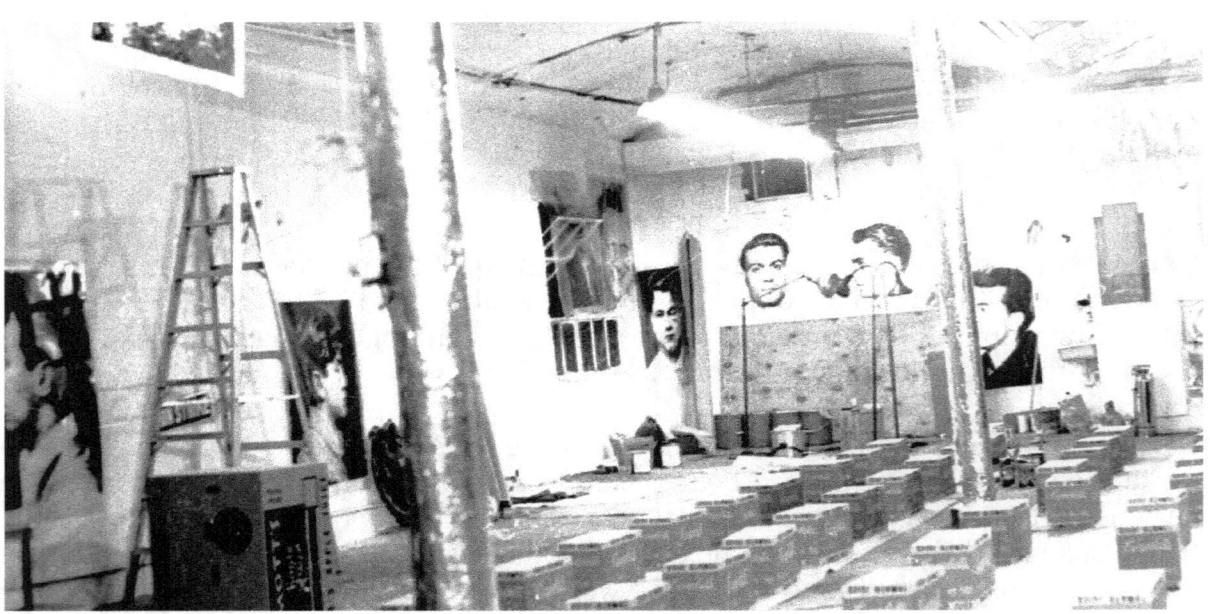

Campbell's Boxes in production at the Silver Factory. On the walls: mug shots from '13 Most Wanted Men'.

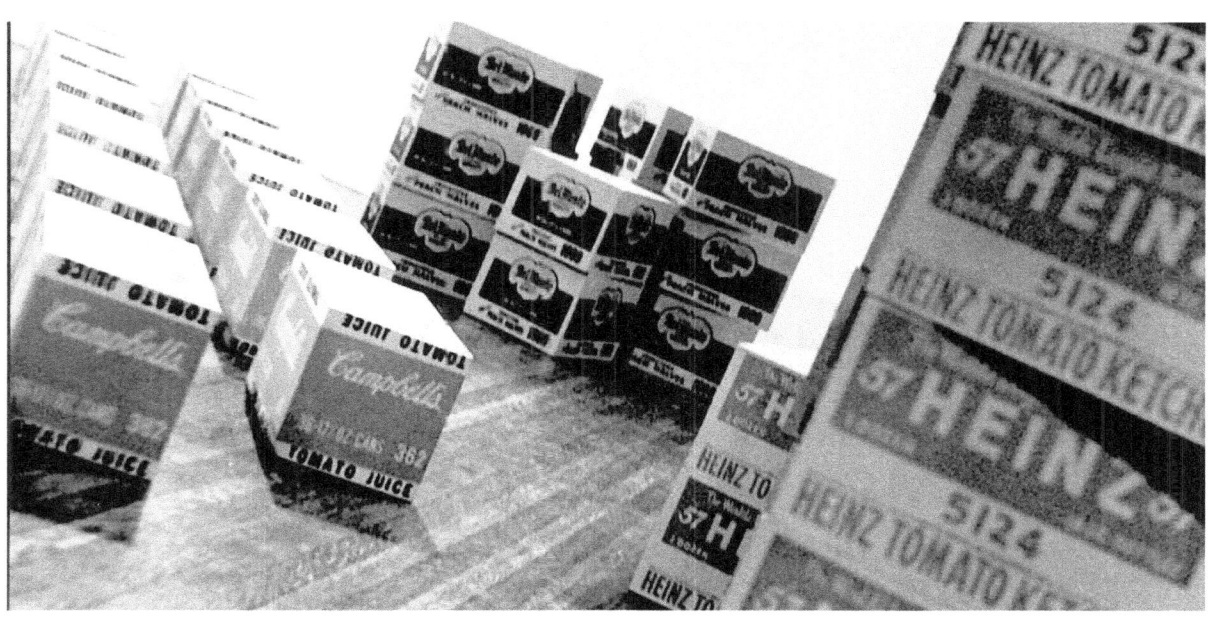

"Like a warehouse." Billy gets creative with boxes just before the big show.

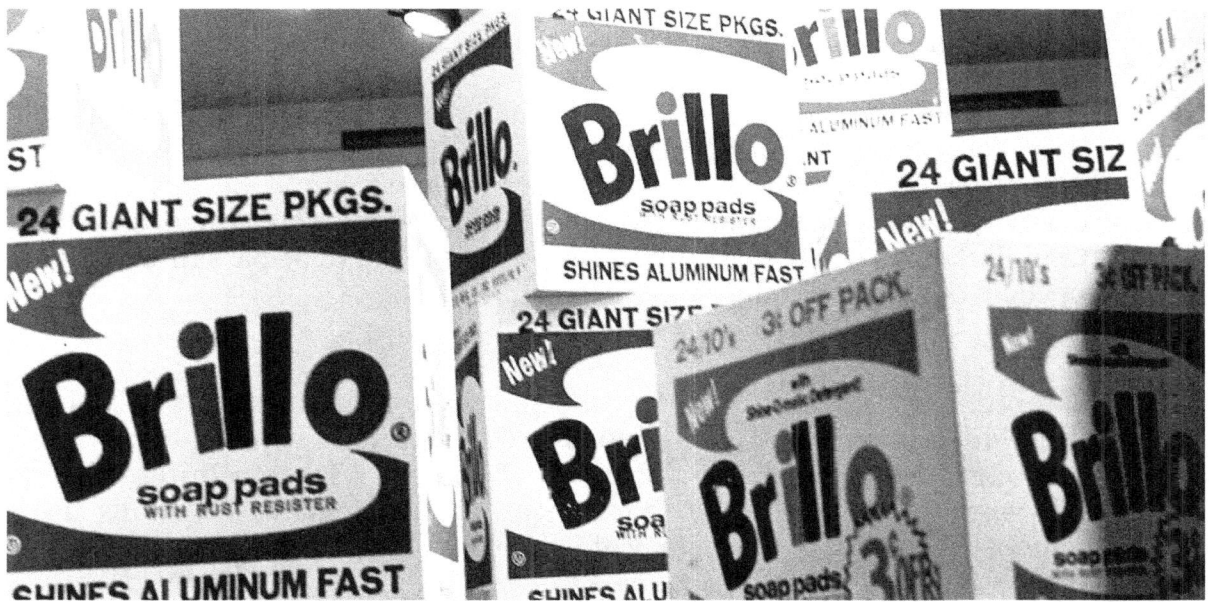

Brillo Boxes on proud display by artist Andy. (Photos by artist Billy Name).

ALL TOMORROW'S PARTIES

And what costume shall the poor girl wear, to all tomorrow's parties?
—Lou Reed

The title refers to Warhol's favorite Velvet Underground song, written by Lou Reed for Nico in 1966. In the early days of the Factory, while Lou and the Velvets were being regularly tossed out of downtown clubs, Warhol and Gerard enjoyed listening to early Rolling Stones and the Supremes as they worked in the front of the loft space, while Billy and Ondine would be in the back singing along with Maria Callas to 'Aida' and Lucia de Lammermoor'. . .

Billy Name: The first gallery as you walked into the Stable Gallery is a diamond formation of Campbell's box sculptures. You have to walk through them to get through the place. It was spectacular! And there was going to be this big party afterward at the Factory—the first big party. Elinor Ward, who owned the Stable Gallery hired Pinkerton Guards and everything, and you had to be pass through them before you could get to the elevator and go up to the Factory.

At his busy Brillo Box opening in 1964, the CBS network and the CBC (Canadian Broadcasting) interviewed Warhol in Elinor Ward's Gallery. Surrounded by mounds of plywood boxes silk-screened with the logos of Campbell's Tomato Juice, Kellogg's Corn Flakes, and yes, lots of Brillo boxes. Warhol, in sunglasses, was his usual deadpan monosyllabic self, to the dismay of feisty CBS reporter Mary Pangalos.

Mary Pangalos Manilla: I had the hardest time getting the guy to say something. And I'd been nominated for two Pulitzers!

Andy and art dealer Ivan Karp with CBS interviewer Mary Pangalos, 1964. (Photo: Billy Name)

News Interviewer
Your art could not be described as original sculpture. Would you agree with that?

Andy Warhol
Yes.

Interviewer
Why do you agree?

Andy Warhol
Because it's not original.

Interviewer *(perplexed)*
You have just copied a common item.

Andy Warhol
Yes.

Interviewer
Why have you bothered to do that? Why not create something new?

Andy Warhol
Because it's easier to do.

Victor Bockris: The Factory opened with a grand party, to which came the Old World and the New World. The Old World was represented by Judy Garland and Tennessee Williams and people like that, and the New World by the early Superstars. What Andy noticed in the middle of the party was that the old people were getting less attention from the press. They were interviewing and photographing the new people, because they looked so fantastic! The party was actually a disaster. Since there were a lot of expensive artworks up there, Ethel Scull and her husband, who were giving the party with Andy, insisted on having a Pinkerton detective at the door downstairs. No one could come in if you didn't have the invitation. This really worked badly. A lot of well-known or important people weren't allowed in and they were very pissed off. People wanted to be there from all these different worlds. Girls were dancing on the tables; Judy Garland started singing. It was a very Warholian thing. His presence, although very quiet, seemed to unleash these people. They were performing for him, to please him... "Me! Make a film about me!"

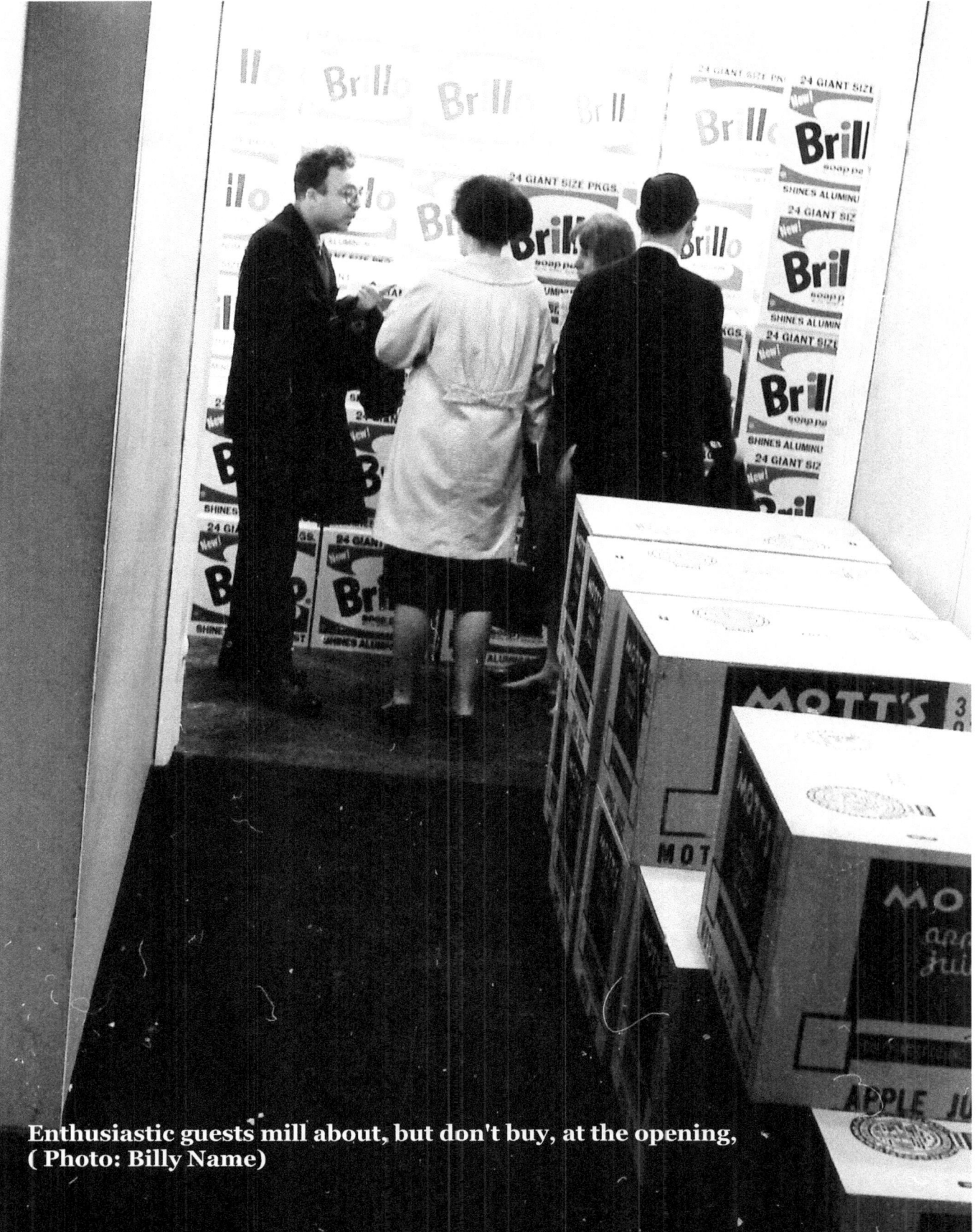

Enthusiastic guests mill about, but don't buy, at the opening. (Photo: Billy Name)

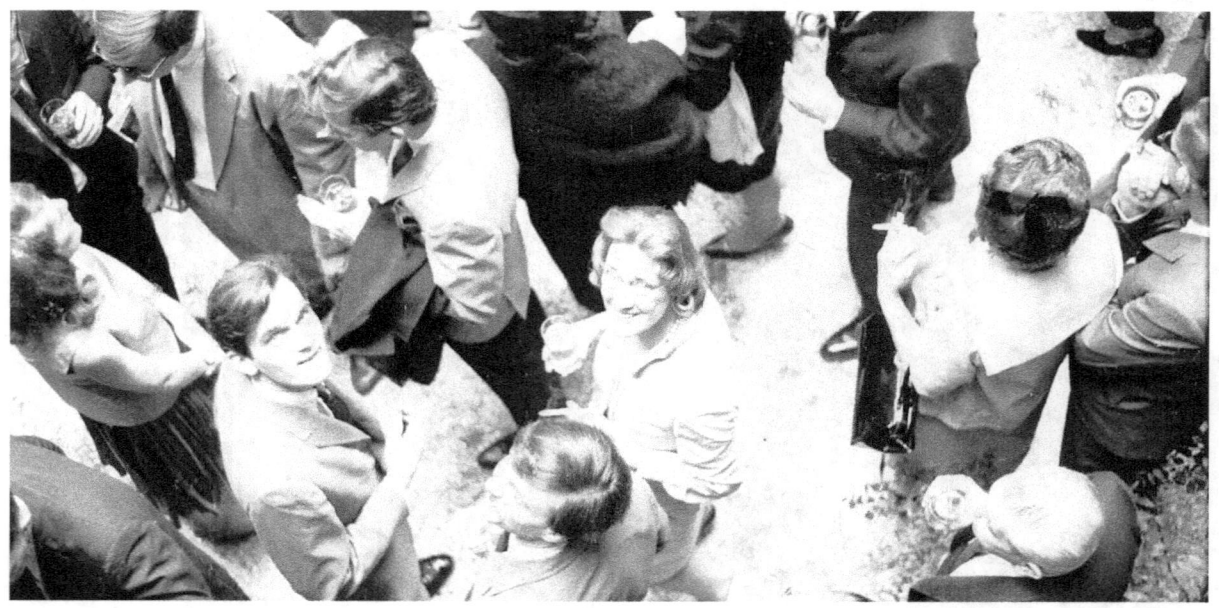

Does everyone have a drink? The lucky partygoes who made it past the Pinkerton detectives. . .

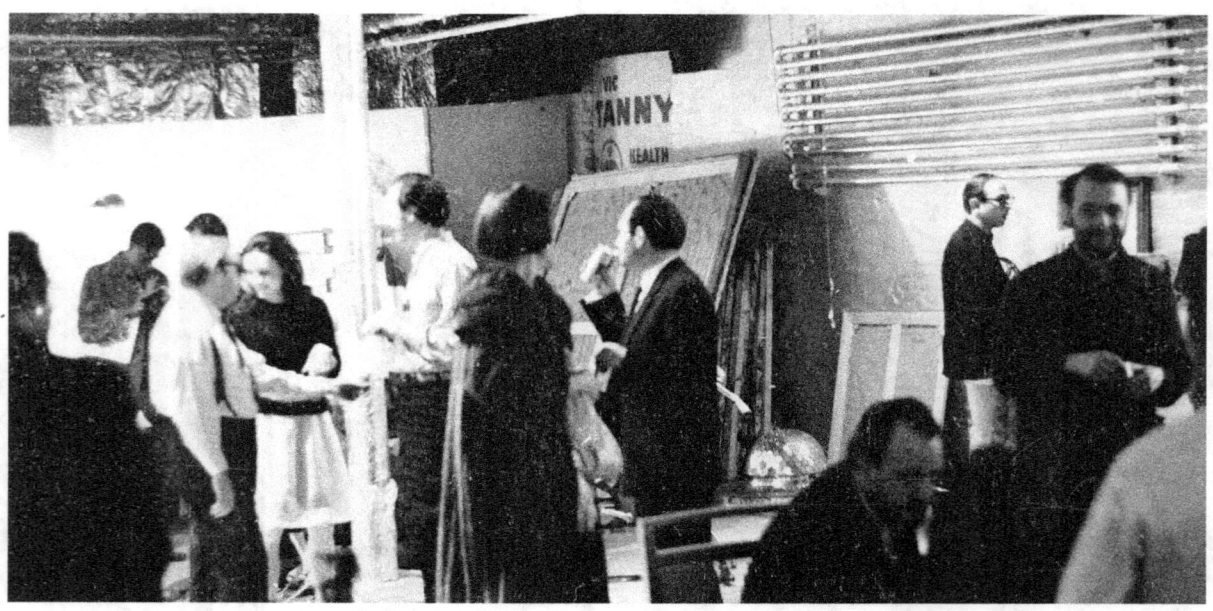

. . . Not surprisingly, no art was stolen. (Photos: Billy Name)

One who got Warhol's attention was a loopy former fashion model we met with in Paris. Dramatically statuesque, slinky (the description 'feline' comes to mind) and extremly outspoken, Ivy Nicholson gives the word 'eccentric' new meaning. In the sixties, she became both muse and menace to Warhol.

Ivy Nicholson: I think about it like the king and his knights. He had the knights and the princesses, and such fun parties. I loved his ideas. He had a couch that was all ripped, from the thirties. Billy Name found it in the streets, but it was one of these wonderful shapes, the prettiest piece of furniture he had. A red velvet couch with rips and tears all over. He filmed on it, a movie called 'Couch'. I don't even remember if I was in it. The couch was so chic. Most people would throw it out or have it reupholstered. Oh no! He just left it the way it was, the pillows falling apart.

The film 'Couch' consisted mainly of people mirthlessly having sex on that infamous couch, though we did use footage of Jack Kerouac doing a handstand on a stool, with Allen Ginsberg looking studiously bored. But Warhol's followers were expected to 'perform'. The cast included Ondine, Gerard Malanga, and Naomi Levine, a lush brunette considered by Warhol to be the first 'underground film queen'. We 'studied' the entire film, and noted that the same people who had so casually fornicated in 'Couch' were photographed by Billy Name at the party, seated on that same grungy, semen-soaked sofa. . . One actor who does not believe he was in 'Couch', Allen Midgette, showed up at the party, but avoided sitting down.

Allen Midgette: At that time I was hanging with Montgomery Clift. He was going to the party and invited me. Monty was very fragile, and I knew that he needed someone to go with him. So, we arrived at the Factory, and it was just a few people from the Factory doing their thing. And across the room there was Judy Garland and Tennessee Williams doing their thing, a little drunk, a few pills, and they're looking into each others eyes and saying, "Oh, you're so beautiful." Billy Name offered me a joint; I smoked it and got, you know, whatever. Then, in the middle of it, the elevator comes up and Rudy Nureyev walks out. This is when he was king of the world. All this time, people all over New York think I'm Nureyev, and I'm saying "No, I'm not." He walks over to me (and asks), "Hmm, are you a madman, or a sexy bitch?" . . . "I'm afraid I'm a madman," I said. Then we joined Monty, Judy, Tennessee, and Judy's husband at the time, and they decided they want to go to the next party already.

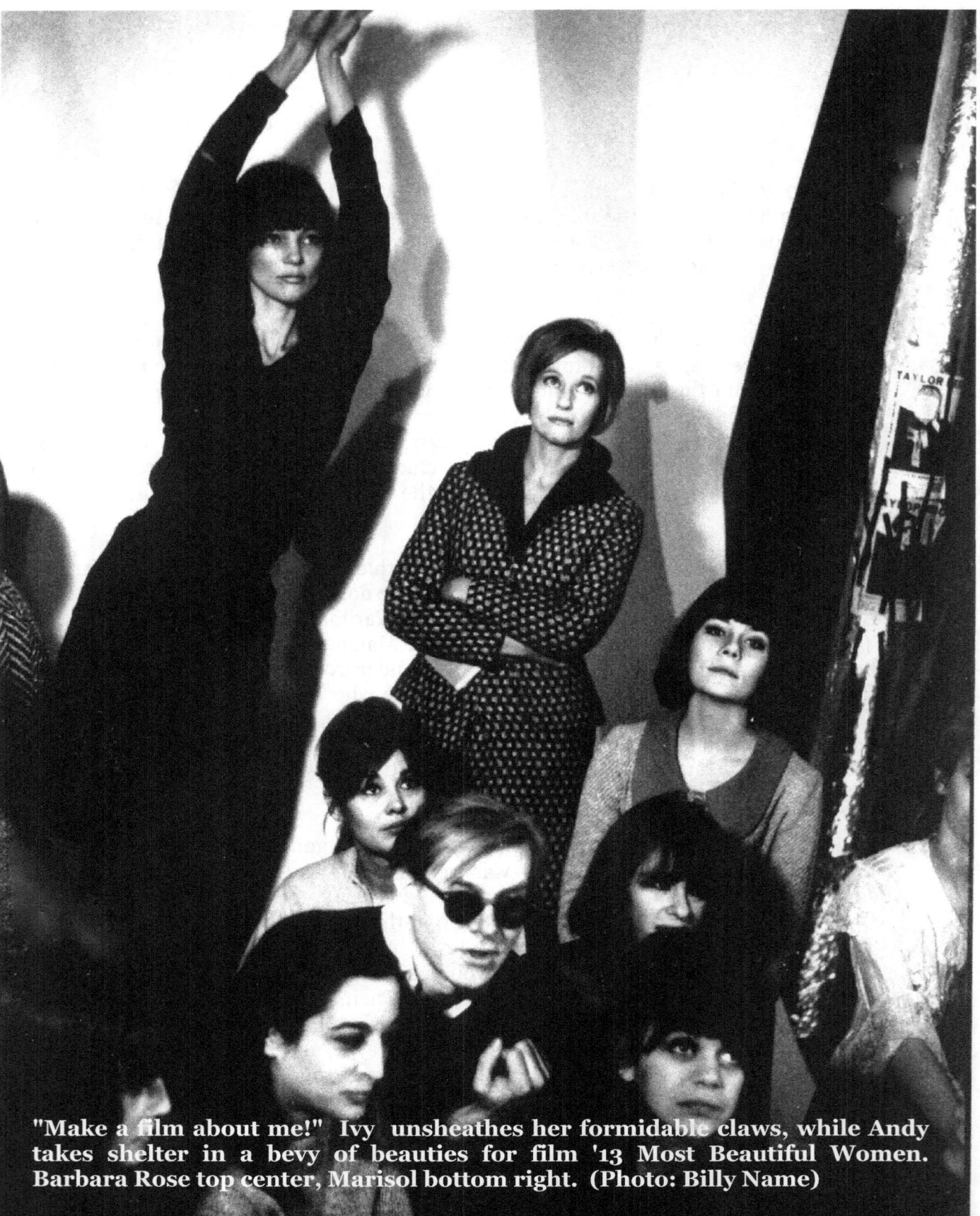

"Make a film about me!" Ivy unsheathes her formidable claws, while Andy takes shelter in a bevy of beauties for film '13 Most Beautiful Women. Barbara Rose top center, Marisol bottom right. (Photo: Billy Name)

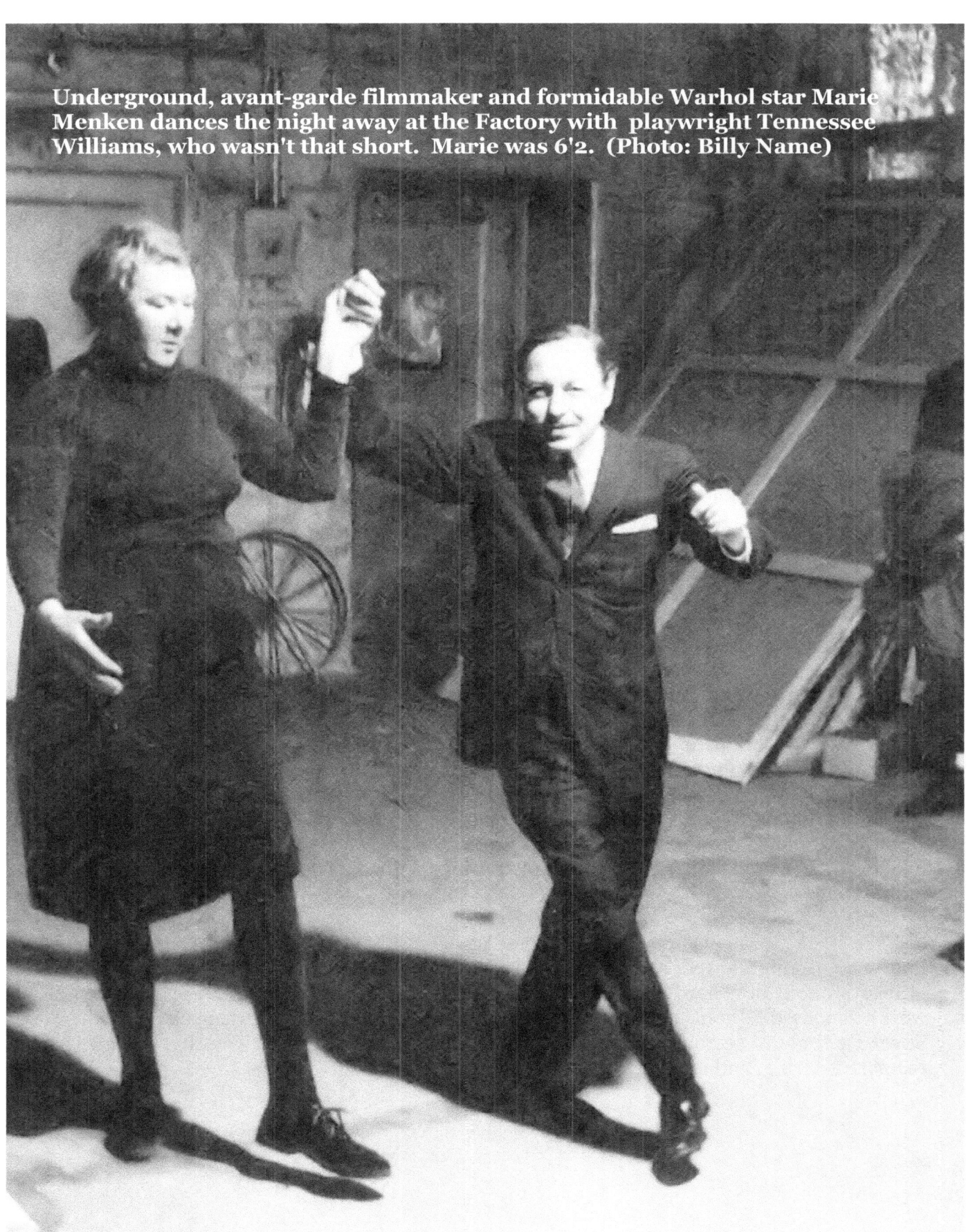

Underground, avant-garde filmmaker and formidable Warhol star Marie Menken dances the night away at the Factory with playwright Tennessee Williams, who wasn't that short. Marie was 6'2. (Photo: Billy Name)

According to biographer Victor Bockris: "People were there until about four in the morning, and went out to breakfast together afterwards. Andy didn't sleep much in those days." So, the first party would have been considered a huge success, but Warhol wasn't about to take the time for a well-deserved nap. His penchant for following the movie magazines, tabloids and social columns had been a lifelong habit. Now, as he started to cut a swathe through the social scene that surrounded Pop art, he found himself in constant proximity to those very people, New York's Upper East Side Uber-WASPS, Philadelphia's Main Liners, Cambridge-Harvard Set, and a raven-haired French heiress, who would certainly never have beaten a path to his grubby freight elevator door.

Ultra Violet: I had access to a certain level of society, which Andy did not, and he wanted to climb the ladder, which he did. He wanted power, over the art, the fashion, the society, the glamour, and he got it. People used to say, "If there's a party and if Warhol isn't there, it's a failure." But the minute he came in, oh, now this is a party. But it's very flat on the surface. It's very mundane. It's very... Oh, I don't know.

Victor Bockris: Andy's attitude towards life is that life should be a party, work should be a party. Everything should be a party. And he really tried to take that mentality into everything he did. It had a double effect, because it worked for him, but it doesn't necessarily work for everybody. A lot of people started trying to live as if they were Warhol people, but they weren't, naturally, so they just sort of fell apart. What Andy was really saying was, the way to live is to make work *fun*, because life is essentially work, and so you make it into a party in some way. He would have people sitting talking to him, telling him stories while he was on the floor painting. Plus, he would have music on, the TV on, and so forth. So, his whole idea was to surround himself with people who could help him get things done quicker, so they could make more money.

Everyone we interviewed, especially those who were with Warhol all the time, talked at length about how hard and diligently the artist worked. It was always about the work. Among the thousands of photographs we used in our film, the denizens of the Silver Factory are seen diligently doing their thing, while Warhol is working, before the party, during, and long after everyone has gone home...

BACK TO WORK

I enjoy my work. When I begin to work on something, it usually takes me a minute to do
—Andy Warhol

Robert Heide: Andy sometimes liked to take liquid speed. After one party, the sun was coming up. We went back to the Factory and there was this famous couch. I was sitting on one end and Andy on the other, and he said, "Oh, gee, I wonder what we should do next?" I said, "Well Andy you're into this Zen emptiness thing. Just do the same thing—Zen with repetition." *(mimicking Warhol)* "What do you mean?" . . . "Just change the colors around, like Marilyn Monroe, with a fuchsia face and green hair, and change the colors on the Campbell's soup can." I felt this little light bulb going on in Andy's head. He liked the idea of getting his ideas from other people. But Andy was a kind of Zen master. I learned a lot from Andy without knowing it, without knowing that I was an acolyte.

Nat Finkelstein: Andy was, in the beginning, a commercial artist. He was the original yuppie. There were three different corporations formed under his name, at least three that I know of, so he wasn't evolving—he was *there*! He made tons of money dressing store windows, and then he decided he wanted to be a fine artist as well. I think Andy was quite focused and quite determined from the minute he got to New York. He had a conversation with this gallery owner (Muriel Latow) and said "I want to be a fine artist, but I don't have any ideas." So, the woman needed to pay the rent on her gallery and said "Andy, supposing I give you some ideas will you pay me two hundred dollars so I can pay my rent?" Andy said "Sure," and she said, "Andy what is it that you like most in the world?" Andy said, "Money." And so Muriel said, "Well, why don't you make a painting with dollar bills?"

On November 11, 2009, Warhol's seminal early silk screen of '200 Dollar Bills' sold at Sotheby's for $43.7 million, three times its estimate, making Muriel Latow one of the least paid financial advisers in history. Latow also said, "Andy, you should paint something that everybody sees every day, like a can of *soup*." Warhol's mother could also take credit. Inspiration would come from her kitchen. Robert Heide called Julia Warhola an "almost spooky presence; there was definitely a pre-oedipal thing about Andy." Warhol's desperate childhood and well-documented obsessions would seem to inform his early art: Basic food staples, money, and death. . . Vincent Fremont, the personable founder of The Andy Warhol Foundation For The Visual Arts, agreed.

Vincent Fremont: Andy's output between the Firehouse and The Silver Factory is what most people know of his work. The Flower paintings, the Electric Chair, the Death and Disaster paintings. What were Andy's influences? I know that he kept thick files of the suicide photographs, Associated Press photographs of car accidents.

Some of Warhol's works were based on AP photos taken by Charles Brown or Ed Wallowitch, who also took portraits of Warhol pal Bob Heide when he wasn't rushing to the next newsworthy event. According to Heide, the handsome, well-endowed Wallowitch and Warhol had an intense affair in the late '50s, which petered out when Edward (who had a drinking problem) suffered a nervous breakdown. Warhol refused to contribute toward his treatment, but Wallowitch held no grudges, and took a picture of Warhol against a wall, upon which had been painted a huge skull.

Vincent Fremont: I think death, or the subject of death starts early on in his work. The Marilyns, you see it all progress, and these were done in the Silver Factory period, with the exception of the Elvises, which started in the Fire House. . . He was a great editor. He didn't pick just any photograph. He didn't pick just any subject.

One subject taken from the headlines: a grieving Jackie Kennedy at her husband's funeral. Billy Name documented Warhol's feverish compilation of 'commemorative' silk screens, which stretched across the floor. In 2011 'Sixteen Jackies' sold for a "bargain" $20.2 million at Sotheby's according to its seller. Here's an idea: Invite Billy Name out to a lunch at one of Jackie's favorite restaurants, buy sixteen of his photos of the 'Jackie' series, then mount them together on the wall. There you go. . .

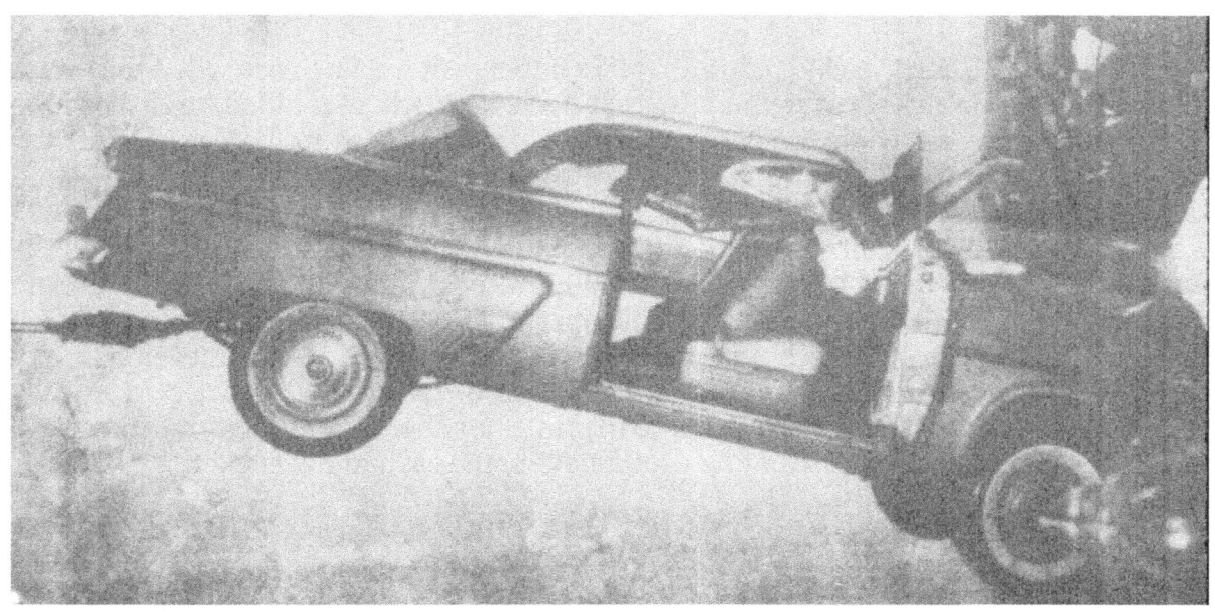

The "Death and Disaster" period, which included suicides jumping from windows, electric chairs, skeletons, and horrific accident scenes taken from AP photos. (Car crash photo: Billy Name)

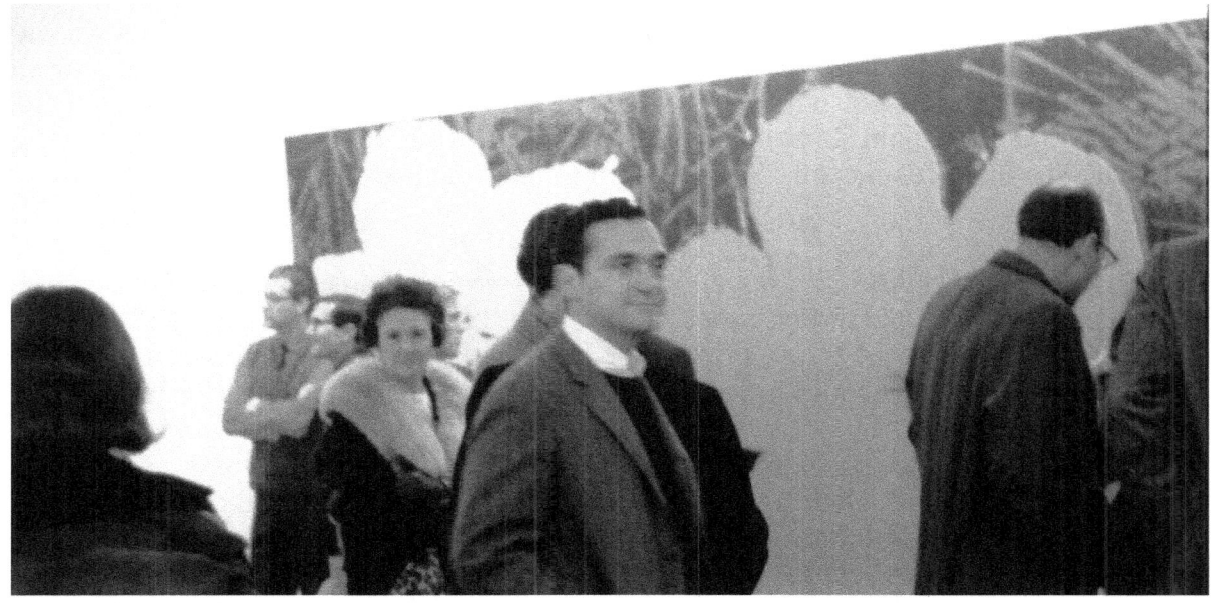

Friendly flowers. . . Gallery goers appreciate a lighter side of Warhol. (Photo: Billy Name)

Billy Name: The early Jackie paintings were not shown in New York when they were first produced, because it was the year that Jack Kennedy was killed, and these are the pictures from her widowhood series. The pillbox hat is from the day that he was shot. They are amazingly haunting when you see them in reality. But no one would show them because they thought it was in bad taste... So, Leo Castelli in New York was then married to Ileana Sonnabend, who had a gallery in Paris. She came to the Factory and purchased a dozen 'Jackie as Widow' portraits. She bought them from me, not Andy. He did not want his bookkeeper to know, because every time he gave the accountant cash, the accountant used it to pay bills, and Andy never had any cash. So Ileana made out a sale note: 'Purchase of twelve (12) Jackies from Billy Name for one thousand dollars ($1000) from Sonnabend' and gave me the cash, which I then gave to Andy so that he would have some cash in his pocket.

In 1964 N. Y. gallery owner Leo Castelli's by now ex-wife Ileana Sonnabend bravely showed Warhol's 'Death and Disaster' paintings in her Paris gallery. Elinor Ward of the Stable Gallery had refused them, and none of his friends wanted "dead people" on their walls. Warhol couldn't give them away in America, but they caused a sensation in Europe, especially the 'Electric Chair'. My personal favorite, 'Green Car Crash', copied from the AP photo, depicts not only a lethal car crash, but on closer look the body of the driver (or passenger), fetchingly hanging from a telephone pole. The paintings multiple images don't translate well to the printed page, but we did license it from the Warhol Foundation to put in our TV series, complete with garish sound effects. Again, not happy folk, but I think Andy might have appreciated the effort. The painting sold in 2007 for $71.7 million. In 2013, 'Silver Car Crash' set a record at $105m. This month, 'Birmingham Race Riot', is expected to fetch $50m.

Taylor Mead With Andy it was about poverty—tremendous poverty. Dinner was Heinz ketchup in a bowl of hot water. Heinz was the biggest employer in Pittsburgh and his father worked for them, I think. So, they had plenty of ketchup to make soup with, or otherwise they would have starved. And Andy of course never forgot that.

Ultra Violet: Andy is the most puzzling person I know. Because he is born in the Pittsburgh ghetto, and when he dies he is worth eight hundred million dollars. So, that has not happened by accident, I don't think. But when you were with him he was so helpless! *(mimicking Warhol)* "Tell me what to do. What should we do? Help, help. Can you do this, can you do that, can you drive the car, can you make the phone call, can you make the painting."

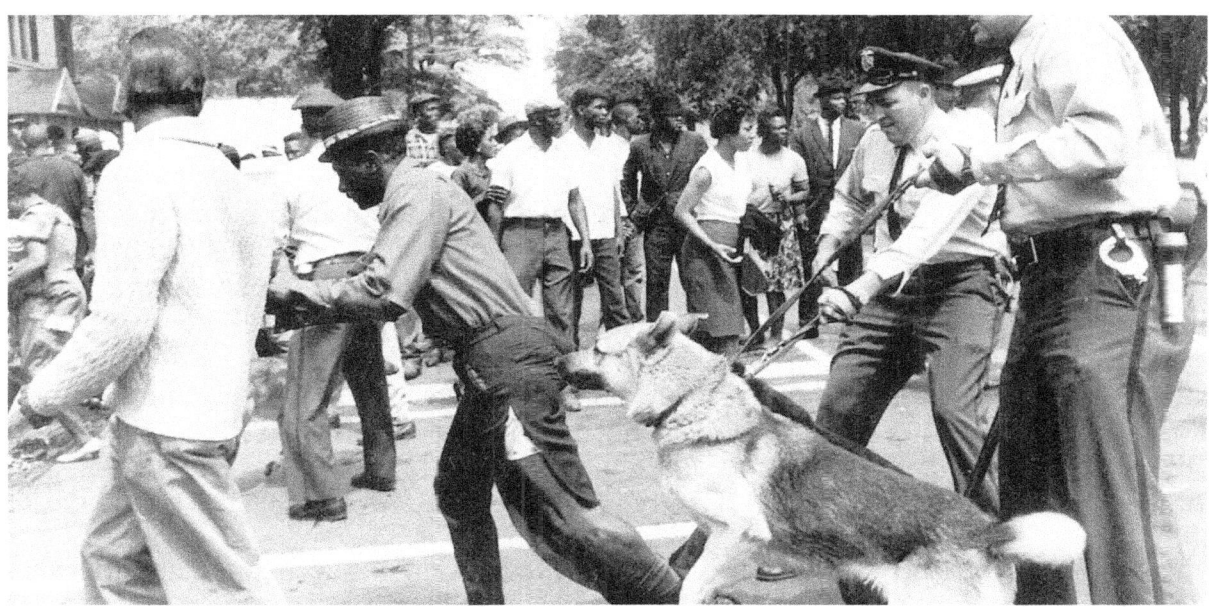

AP photo of Birmingham Dogs, from which Warhol created his iconic early painting, part of the "Death and Disaster" series. (Photo: Charles Moor, 1963

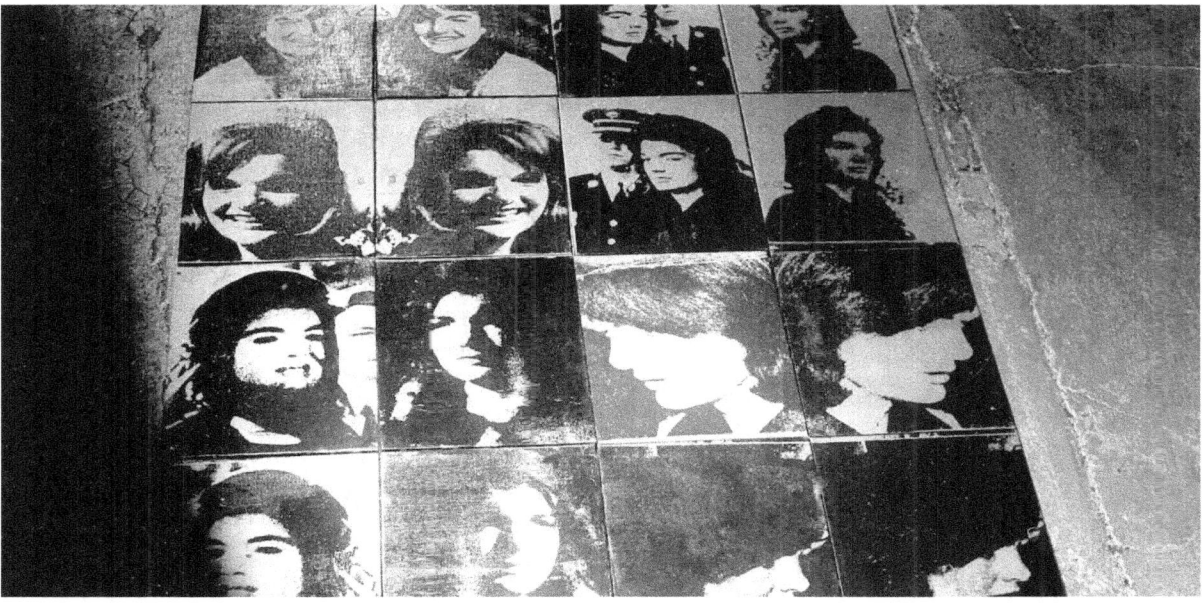

'16 Jackies' grace the floor of the Silver Factory, reproduced like faces of saints in the Byzantine Catholic churches of Warhol's youth. (Photo: Billy Name)

Andy Warhol (to gallery owner Muriel Latow, 1962) I've got to do something that will have impact, that will be different. I don't know what to do! Muriel, you have fabulous ideas. Can't you give me an idea?

Ultra Violet: If you talked to him, he never had anything to say. If you're next to a genius, they have a philosophy, which they can express verbally. With Warhol, it was, "Oh, aaah, gee." So ambiguous. Who was he? Was he a total genius who was saving his energy for the brainstorm, and then delegating to people doing all the work?

Billy Name: Andy actually did work, you know (*laugh*). He did everything; he was a workaholic. . . 1963 into '64 he had been silk screening the Marilyns, the Dollar Bills, the Coke Bottles, the Soup Cans, doing Box Sculptures, the Jackie Kennedys, the Thirteen MostWanted Men. If Andy needed to take a break, he'd lie on the desk.

Victor Bockris: Andy had been commissioned to do a piece for the American Pavilion at the '64 World Fair in New York. He delivered a twenty-by-twenty foot black and white mural called 'The Thirteen Most Wanted Men', based on a series of mug shots. The Governor thought the mural might be insulting to some of his Italian constituents, since most of the thirteen criminals were Italian, and demanded Andy change it. So he and Gerard went and painted the wall silver. The next day the New York Times featured an article about how many people had been robbed at the Fair.

The influential architect Philip Johnson had asked Warhol to do a mural for the Pavilion, to be installed alongside works by Robert Indiana, Robert Rauchenberg and Roy Lichtenstein. Johnson fought Warhol over his vision of using criminal mug shots to represent America, as did demogogic Robert Moses, the fair's president, as did a horrified Mayor Robert Wagner, who heartily agreed with Gov. Rockerfeller. In an effort to 'clean up' New York before the fair, police raided downtown avant-garde theaters and those screening underground films, including Jack Smith's 'Flaming Creatures' and Warhol's 'Newsreel', which was never recovered.

Taylor Mead: I admired Andy as a revolutionary, a Voltairian from a literary point of view. I thought, to take a 25-cent can of soup and make it a painting that starts at 2,000 dollars was a great stroke of genius about American culture. So, as a scholar of Voltaire, I was very excited to be going to Andy's house. Even his mother came downstairs. They used to say he kept his mother in the basement. That's not true! She brought us little sandwiches, and Campbell's soup.

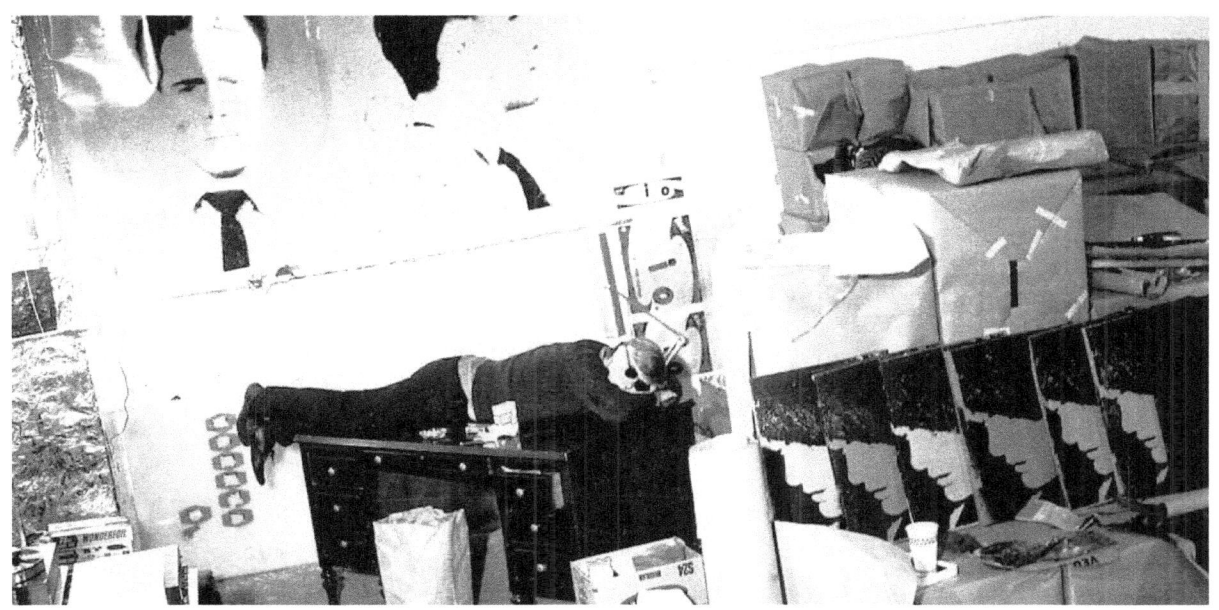

Workaholic Warhol takes a break. Jackie Kennedys are in foreground, one of 'Thirteen Most Wanted Men' in B.G.

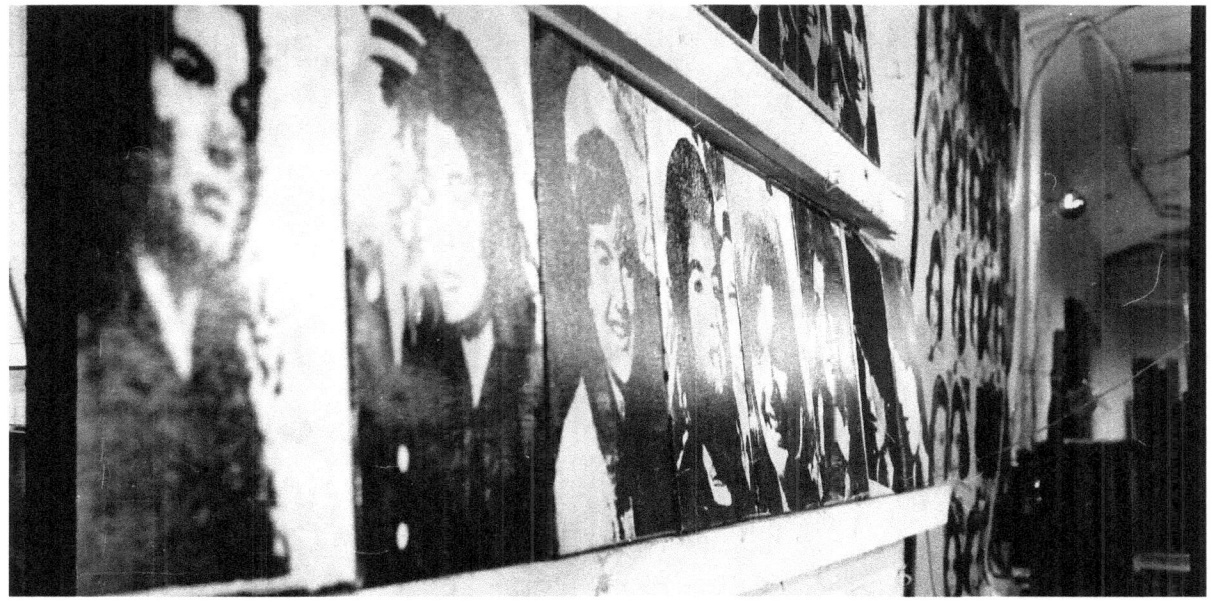

Jackie paintings displayed on Silver Factory Wall. In May of 2014, a group of silk screens and prints were the subject of a remarkable exhibition at the Blain/Di Donna Gallery in New York. (Photos: Billy Name)

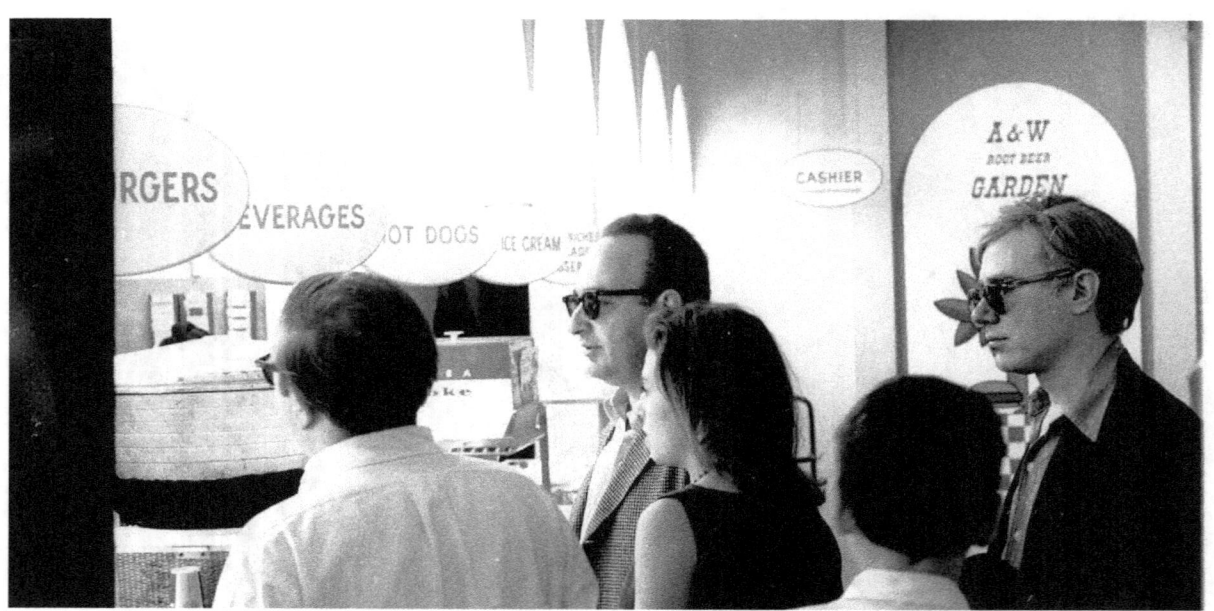
Andy at the World's Fair in New York, 1964, with his dealer, Ivan Karp, in profile. 50 years later, '13 Most Wanted Men' would be museum-exhibited on the very fairgrounds it had been censored.

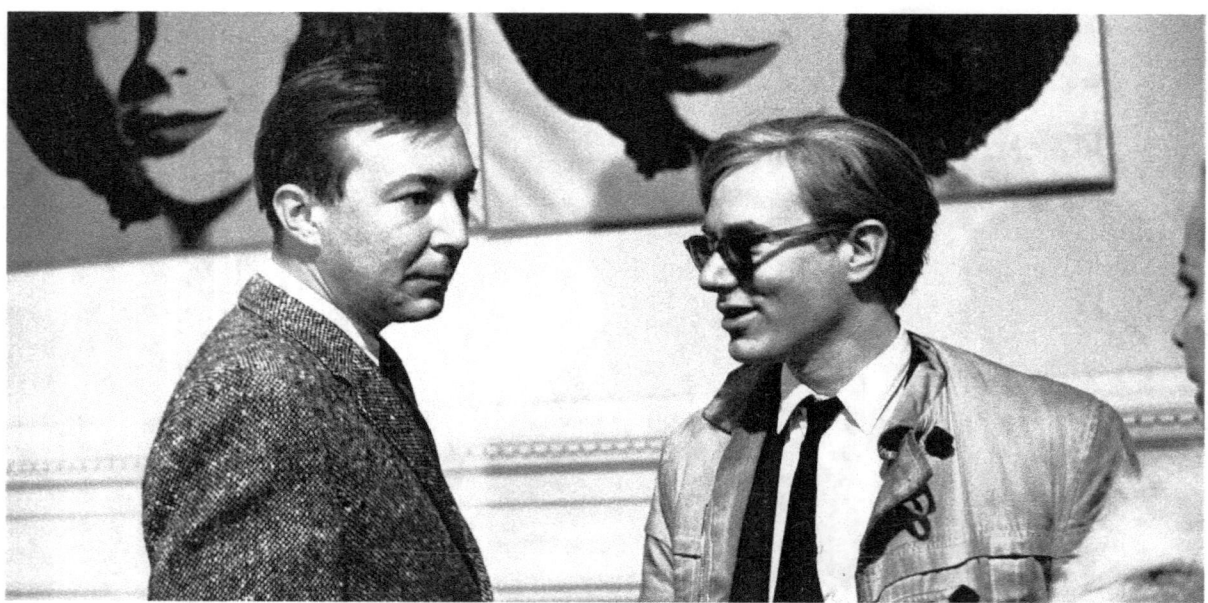
Jasper Johns, pre-eminent figure in art (American Flags) visits with Andy at the home of Henry Geldzahler. Ultra Violet on right. (Photos: Billy Name)

Louis Waldon: Andy had seen me on Broadway, in a play called 'Ballad of the Sad Café', and he came with Taylor Mead. Andy really wanted me to join the Factory. They were starting to make movies. So, I was having a vacation out in Fire Island and I ran into Andy. "Oh, we're making a movie. Come on over, be in it." No script, nobody knew what to do. Andy looked like he was lost. I said, "Oh boy, I can't work with these people." I had never worked without a script. But I had always wanted to do improvisation. So, one night, Allen Midgette, one of the actors, came over and said, "We're shooting a movie right now; he wants you in it." I said, "I can't do it." My neighbor had painted a big design on my back for this new restaurant.

The late Louis Waldon (1934-2013) did not become a de facto part of the Factory until well into the sixties ('Lonesome Cowboys', 'Nude Restaurant'), but he was still a big part of that downtown scene, so we took artistic license (as usual) and put him and his hilarious stories in the first episode of the television series. Though a relative newcomer, Louis made a lasting impression on New York's avant-garde theatrical directors... Jonas Mekas, revered "patron saint" of underground filmmakers, also remembers the period well, though he's older, because he *was* the avant-garde.

Jonas Mekas: It was the kind of cinema that one could do by oneself, or just with friends, beginning with the Cassavetes piece 'Shadows'. Andy came in at that very exciting time for cinema. I remember him talking."I want to make films. I'm making a film." He got the bug. So, we began screening films at the Filmmakers Showcase in '62, '63, and that's where a lot of early Warhol films were shown. At first, he made a series of 'Kisses', usually projected before our main program. That is also where 'Sleep'* was premiered in, I think, 1963, and everybody said, "Who could sit through a six hour long film?" Andy was there, so as a joke I got a rope and tied him to the chair. I said, "You should see it yourself, you better not leave." At one point I went to the projection room. I came out, it was like an hour later, and Andy was gone.

Ivy Nicholson: When he made 'Empire' with my ex-husband John Palmer, I told Andy I didn't really get it. Maybe he did it for the publicity. I said, "I want movies about sex and love." And, boy, soon it was all sex and love. That was the way he was—everything was exaggerated. He posed for one year for a portrait I did of him, an oil painting. It was just another excuse to see him when I didn't necessarily make a movie with him that day. I could go and paint him, and be near him. But with true love that's the way it goes... He loved my tantrums. He loved everything I did. He would say, "Oh, why don't you go up and down the aisles and start yelling?"

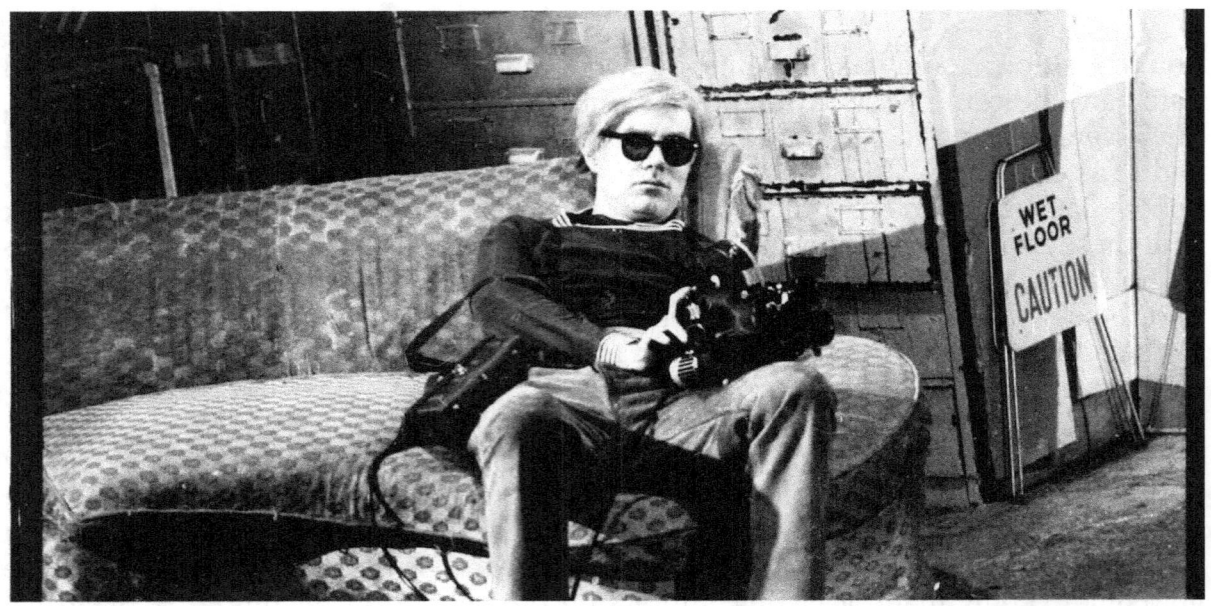
Caution, man at work! Andy tries out his new camera.

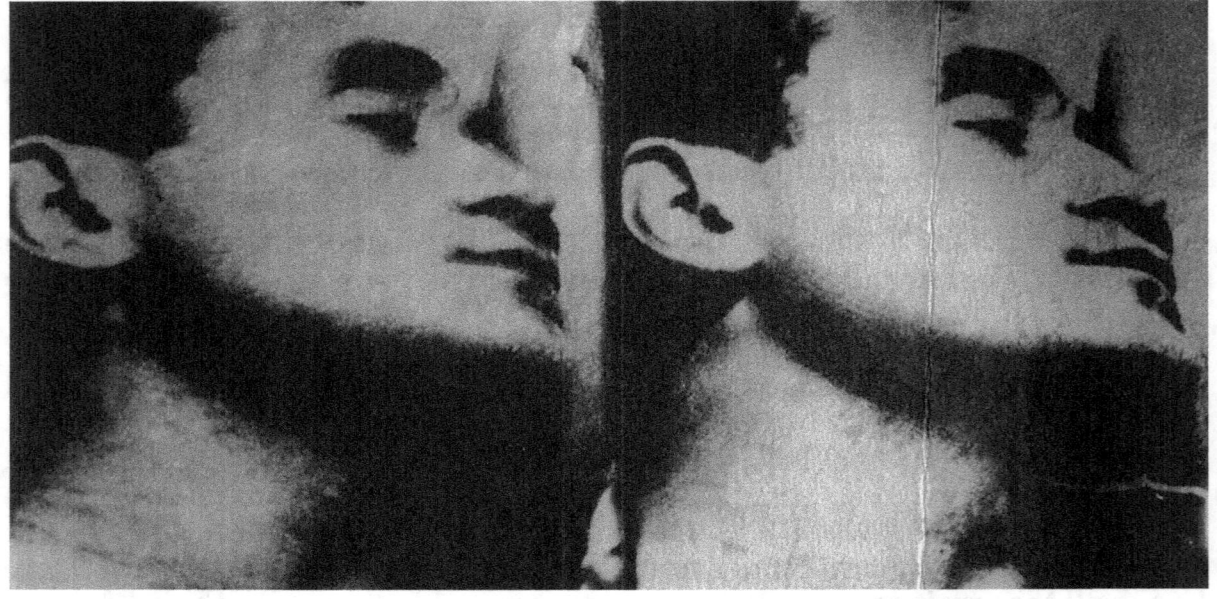
'Sleep' (1963) with poet John Giorno, was one of Andy's first films. (Photos: Billy Name)

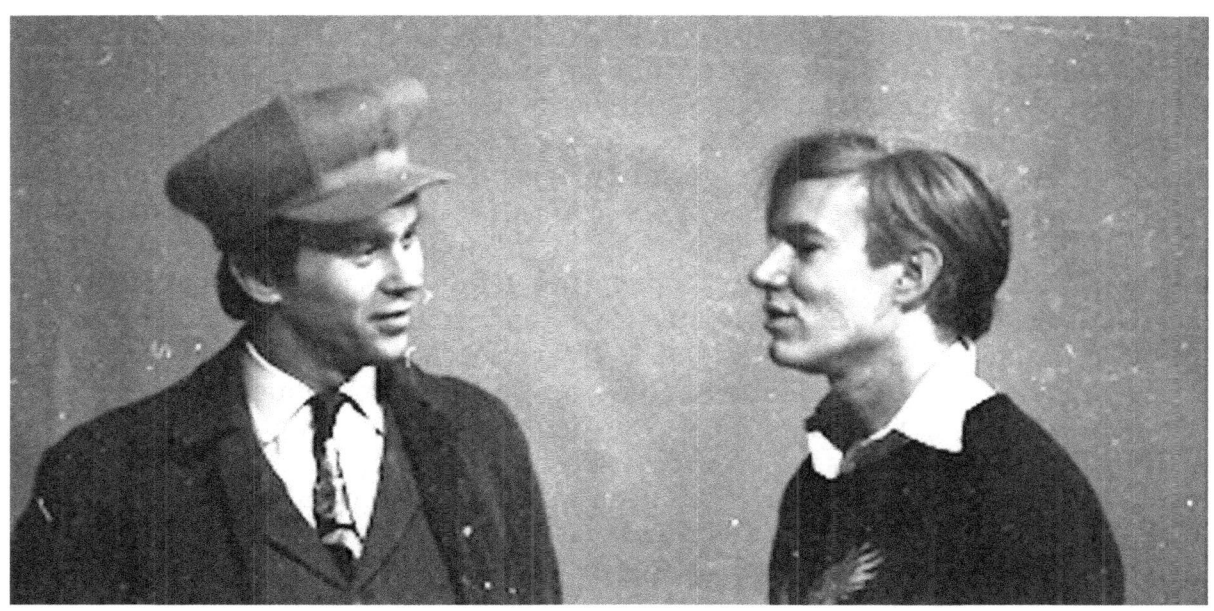

Young, beardless, Off-Broadway thespian Louis Waldon meets Andy Warhol. Louis would go on to have an acting career spanning 45 years.

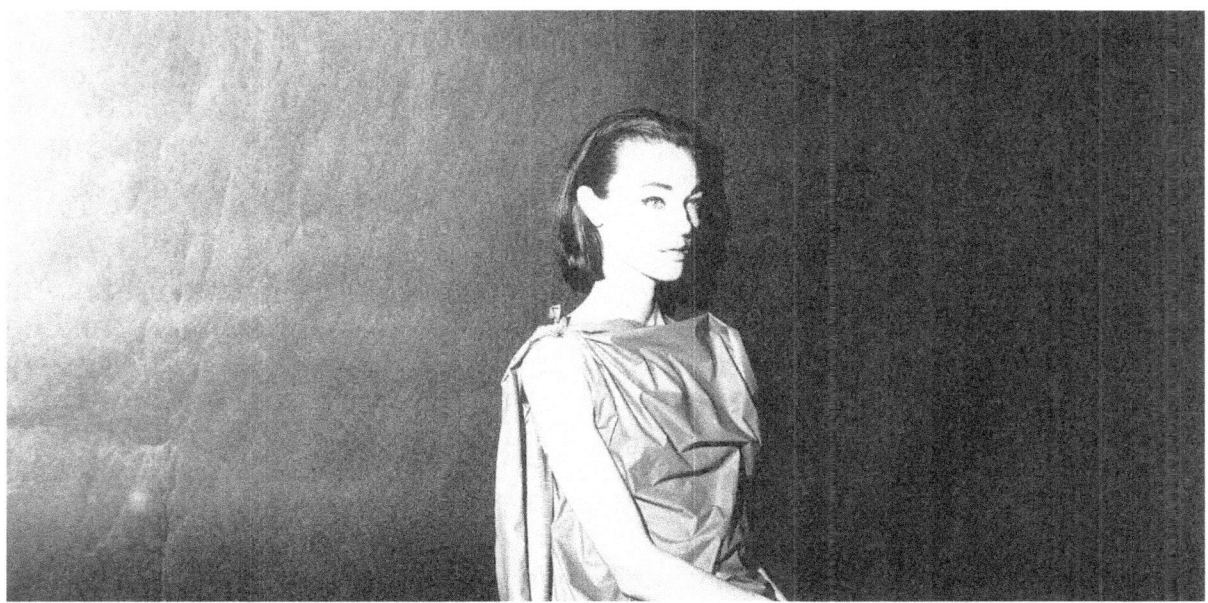

Fiery fashion model Ivy Nicholson, in a rare docile moment, sits for a Warhol Screen Test. (Photos: Billy Name)

Jonas Mekas: I can tell you about 'Empire'. A young man by the name of John Palmer, who later made a feature length film, was helping me on 'Film Culture Magazine', taking packs of the magazine to the post office, which was in the Empire State Building. At one point, as we were approaching the Empire State Building, we stopped to admire it, and John says, "Ah! This would be a perfect film for Andy Warhol." Andy said, "Yes! Let's do it, let's film it." Andy decided, or maybe both of them decided, that we should start filming early before sunset, then go all night until sunrise. I was asked to be the cameraman because Andy was operating only with a little Bolex that took two minutes and forty-five seconds of film,. I decided to use one camera that took thirty minutes of film. So we spent the night eating sandwiches in the Time Life Building on maybe the thirtieth floor. I kept shooting and changing the magazine, and that was the film. A month later, we opened it. The first screening took place at what was known as City Hall Cinema. They had about three hundred people, and they came with sandwiches, some came with sleeping bags *(laugh),* and at the end we had some forty or fifty people. Still, that was not bad at all.

In Paris awhile back, 'Empire' was screened on the wall of a building during '*Nuit Blanche'*, where hardy Parisians stay up all night trudging from one exciting art venue to another all over town. Well, we started filming the screening of Warhol's opus, and soon a bunch of news cameramen showed up to interview all us hip night revelers. A weird brawl broke out in six languages over the value of Warhol's art, which then segued into drunken diatribes over everyone else's art, the *ennui* of Empires, the imperialism of America, blah, blah. The evening finally ended with everybody sharing wine and whatever, and nobody watching the film, as the stately Empire State Building slowly revealed itself to the breaking dawn.

Gerard Malanga: At a screening, Andy would usually be a bunch of giggles. He would just love it. . . So this was one of Jonas Mekas' touring cinema things, and we were premiering 'Empire' for the first time. It was eight hours—no—it actually was almost twelve hours, and at some point people started throwing paper cups at the screen, and voicing their opinions out loud. All kinds of weird shit was going on, and Andy turns to me in the back of the theatre and he goes, "Oh my God, do you think they did not like the movie?" And I do not know if Andy was putting me on or what.

Taylor Mead: With Andy they shot twelve hours of the Empire State Building and everybody thinks, "Oh, that's another Andy Warhol film." They do not know that they (the films) had characters, stories and people in them, and all kinds of locations and the camera moving. But no, we are buried under the Empire State Building. >

It's the conception. Andy was not just a conceptual artist, he was also very humanoid, a humanoid. I don't know if he was human; he didn't want to be human. When we went to a Broadway show, he wanted a robot to play Andy Warhol.

In 1962, Warhol had discovered diet pills, which kept him going through his usual twelve-hour workdays and nightly social marathons. The amphetamines also curbed his appetite, so by eschewing food and sleep, Warhol achieved his goal of "becoming a machine," and endlessly duplicating his product. His favorite film of 1964 was called 'The Creation of the Humanoids', in which the survivors of World War III solve their labor shortage by creating humanoid robots. When the hero and heroine discover themselves to be machines, Warhol was thrilled with the film's "happy ending."

Ultra Violet: I saw in the Factory all kinds of canvas and stretchers, turned back, so you couldn't see the front. I asked Andy to see one, and it was a flower painting, in a series. I said, "I would like to get one of those," which we sort of did together. Andy said, "What color?" And I said, "One flower should be violet." He opened a huge gallon of wall paint. and we did it. Then he said, "What color should the other flower be?" And I said, "Of course, the complimentary color." . . . "Which is what?" said he. "Orange," said I. So we did one violet flower and one orange flower, with a black and white grass background—which he *sold* me. Artists never, *ever* give you anything, because it's their children. I forget if it cost $500 or $2,000, but you know, nobody wanted his art work at the time. They are blind; they are blind in the art world.

Oh, Ultra you are so right, and so rich. I always look forward to my visits to your spectacular Upper East Side duplex penthouse. Well, maybe I'll be *uninvited* after this, because she did tell me to keep my mouth shut. ("But I'm a writer," I whine.) Actually, Ultra's expansive aerie is perched on the roof above the penthouse floor, accessible only by helicopter or a private stairwell, upon which were displayed posters, and they were many, of Ultra in her glorious purple heyday. What a classic beauty. Central Park and the city is spread out beneath her aristocratic feet, with endless views from every window. A huge wrap-around teak deck filled with a forest of trees and shrubs offer a quiet haven from the rigors of 5th Avenue life. . . But back to the "blind art world" and Ultra Violet's prescience. Her custom-commissioned Warhol Flowers painting fills the enormous living room wall of her house, and is certainly a conversation stopper. . . So, Ultra got her fabulous Flowers, and Billy got his photographs, and an invaluable insight into Warhol.

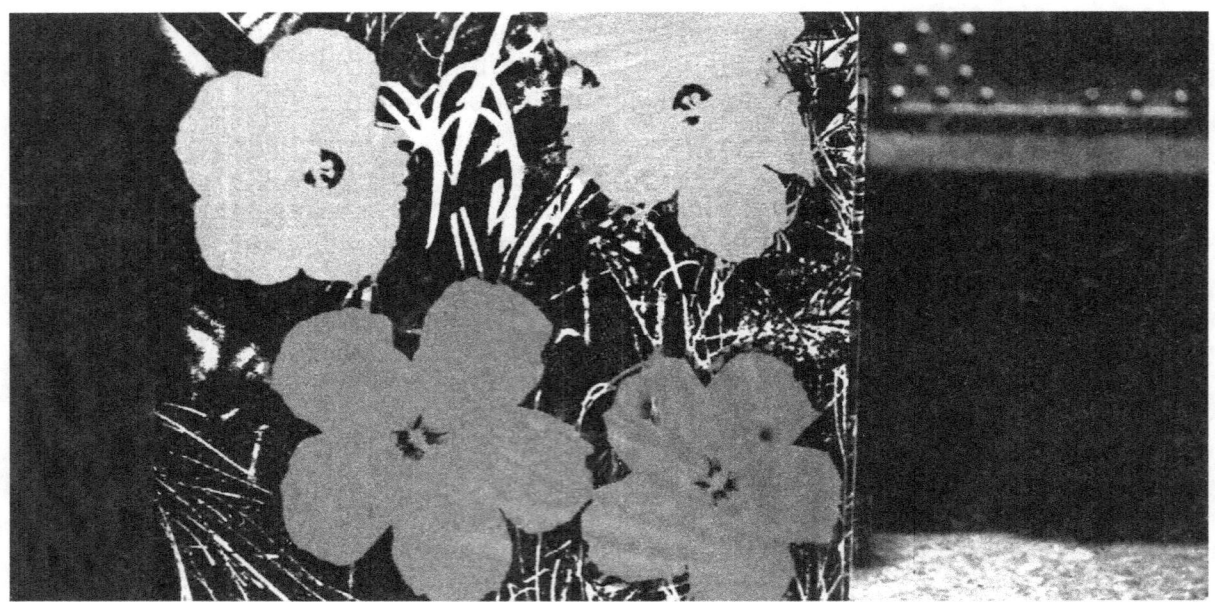

"An artist is sombody who produces things that people don't need to have." Andy Warhol's soon to be famous Flowers await a savvy buyer.

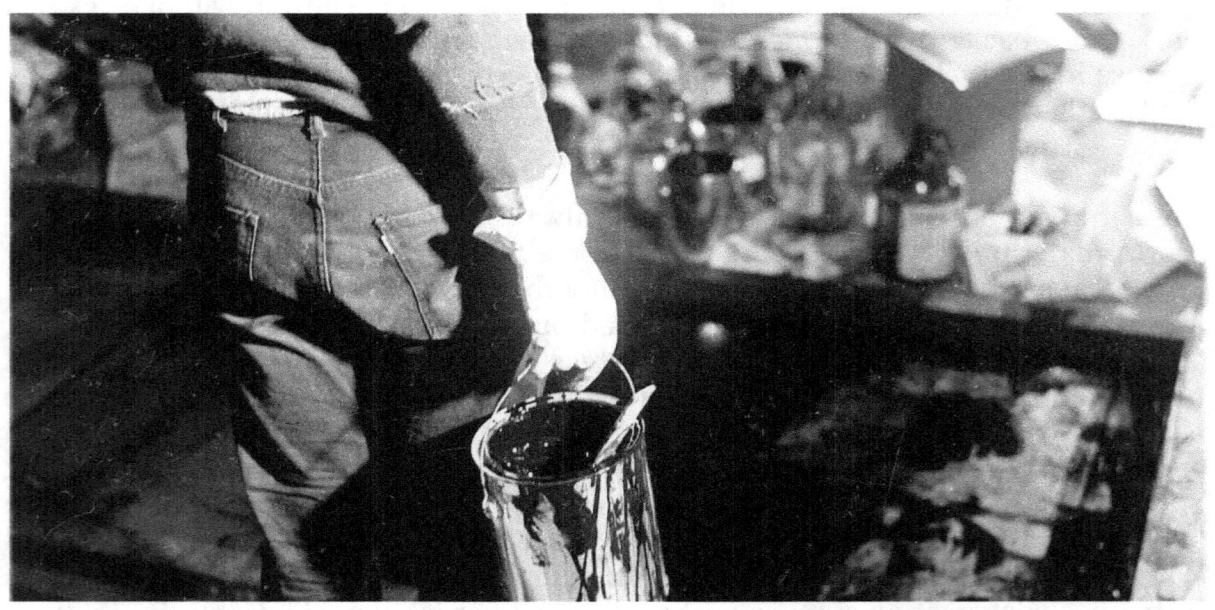

"I never wanted to be a painter. I wanted to be a tap dancer." Andy carries his can.
(Photos: Billy Name)

Billy Name: Well, Andy was a Zen master from the 'dissolving' school... the school of 'dissolution', which allowed confusion and chaos to occur in a semi-controlled situation. Andy's significant impulse which affected people was 'synthesis'. If you had an opening in an art gallery and Andy came in, all of a sudden the entire gallery would be galvanized in a 'synthesis' sort of way. Everyone felt the same electricity and fusion. And it was an inspiring fusion. It was something that allowed people, all of a sudden, to be just who they are.

Mary Woronov: What Andy needed all those people for was because Andy is not stupid—he knows that out of chaos comes art. He needed those people because they didn't think in a little box like my dad and my mom. They thought *way* off the map! And the further off the map you have people thinking around you the more artistic you can be, because it is not real and it's not bound and tied up. And that was why we were all there... Well, that and drugs.

Peter Scheldahl, art critic for The New Yorker, would, I feel, agree with Mary. In May 2000 he reviewed the show 'Women of Warhol: Marilyn, Liz and Jackie', and sensed "a radical artist stepping ashore from the foundering vessel of twentieth-centry taste, without so much as wet feet." Scheldahl added, "When Warhol burst upon the world in the early sixties, he was immediately taken to be a decadent mocker of high-cultural traditions... Critics at the time drove themselves crazy trying to adduce an ironic attitude in Warhol's enterprise." It's a really great article. The accompanying photos came from the art collection of Jane Holzer, who was not stupid either.

Andy Warhol: Beauty is a sign of intelligence.

Warhol's women had a special place in his heart, but of all the human flotsam that swirled about Warhol in those productive Silver Factory years, three young men emerged to become the vital components that Warhol would need to create his 'Dream Factory', based on his own unique take on the Hollywood studio system. Since Andy and company were hard-core New Yorkers, they favored a downtown 'beatnik' uniform in the early years, dressing alike in black jeans and the Breton-striped boat necks worn by French sailors—*tres conceptuelle*. At one point Gerard Malanga even died his hair ash blond to match Warhol's wig. These three energetic lads, with the help of copious amounts of amphetamine, would form...

...THE TRIANGLE

Andy completed us.
—Ondine

Victor Bockris: Andy's Factory always worked with a triangular group at the head. It comes directly from the family. He treated the boys the way his mother treated him and his two brothers. The idea is to keep each person in competition for your attention. "Who loves me most?"... "Me, me!" ... "No, me!" This is exactly what happened. These people were young and easy to manipulate. They wanted the attention. When Andy gave you his attention, it was like a drug. He would shine his light on you. It made you feel like he was really only concerned about you. He'd make you feel beautiful, which wasn't so hard because many of them were beautiful. In those early days, before the thing became so big, where I think he lost control of it, there was just a little tight group.

Billy Name: It sort of started out in that old New York Eurocentric way of an older artist keeping younger artists. The other artists had pretty boys around, but it was the tail end of that culture of that era. For instance, Andy and I would often go to Rauchenberg's studio, and his boyfriend was a dancer in Merce Cunningham's Dance Company. The arts culture was integrated like that. Gertrude Stein was still the queen of literature, with that whole hashish Alice B. Toklas thing, and a person having a younger lover or someone they were keeping was still going on, so that's how I started out my relationship with Andy.

Victor Bockris: Andy relied upon Billy, and Billy was certainly reliable. He was the only one allowed to live at the Factory. He was the gatekeeper, the key man. In those early days, before the life ravaged him, he was just extraordinary. He was part of the Judson Dance Company, closely associated with those people at the Judson, with Merce Cuningham and John Cage, the avant-garde. That was a door to another world, into which Billy took Andy. He also became a great photographer. I would argue that Billy Name was one of the great photographers of the sixties, in terms of capturing the movement and the spirit of that world.

Robert Heide: I first met Billy Name, whose name was Billy Linich, at the San Remo, a bar on the corner of Bleeker and Macdougal. It was quite a mix of people, a lot of the theater crowd. It wasn't just gay. I became quickly infatuated with him because he was so stunningly interesting and beautiful, so we wound up getting together, having an affair. Billy might put it another way, but that's the way I saw it. He was interested in Existentialism, and we talked a lot about that, and 'being and nothingness', being there.

Billy Name is still 'there', and sometimes having a simple conversation can give one the feeling of falling into a rabbit hole. As a Buddhist far more evolved than myself, his altruism toward his fellow beings, even when they are complete dirt bags, can be unnerving. ("Hell is other people," to quote Sartre.) But Billy has fond memories nonetheless. Of his salad days spearheading the 'A-heads', the Silver Factory's hyperactive amphetamine rapture group, we were to discover that he had perfect recall, and unlike some others, was not prone to hyperbole.

Billy Name: Andy and I had been lovers, but when he got this new space, we became *so* involved with the creation of what became the Silver Factory. . . And because he had just started doing filmmaking, he gave me a still camera and said, "Billy, you do the photography. I'm just going to make films now."

Victor Bockris: The way Billy became a photographer was classic of the way Warhol worked. Andy bought himself a camera in early '63. But in those days, having a camera was cumbersome. After using the camera a couple of times, he gave it to Billy. From that moment, having never taken a picture, Billy Name made his own film, and developed the pictures, the whole bit, from beginning to end

Warhol: My idea of a good picture is one that's in focus and of a famous person.

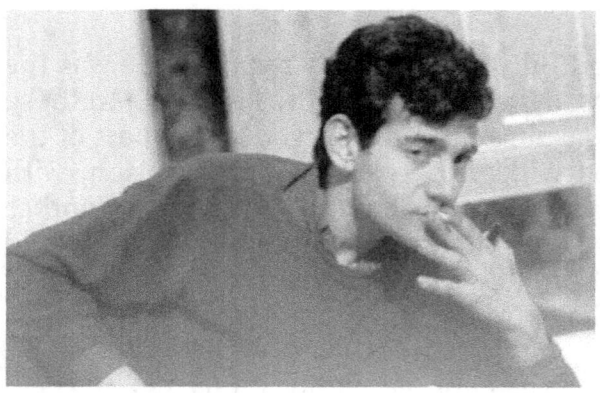
Ondine, the "King's Court Jester" (Photo: Billy Name)

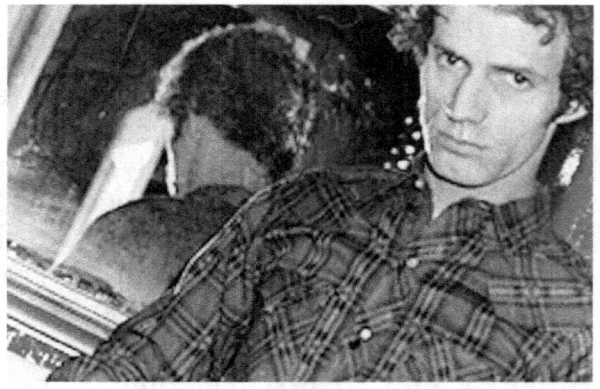
Factory Manager and 'gate-keeper Billy Name, in a self-portrait

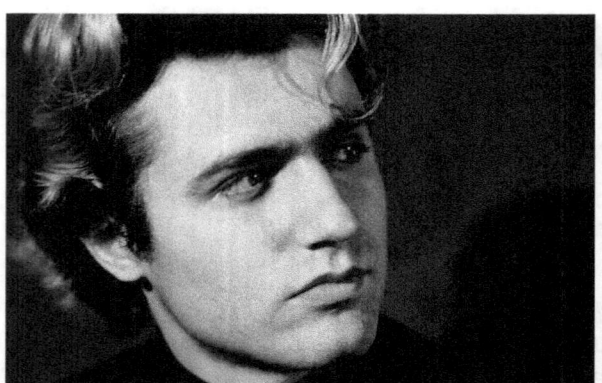
Gerard Malanga, "The Prime Minister" (Photo: Nat Finkelstein)

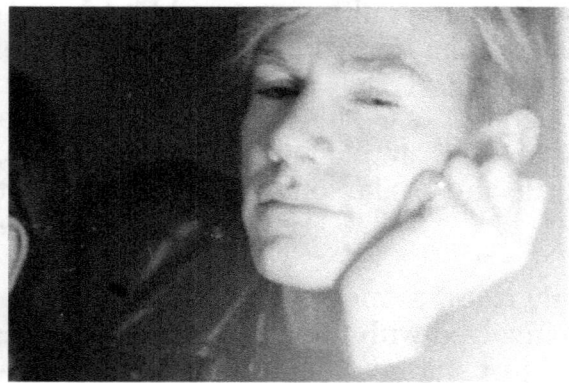
The King of Pop Art. (Photo: Billy Name)

Louis Waldon: Oh, Billy was definitely on the scene in New York. He would hang out at your place, and smoke Camel cigarettes. He would take the silver paper out of the pack and paste it on the wall, do a whole wall with silver. That was where the Factory came from... Gerard was also around. And always with girls.

Gerard Malanga: The *girls*? Well, I guess I had a few girlfriends during that time. But it's not something that meant anything. It was just the way things were.

Victor Bockris: Gerard was devoted to Andy. The thing, the most important thing that Gerard walked a thin line on, was that he was actively bisexual, but primarily he was just heterosexual. He was the Factory stud; he really did have sex with all those girls who came to the Factory.

Nat Finkelstein: As far as Gerard is concerned, he was the person who gave the Factory its impetus. Gerard was the pretty guy who went out. He was never gay. He was *fake* gay. You can be pseudo gay but Gerard was never ever gay. He brought the girls up. And to a certain extent Gerard was the person who was the intermediary between Andy's group of people and the Beat poets.

Billy Name: Gerard started to work as Andy's assistant, and because of his ties in the world of poetry he started getting Andy connections into that world. He would go out with Andy to a cultural occurrence acting as if he was Andy's boyfriend, because they all had young boyfriends, so Gerard acted like Andy was keeping him. I recall I got a bit pissed off with this, because he was pretending. You see, Gerard knew how to social climb, but it wasn't a pretentious thing; he just knew how to manipulate things to get his position in the world. We all did that when we had the opportunity.

Gerard Malanga: I met Ondine at the Factory through Billy. Friday night we would go on this all-night binge. We would start at someone's apartment—there was probably amphetamines going around—and end up going out in the morning looking for a luncheonette to be open. The 'Dawn Patrol'... I was the youngest in the group, so I never thought of myself as running the show. I always felt a part of the show—it had a life of its own. Andy was very open to ideas and activities, so we'd go to a party or a gallery opening, or a concert. Andy would just go home, if nothing was doing.

Andy Warhol: Isn't life a series of images that change as they repeat themselves?

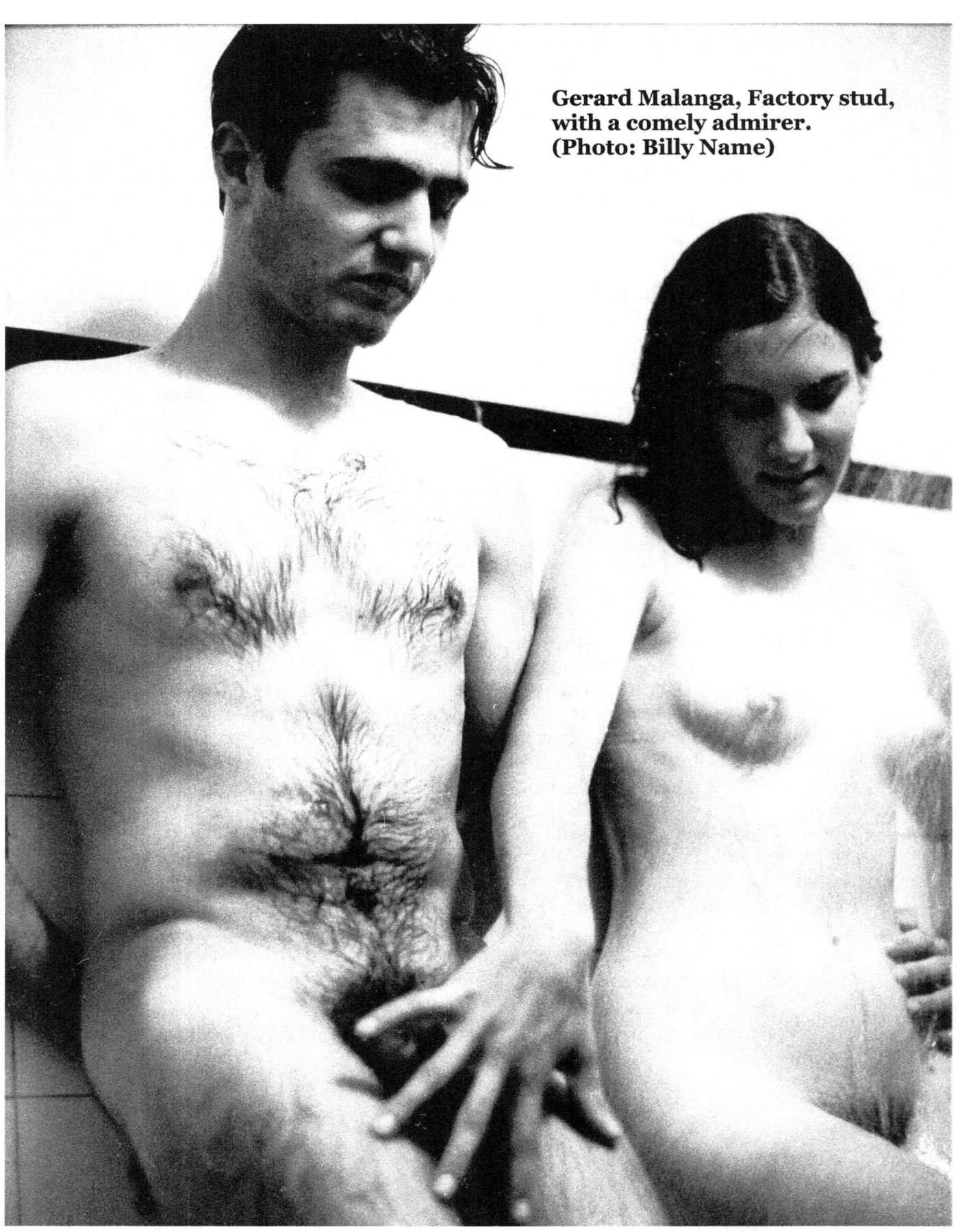

Gerard Malanga, Factory stud, with a comely admirer. (Photo: Billy Name)

Mary Woronov: Gerard and I were sitting down on this tacky little dirty couch and he said, "You should stay because we are doing screen tests. This will be the beginning of movies for you." He didn't say "you and me", and I didn't find out until later. He was so secretive in a way. Gerard knew that Warhol was going into movies, and he wanted to be *the* male lead. He realized that he needed a counterpart, a female, and I was it! . . . Gerard didn't really like the other guys who hung around Warhol—Billy, Ondine. He was like, "Uh uh, no, no!" It would ruin his image. . . But Ondine was probably the best camp actor I knew. I once did a play with him, and he would say something, obviously being gay, but looking totally masculine. A minute afterward, I would say the same thing, obviously being feminine, but acting very masculine. It was a weird complementing thing. From that moment on, Ondine and I were totally connected.

Bibbe Hansen: You could never leave anything at the Factory. Ondine would take it and scissors and needle and thread, and staples and Lord knows what, make it into some article of clothing. So somebody was always furious. I would just think, "Why would you leave a cashmere sweater lying around here? You know that Ondine is going to make it into a turban." He would speed madly all night. I remember one time, apparently no one had left anything that he could work with, and we came in and he was wearing an outfit made entirely out of greenish grey trash bags, which completely predicts the whole punk fashion craze by many, many years.

In the sixties, filmmaker Bruce Torbet put together a uniquely revealing collage of daily life in the Silver Factory entitled, 'Andy Superartist'. It was also riotously funny. We licensed copious clips, including a star appearance by Ondine, the 'Clown Prince' of the Factory, whose lupine grin could be frightening to newcomers, but his amazing Romanesque profile clearly belonged on an ancient coin. Here, he meticulously paints Warhol's nails with a bottle of polish, mouthing the words 'Polish', Warhol's nationality (Well, Rurethania, but why quibble; it was on the border). Meanwhile, a spry young nautically-clad Billy Name, rail thin and painfully hip, hazards a grin as he arranges a stack of Warhol's gallon-size paint cans, which Warhol will lug about like any day laborer. . .

Andy Warhol: I suppose I have a really loose interpretation of 'work', because I just think being alive is so much work at something you don't always want to do. The machinery is always going, even when you sleep.

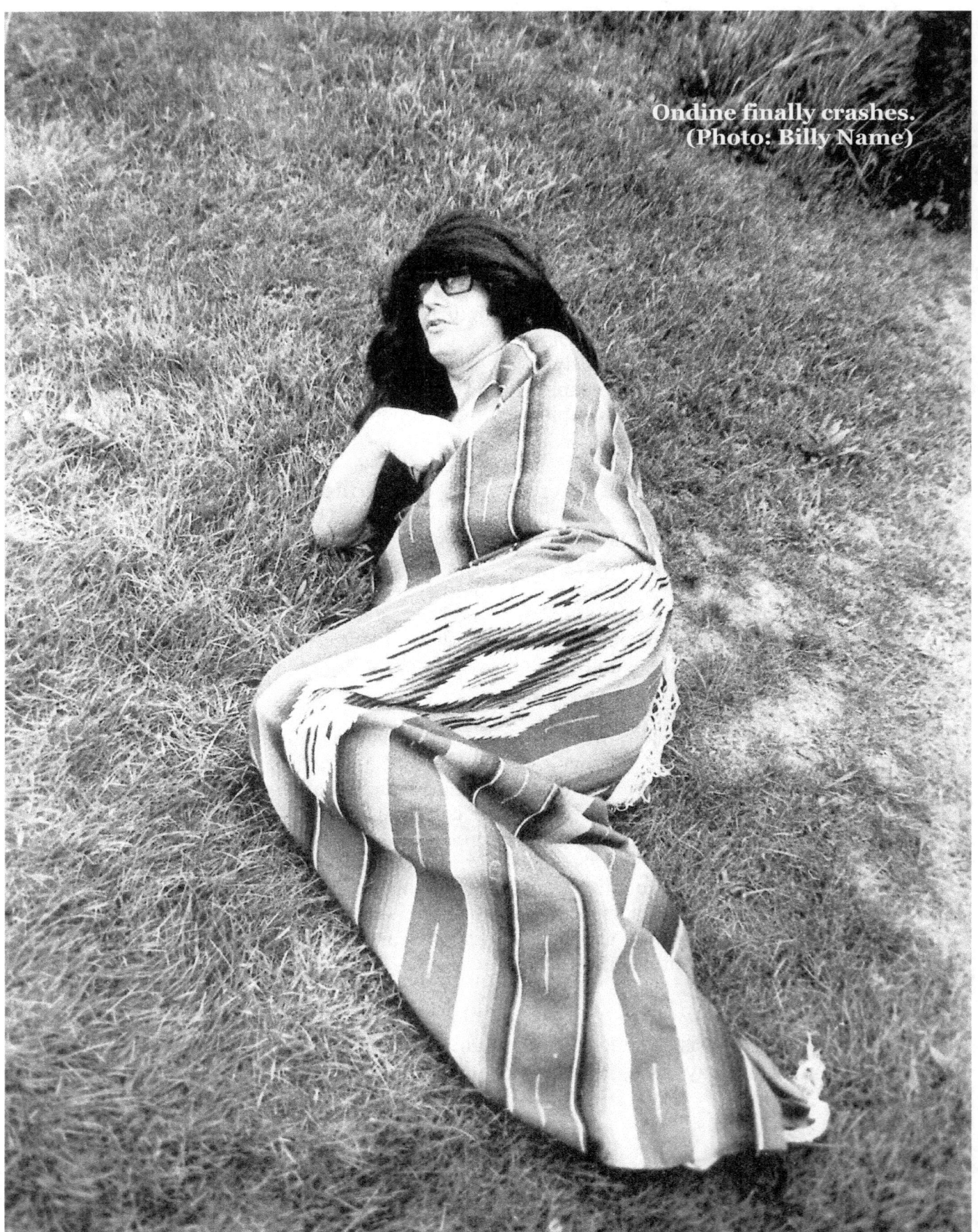

Ondine finally crashes. (Photo: Billy Name)

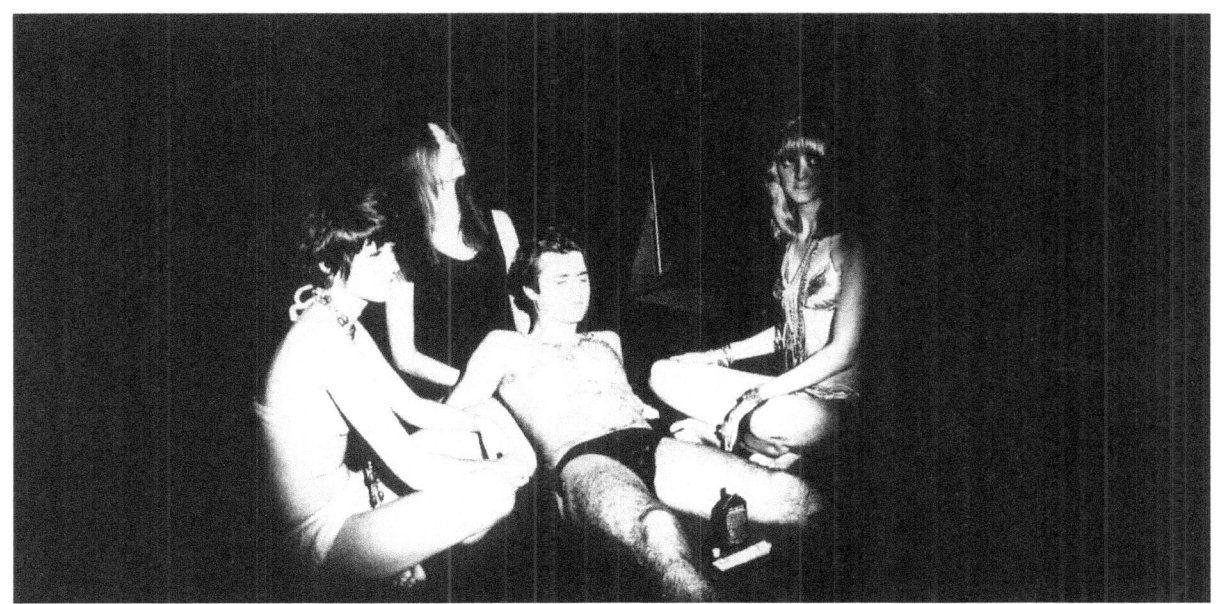

Three's a crowd, or, as Andy would say, "a party." Gerard and the girls get tantric at his 'Nair' party. They used the hair remover all over his body.

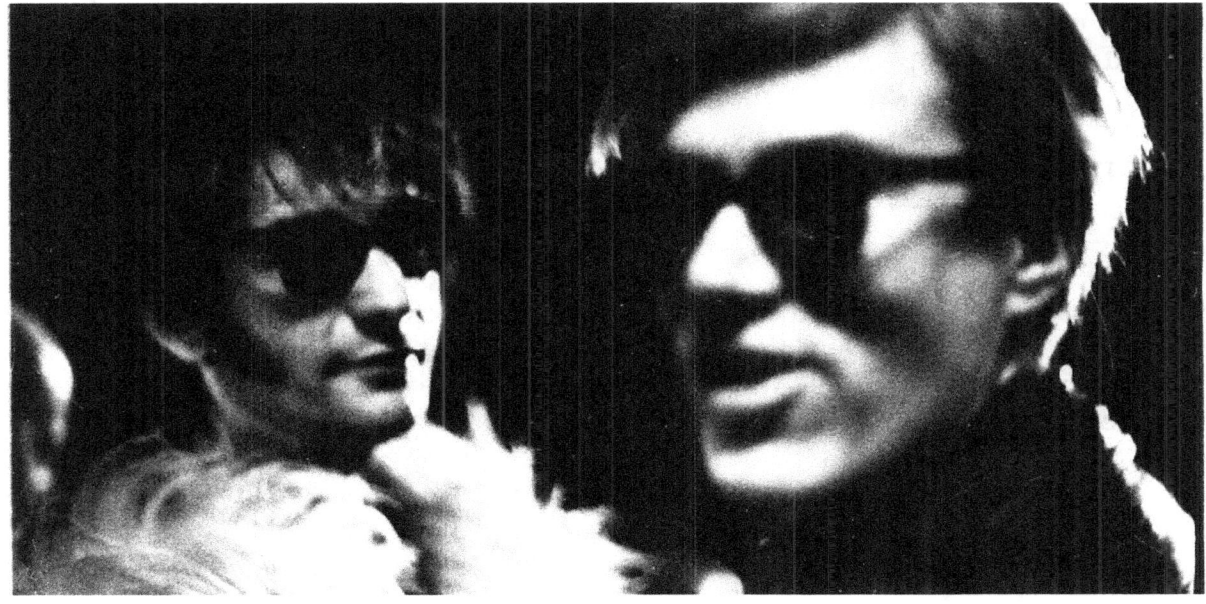

Night owls Ondine and Andy frequent Cheetah Disco. (Photos: Billy Name)

Billy Name: Andy thought Ondine was fabulous. Ondine, whose real name was Bob Olivo, was not part of the Warhol Factory as someone who worked there. He was my buddy from the amphetamine crowd. He was the grand flame, the screaming faggot who was a combination of Oscar Wilde and Laurence Olivier. So Ondine didn't come in a worker, like Gerard, or a technical facilitator, like me. He came in as a Greenwich Village star, ready to be a star of Warhol movies.

Allen Midgette: I knew Billy Name from Italy, before he met Andy. I'm working as an actor in Spoleto, and Billy's the lighting designer for various plays, with great success. Billy had come back to New York, into this little darkroom, and he offered me a joint. I smoked it and got. . . you know. At the Factory, people immediately assume that, oh, you're an actor and you really want to be in Andy's movie, which is absolutely not true. Billy and I had worked in Italy with Bertolluci and Passolini. I mean they did a professional job! After that experience, I could never really want to do anything but. . . So, who were we talking about?

Not surprisingly, we unearthed film of Billy rolling a joint, sharing his bounty with Ondine and Allen Midgette, and it's right out of 'Reefer Madness', all jittery and swooshingly hand-held by Danny Williams, Warhol's tormented young boyfriend from '65 to '66, who disappeared under mysterious circumstance, an apparent suicide. His work reminds one of a Francis Bacon painting. The transgressive quality of the film may have dissipated in the smoke of time and medicinal marijuana, but back in the early sixties smoking pot with friends was a real bonding experience. It still is, except that now people my age really *do* use it for assorted ailments. This is so not fun to talk about when you are high.

Victor Bockris: Billy, Gerard, Ondine, '63, '64. These three guys were basically supportive of each other, on the same trip. They called Gerard the Prime Minister, and Billy was, of course, the Manager of the Factory, and Ondine was the Fool, the king's court jester. Henry Geldzahler, assistant curator at the Metropolitan Museum, put it well when he compared Andy's world to the court of Louis XIV, the Sun King, and for this particular period, as Ondine said, "Every moment was the right moment." They were all there for Andy. They took it seriously—*This is a cause, this is an artistic cause*. And they were going through his last great painting period.

Andy Warhol: I just do art because I'm ugly and there's nothing else for me to do.

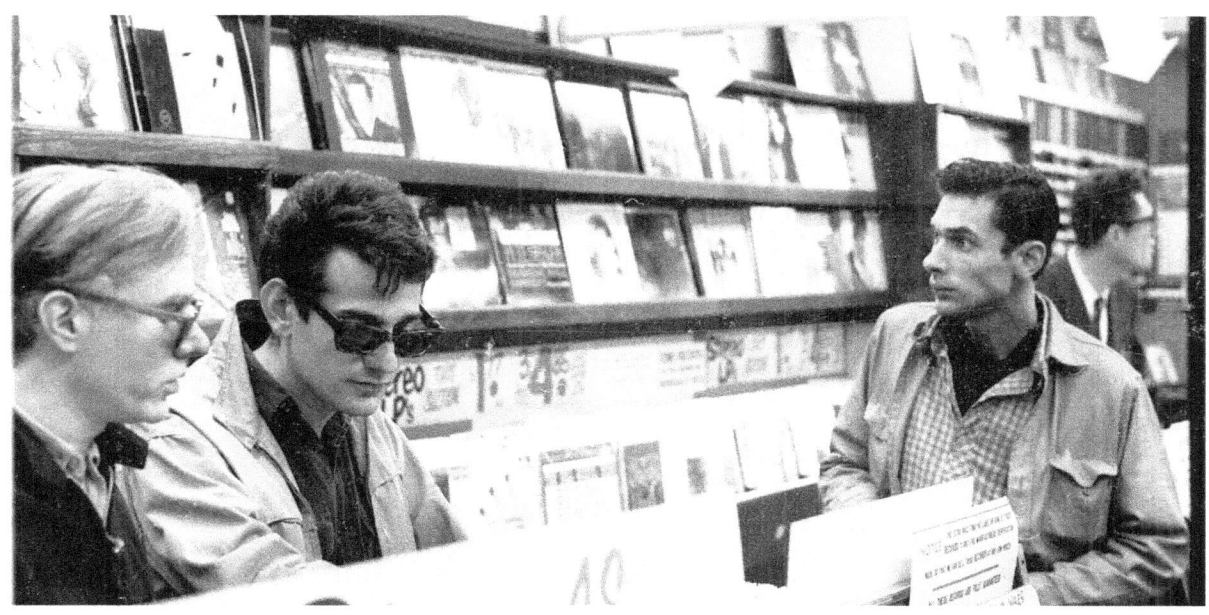

Andy, Ondine, and Billy's boyfriend Jimmy Sullivan cruise a music store for Marie Callas records.

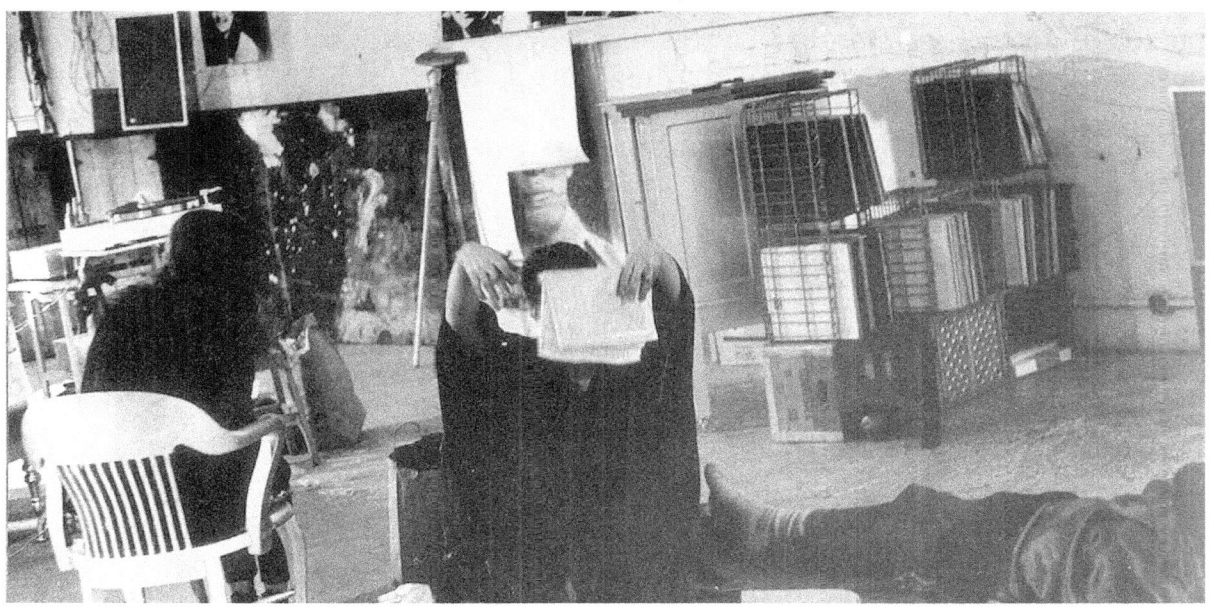

Ondine (center) and friends relax and listen to their favorite music. Note record player at left. (Photos: Billy Name)

As you may recall, Warhol had created the Flower Paintings on the advice of his friend, art curator Henry Geldzahler, who was tiring of all those Death pictures, and suggested he try something living for a change. Warhol, as ever, was open to suggestion. Geldzahler leafed through a magazine and stopped at a centerfold of flowers. Eureka! Warhol immediately began to make silk-screens of Patricia Caulfield's friendly photograph of four poppies. She later sued, and Warhol was put through a long costly court case, which was eventually settled. He had to pay.

Andy Warhol: I've decided something. Commercial things really do stink. As soon as it becomes commercial for a mass market it really stinks.

The Flowers were exhibited in 1964 at the Leo Castelli Gallery, and sold out. Warhol claimed to like them because they "looked like cheap awning." A few months after, the cheerful Flowers were given their 'Vernissage' at the Sonnabend Gallery in Paris to Gallic accolades. Henry Geldzahler had been right: At that propitious moment, his favored artist had been duly crowned the 'King of Pop Art', and was the giddy recipient of the royal treatment from the enthralled French, who had long since decapitated most of their own. At which point, Warhol majestically declared, to the horror of his art dealers, that he was officially 'retiring' from painting. He would have a grand retrospective the following year of works from '62 to '64 (so it may indeed have been a wily move to raise those prices), but following the wild success of the Flowers, Warhol would only make art as needed, reproducing silk-screens or portraits to finance his budding film career...

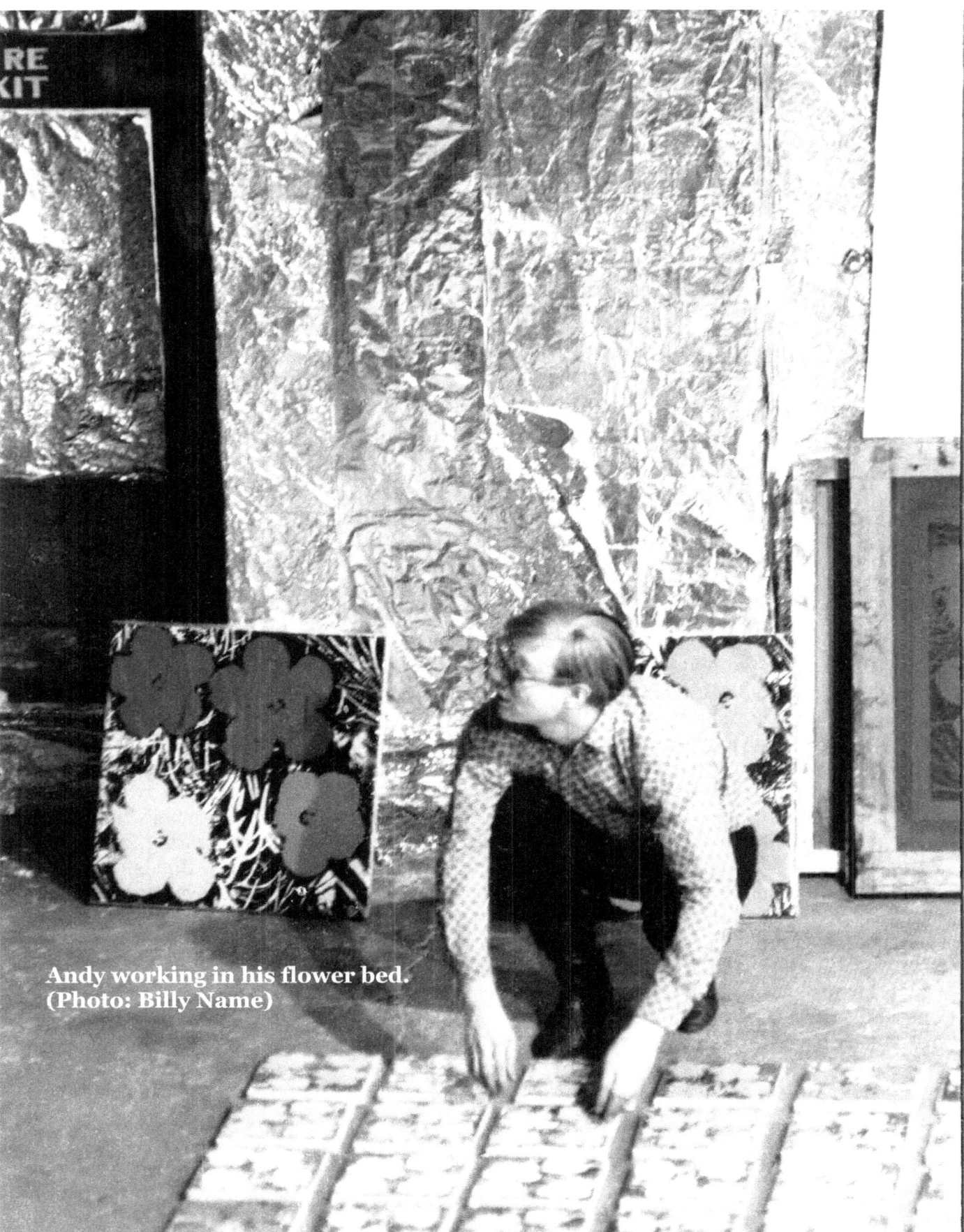

Andy working in his flower bed.
(Photo: Billy Name)

ANDY MAKES MOVIES...
THE SILENT ERA

There is the possibility that new techniques are being explored, that other filmmakers can benefit by those techniques.
—Willard Van Dyke: Curator, Metropolitan Museum of Art

We found early sixties news footage of Willard Van Dyke, who had used Warhol's film 'Sleep' to make his point. He didn't bother to mention that Warhol had been inspired to make 'Sleep' from the memory of shyly watching his first boyfriend sleep, while his lonely immigrant mother wandered the halls, wondering what he was up to. According to Warhol biographer Victor Bockris, he would often resort to locking Mother Julia in her bedroom, until finally relegating her to that damp basement, where she would reside, despite what Taylor Mead remembers, for the next twelve years. Disappointingly, Van Dyke didn't go into the Gothic aspects of Warhol's first film noir. Instead he chose to expound on the "painterly aspects of the lighting." He also interviewed a young Jonas Mekas to talk about underground movies. Jonas told him then the same thing he told us half a century later: "Warhol was an avant-garde genius." This is vintage Warhol, those endless silent movies of '63 and '64, before the 'advent of sound', where the most likely accompaniment would be the audience snoring. To make time feel like it was really crawling, Warhol had insisted that these early silents be projected at 16 frames per second instead of the usual 24 (which gives an illusion of slow motion). According to Jonas Mekas, these films "celebrated existence by slowing down our perceptions." When we screened some of them, we celebrated their existence with Moroccan hashish. You want time to stand still? Highly recommended...

Jonas Mekas: The *real* Warhol began with 'Kisses' and 'Sleep', yes. That was a period when art and the time element became important, like LaMonte Young playing a single musical note for six hours. So Andy was not an amateur or naive artist; he was in touch with everything that was happening in all of the arts. Andy adopted and used and transformed, in his own way. That is why, the six hour films. By the way, the man sleeping was the poet John Giorno, and I heard that he still had the mattress in the attic *(laugh)*. It will be auctioned probably, at Sotheby's.

'Sleep' was first screened for Jonas in artist Wynn Chamberlain's Bowery loft, which was fitting since Warhol not only got art ideas from his friend, he'd also lifted ten rolls of 16mm film that Chamberlain had purchased to try his own hand at making an avant-garde film. One fine day, Warhol came for a visit to Chamberlain's country house. Later that day, Chamberlain walked in on Warhol, who was merrily using up all ten rolls to shoot his boyfriend at the time, a soundly sleeping John Giorno. I watched that film without the benefit of hash, and it was almost enough to make me give up movie-making altogether (Chamberlain didn't try again until 1969). But what do I know? What I do want to know is, how did Giorno get to keep that mattress?

Billy Name: Andy and I went to some sessions of Jack Smith filming 'Normal Love' on Lower East Side rooftops. For the first time Andy saw that he didn't have to pre-conceive a film, you could just make it happen, because Jack Smith was basically conceptual; the focus of his images were his characters. Andy saw that he didn't have to direct people, he didn't have to have a script, he could just make a film of what was going on. But he did not find his own style of filmmaking until he said, "I am not going to do hand-held anymore. I am going to put the camera on a tripod. I am not going to move, I am just going to load the film and turn it on and off." That became what we called the 'Kiss' series, the 'Screen Test' series, the serial art films, and they were simply these still-life portraits of a living person.

Mary Woronov: But I think for Warhol the screen test was *not* that. I believe that Warhol was afraid of people. For this guy who is afraid of people, to finally have this person sitting in front of him, looking at him! But it wasn't the person; it was the *film* of the person, and he would become close, whereas with real people he couldn't achieve that. So he was actually sexually fantasizing, sexually fascinated, and that is why the screen tests kept on happening. We used to watch them and we would be all *bored* out of our minds, and he was like, "Hummmmm, Hummmmmm."

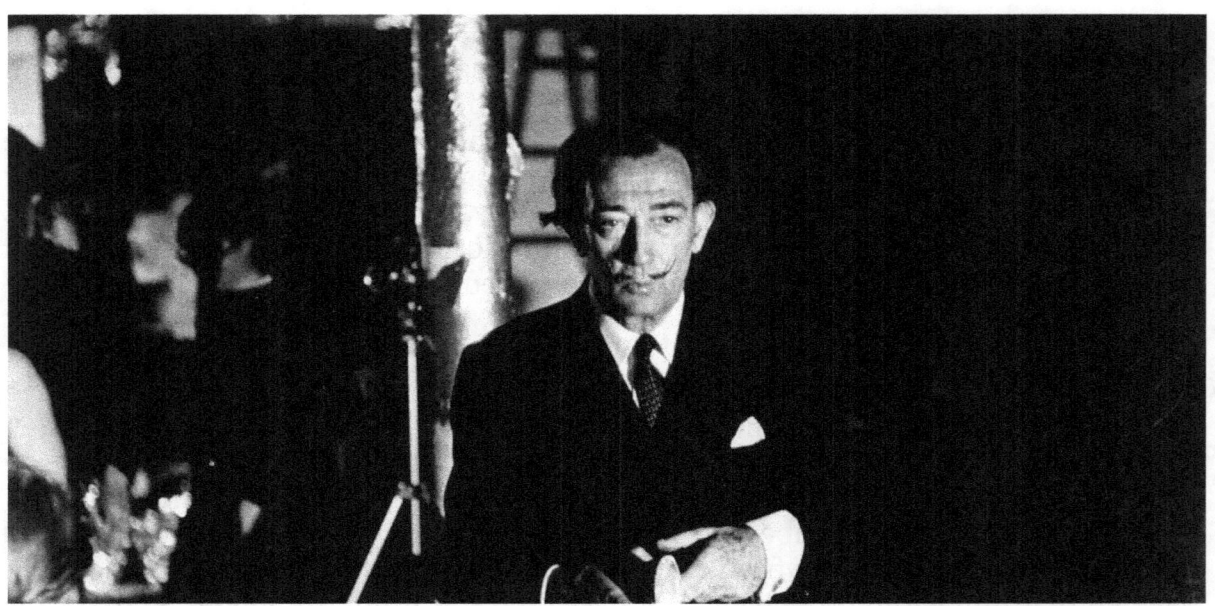

A tense Dali under pressure during his screen test. From the artist, Warhol learned the use of public visibility. At the Dali Museeum in St. Petersburg, Fl. 2014, 'Warhol: Art, Fame, Mortality'.

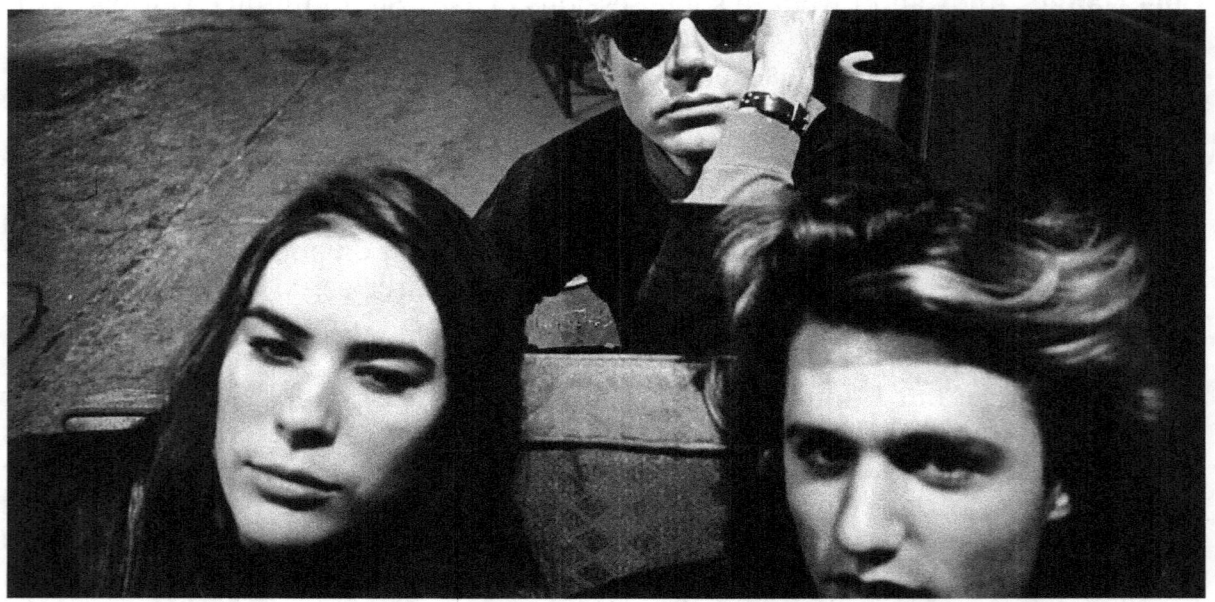

Mary and Gerard try to stay awake by grading the subjects of assorted screen tests. (Photos: Nat Finkelstein)

While Warhol sat glued to the screen, mesmerized and, according to Mary, mentally masturbating, his subjects would squirm. Mary and Gerard and the others waited for the occasional on-camera breakdown, which could supply some entertainment. They also relieved the tedium by grading everyone who wound up on camera, and anybody who showed up at the Factory was fair game, even underground film luminary Jonas Mekas, who, surprisingly, twitched and grimaced throughout his own screen test. . .

Jonas Mekas: There used to be a chair, and a Bolex (camera), a motorized Bolex, and anybody new who came into the Factory was asked to sit there, perhaps for two minutes, forty five seconds of film. They were called 'Screen Tests', about four hundred or so of them, and, interesting what happens, when some people would sit there. You don't know what to do. Some begin to argue and fight, or dance with the camera, or make faces. They are just by themselves, there is no cameraman, the camera is running, and there is you. What do you do, when you face the camera?

Mary Woronov: Gerard said, "Do a screen test," and I am immediately paranoic. I think, "Well, there is no film on the camera, they're playing a joke on me." So, okay, should I show them, just get up and walk away? But maybe there is film there. I saw Salvador Dali's film, when he struck this pose, but he couldn't hold it, so he started to crack. . . We used to play a game with these screen tests. We would judge them, a test of whether someone has a soul. If they look at the camera and nothing comes through, they are soulless, and get a ten; otherwise they get a one or whatever.

Gerard Malanga: You can't really have a narrative without sound I don't think. You can in literature but it is a different idea for film. Certainly from the visual aspect, the idea of a static image taking on a moving image, it was just another appendage to what he was doing with the paintings.

Huh? Well, Gerard, I guess that discounts all the great classic silent films made before the advent of sound. In my humble capacity as a sound designer for a couple of decades, I've helped restore a few classic theatrical silent features for television with an 'M&E' track (music and effects), but the story itself, the narrative, certainly remains intact. The non-narrative style in movies would be, as film writer Bilge Ebiri of New York Magazine claimed, "the cinematic equivalent of how, say, Beethoven had structured his symphonies." Of course Ludwig was stone deaf, but still. . .

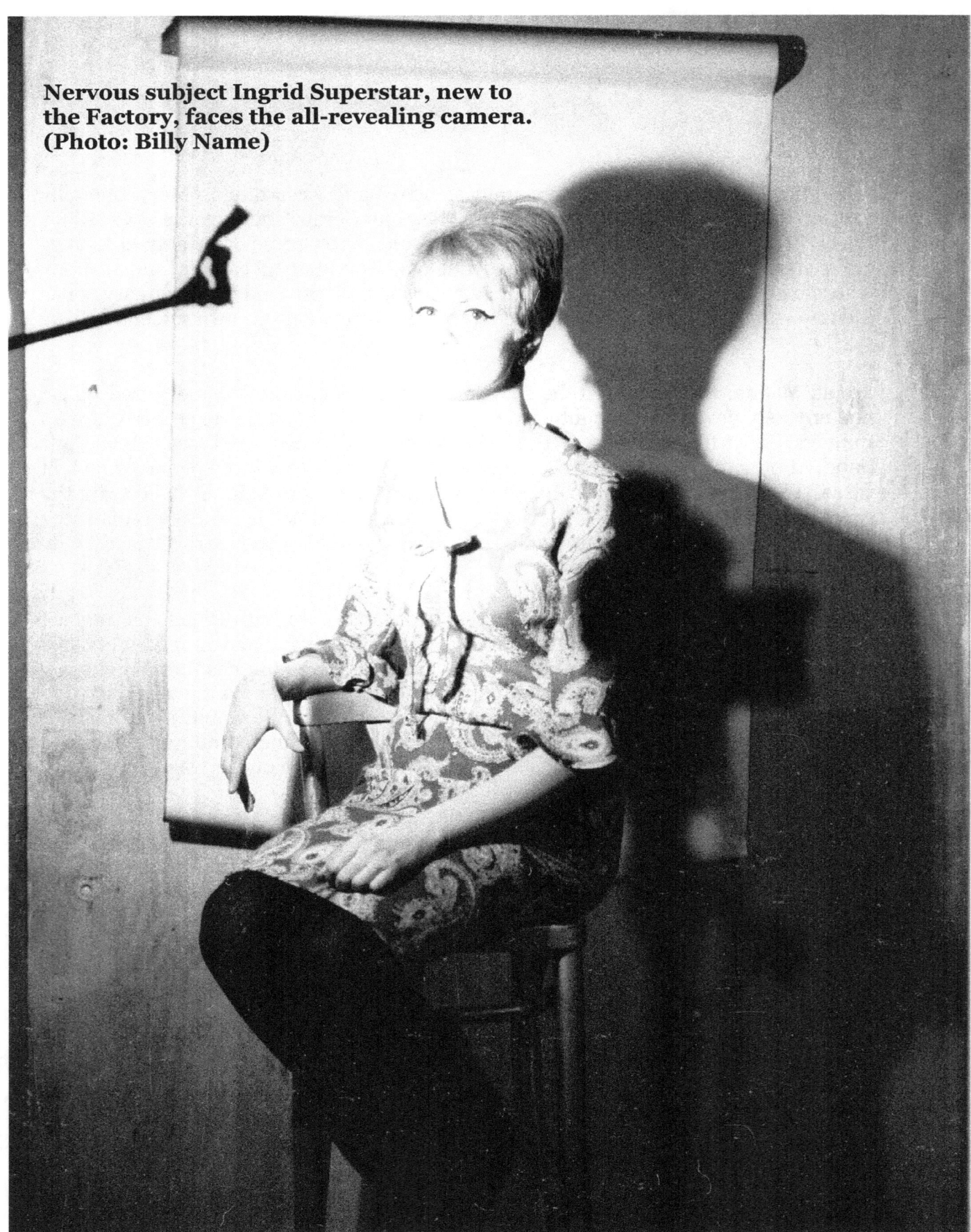

Nervous subject Ingrid Superstar, new to the Factory, faces the all-revealing camera. (Photo: Billy Name)

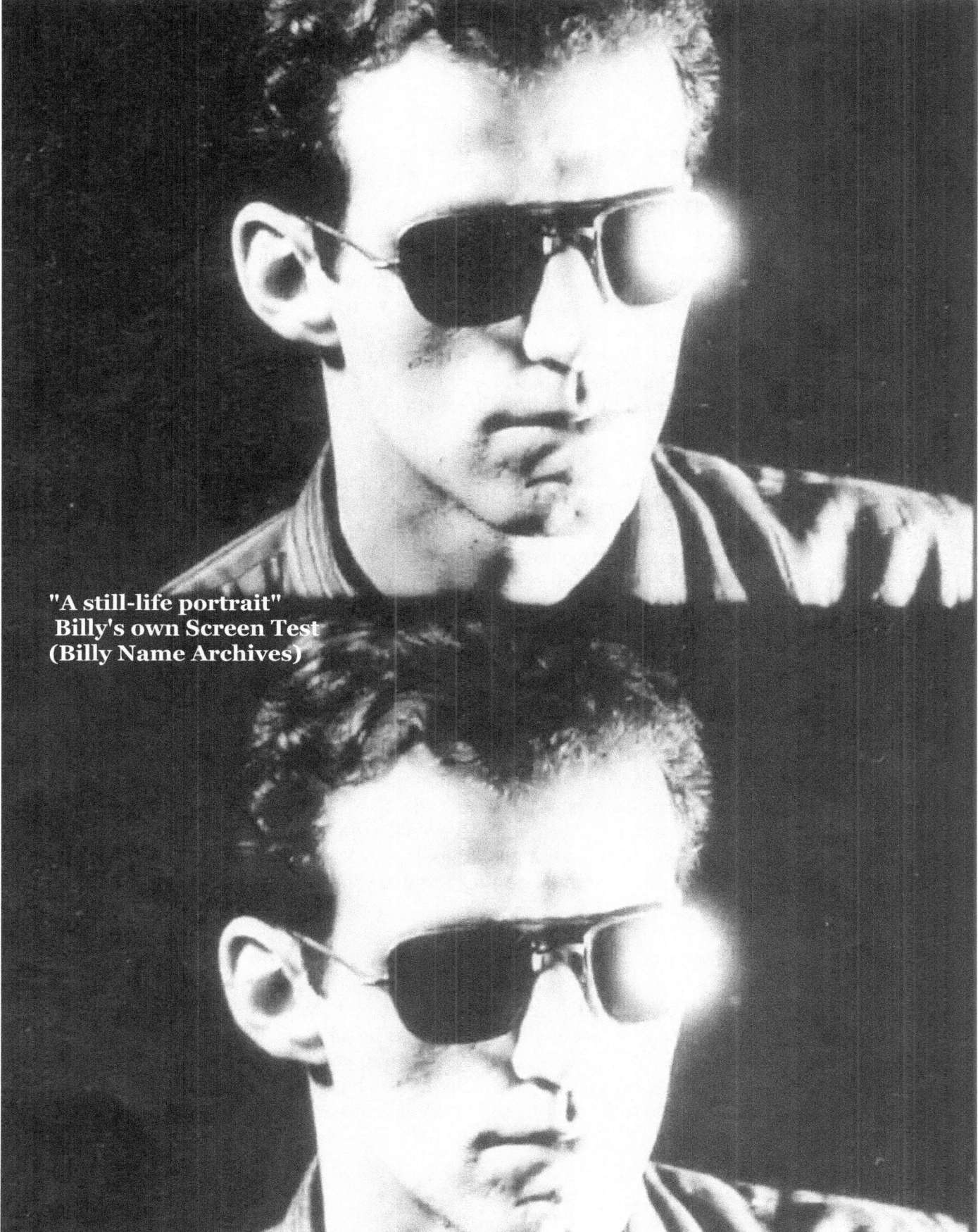

"A still-life portrait"
Billy's own Screen Test
(Billy Name Archives)

Ultra Violet: Every day we were filming at the Factory, the crowd coming in and out. One day Andy said, "You have to be there at noon." The movie was titled 'The Life of Juanita Castro'. She was the sister of Fidel, and there was quite a group of people. We were just sitting, wallpaper-like, and Juanita was screaming and yelling. Marie Menken played Juanita Castro, and she was very good, very explicit. No script of course, but how she could carry on! That was the first time I was on film, which was a bit embarrassing, twitching your lips and what have you. The next day, on a sheet of fabric, we would see what we had done. I think that's what captivates people about those Warhol movies. To be on screen is some kind of a revelation, and you can see who you are. . . What I love about his movies, it's really *Cinema Realité*, as opposed to Godard. That would be *Cinema Vérité*, which is, whatever.

Ultra Violet, who as I mentioned is *Francaise*, actually snorted with derision when talking about Jean Luc Godard, revered 'Father' of the New Wave in France, famous for such films as the marvelous 'Breathless', with Jean Seberg and Jean Paul Belmondo. Well, here I was, editing the 'Factory People' documentary in Paris, for French television with, hello, a French editor. My apoplectic editor threatened dire consequence if I left Ultra's comments in the show. The comment stayed; the editor didn't. *C'est la vie. . .* We also cheated a bit here (what, again?) since this 'Juanita' wound up a 'talkie' (1965) with playwright Ron Tavel taunting the throng of actors into improv. The film is hilarious, but it's an uncomfortable humor. In Castro's Marxist 'paradise', homosexuals were imprisoned and tortured. His wealthy siblings left, settling into NYC, and Juanita wound up working for the C.I.A. *(Viva la vida!)*. While 'Juanita' had a voluble cast, Warhol continued to focus on single characters with the screen tests. Earlier, he'd practiced his silent 'technique' on longtime friends like Emile de Antonio. Erudite when he wasn't drunk, Emile's elite inner circle included avant-garde couples John Cage and Merce Cunningham, Jasper Johns and Robert Rauchenberg, where Warhol longed to belong. But when 'De', as Warhol affectionately called Emile, saw the finished film (January '65), he called his lawyer.

Billy Name: Emile de Antonio was a documentary filmmaker who was one of the first to tell Andy '*how*'—Andy would ask him *how* to make the camera work. Emile's most famous work was the McCarthy hearings, which aired on CBS. He was a real butch heterosexual who drank whiskey all the time. So he said, "Why don't you ever do a film of me?" And Andy said, "All right, I'll do a film of you if you drink a bottle of whiskey on the camera." And Emile said "OK." Soon, he's lying prone in the stairwell. But after he died, his estate wouldn't allow the Warhol Enterprise to release the film.

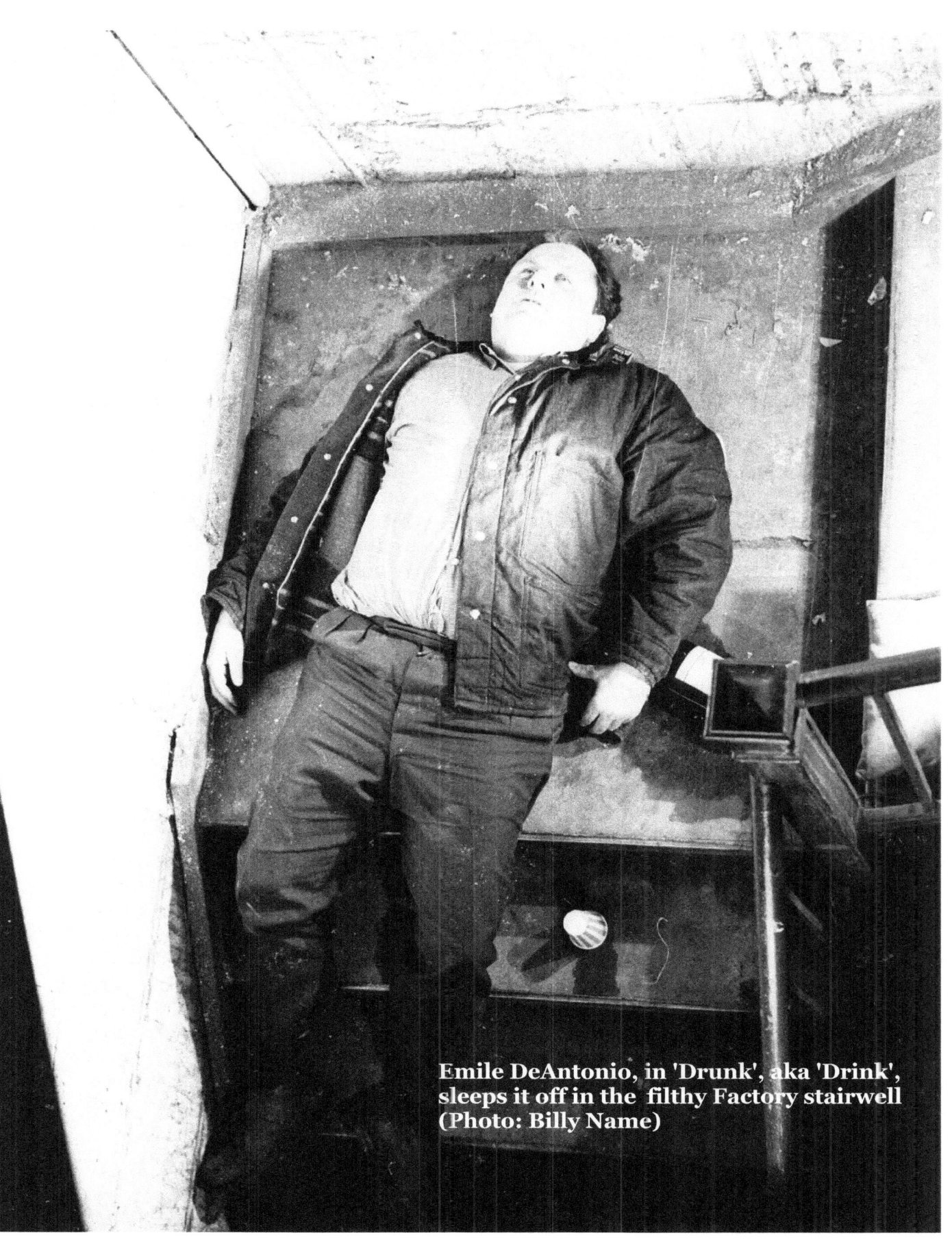

Emile DeAntonio, in 'Drunk', aka 'Drink', sleeps it off in the filthy Factory stairwell (Photo: Billy Name)

Gerard Malanga: None of them were real actors, none of us studied acting. I mean, I never really considered myself an actor even though I was in some of the movies. . . Certainly one of the great Superstars of Andy's movies was Marie Menken, who was a filmmaker in her own right, and there was Ondine, who was just wonderful spontaneity. Of course, one of the greats of all times, luckily still with us, was Taylor Mead. Taylor was initially more of a trained actor but totally out of the ordinary. I would put those three on the top: Marie Menken, Ondine and Taylor Mead.

Taylor Mead: There's a town called Tarzana, outside of L.A. And I thought—I think it was my idea—that we should make a movie where I'm Tarzan. Andy loved for people to suggest something to him, spontaneously. So, we made 'Tarzan' and the Beverly Hills Hotel pool was my crocodile infested lagoon. Dennis Hopper was my stand-in. If I had to climb a tree to get a coconut, I'd hand Dennis money on camera and tell him to go climb the tree. And he was a young, he would climb these horrible coconut trees. It was a great deal of fun. I think I edited it and put on the music. We used every inch of film. There were no double takes. It was impossible in the sixties to do a scene twice, except for Hollywood people. We only showed it a few times, and the art critics said, "We don't want to see any more two hour films of Taylor Mead's ass." My sarong kept falling down while I was climbing the trees.

We watched Taylor and Warhol's film,'Tarzan and Jane, Revisited. . . Sort Of" in its entirety, and peed our pants. So, of course we licensed lots of the footage of Taylor and Dennis Hopper in his youthful, chest-pounding, loin-clothed glory. They shot it amid the luxurious foliage of the Beverly Hills Hotel pool, where Warhol's favorite film goddesses had often preened. His 'goddess' in this film, the big-busted brunette Naomi Levine, cavorts in the sea, her enormous breasts floating like buoys. She also takes a languid bath with Taylor Mead, thus earning them the dubious credit of being the first actors to strip for a Warhol film. If you get the chance, stop by the Warhol Museum in Pittsburgh and ask for it, or wait for a holiday screening at New York's Museum of Modern Art. Otherwise you'll have to settle for our film, and those few moments of fabulous. . . After the Tarzan film, Naomi's neediness began to get on Warhol's nerves. Though she stayed in the picture, Warhol soon made friends with the quintessential big-haired blonde, Baby Jane Holzer (Girl of the Year '64). Jane reminded us that she was probably the prototype for Warhol's 'Screen Test' Series, when he suggested that she "Look at the camera and don't blink your eyes." Well, Jane, the only frames I licenced were when you blinked—otherwise it 'sort of' looked like a lovely photograph. At the museum rate of hundred bucks a second, nuh uh.

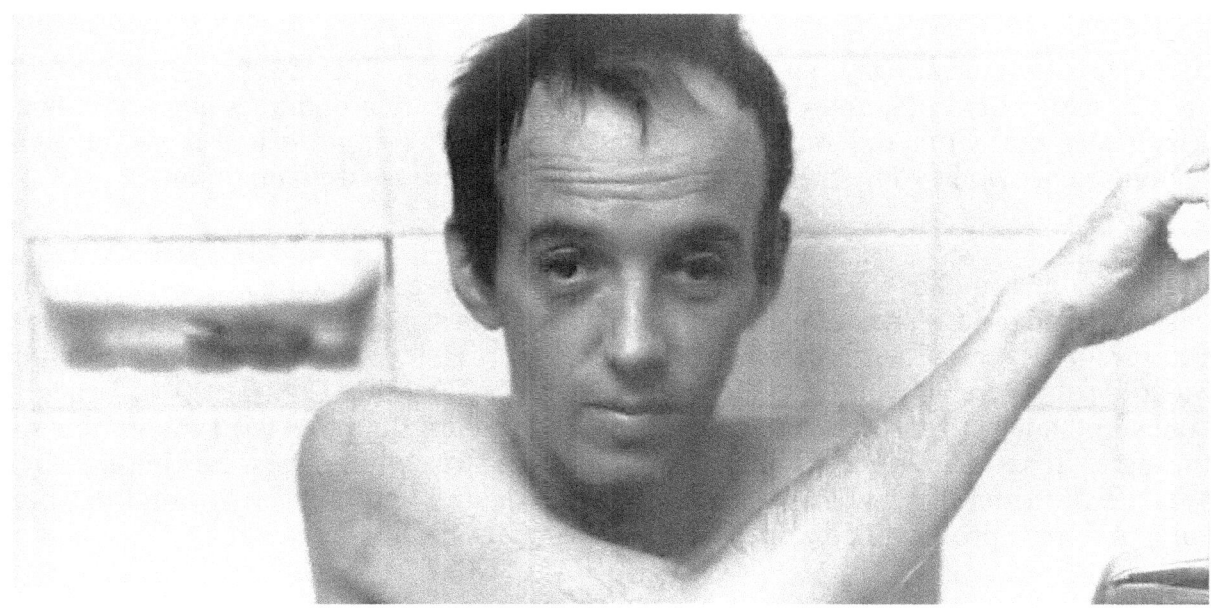

Warhol superstar Taylor Mead eagerly awaits his bathmate, "first underground film queen" Naomi Levine, in 'Tarzan and Jane Revisited... Sort of'.

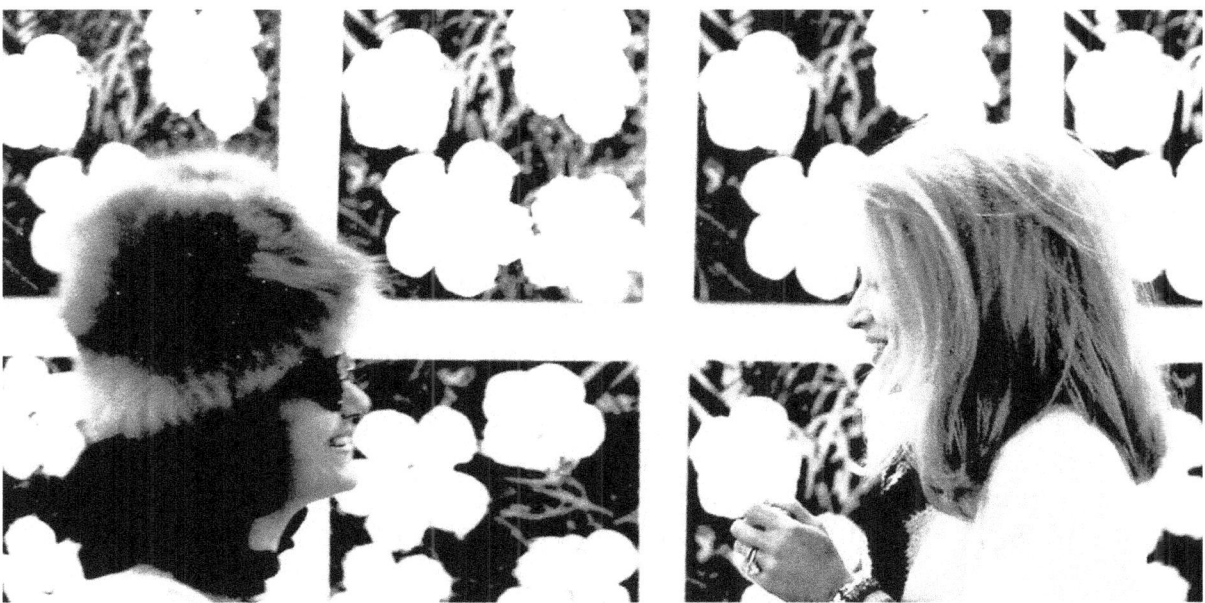

Furry-hatted Naomi Levine greets the new Warhol 'Girl of the Year', fluffy-haired Baby Jane Holzer, at the 'Flowers' opening. (Photos: Billy Name)

Jane Holzer: Andy always let other artists do their thing. He was very generous and gave much of his time, and of himself, to other artists. He had a genius and talent which was totally misunderstood and underestimated. You never had to go through the tense part when you were on camera with Andy, because it just happened.

For our film, we chose some outstanding Warhol Museum footage of Jane Holzer, who also starred in Warhol's 'Batman/Dracula'. She's swinging upside down in the vampire bat segment with Allen Midgette, as Robert Heide tends to her mane. Taylor Mead does pratfalls, while a saturnine Jack Smith ('Flaming Creatures') as Dracula stalks and sucks. I never figured out the naked guy on the table with the jumble of tubing attached to his balls, but Ivy Nicholson can usually be seen lurking nearby. When I first met Ivy in Paris, I could picture her drawing blood if I didn't get her some red wine pronto. The word 'Diva' translates into every language.

Victor Bockris: Baby Jane (Holzer) witnessed the Factory turning into a perpetual 'Happening' with some degree of alarm, though she thought some of the drugged-out performances "brilliant". Baby Jane became Andy's first Superstar. He escorted his beautiful young Park Avenue socialite to openings and parties, attracting more attention from the press. Andy loved the press.

Jane Holzer: Andy was just just standing there in the middle of it watching the whole thing happening. I don't think he believed at the time that it was happening, but he had some sort of genius putting it all together.

Andy Warhol: You have to be willing to get happy about nothing.

Ivy Nicholson: Andy and I met at a cocktail party in New York. I was kind of looking for work—I did something naughty in Europe, but I can't speak about it. . . Jane Holzer was there, and Andy and I were looking at one another like animals, like "Wow! Who is he? Who's she?" Andy told Jane to go over and tell me that I could be in a movie next week! Just like that! He did intrigue me from the first moment, the first taste of the movie. It was called 'Wives of Dracula' on the Peabody Estate, and we had the limousines taking us there of course. . . You can see it in that movie; I am looking at Andy and falling in love with him. That was with Jack Smith and Jane Holzer and Naomi Levine. No dialogue, no script, just running around saying anything we felt like saying. Andy did one head shot of me with blood dripping out of my mouth, and you can see that I am falling in love more and more with him.

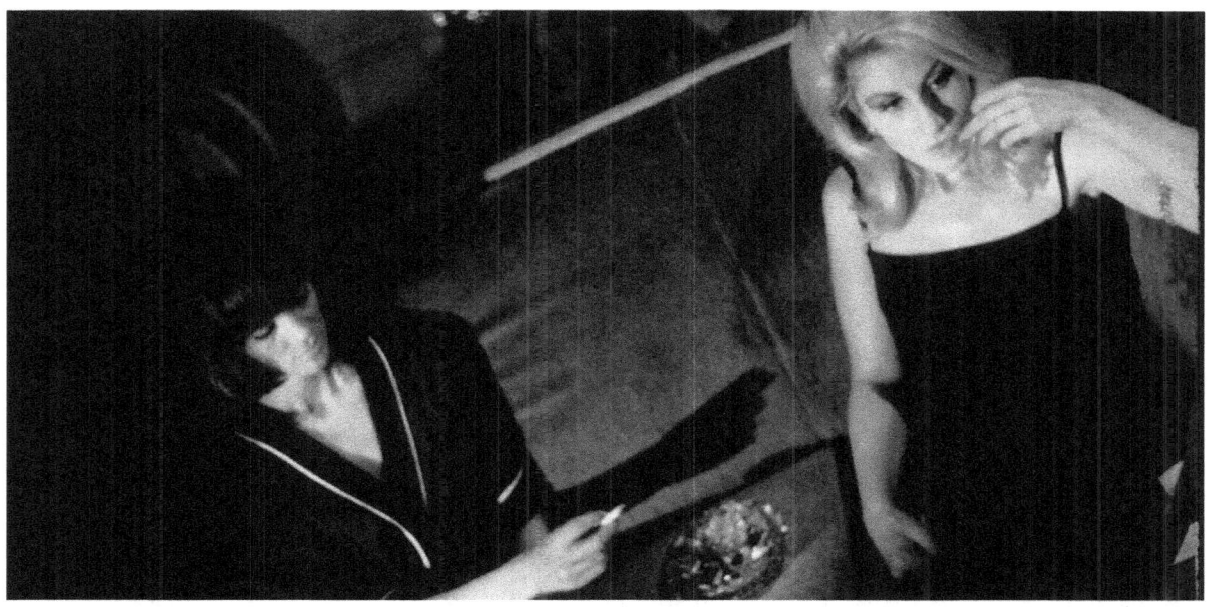

Ivy Nicholson & Baby Jane Holzer take a break on the famous couch between takes in the filming of 'Batman/Dracula', in 1964. (Photos: Billy Name)

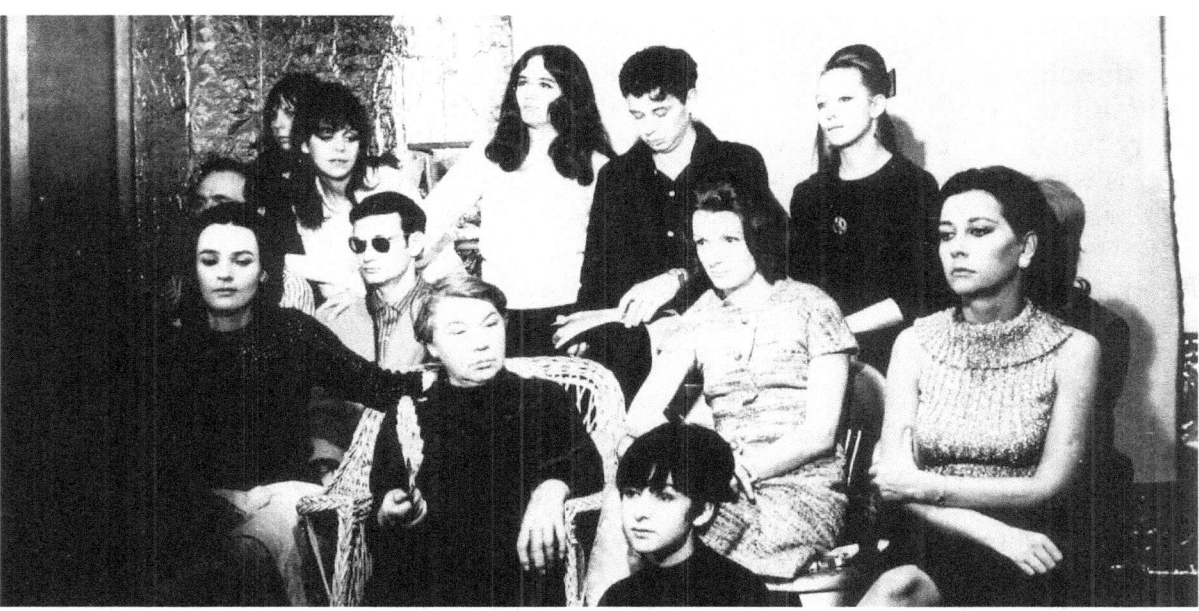

Group Therapy. In Warhol's 'The Life of Junita Castro', star Marie Menken sits at the center of her notorious 'family'. Ron Tavel, the screenwriter, is top center. Ultra Violet sits "wallpaper-like" at the far right.

It seemed that Ivy was not the only star in love with Warhol at the time. The temperamental Naomi Levine, sensing a change in the frustratingly passive Warhol, and jealous of newcomer Jane Holzer, became more demanding of his time. She began to abuse him, according to others who were there, at one point even trying to yank off his precious wig. Well, that was the straw that broke the camel-smoker's back—Billy Name firmly slapped her and threw her out, setting up a scenario that would oft be reenacted in the Silver Factory chronicles... Allen Midgette, so good at mimicking Warhol, always tried to keep a cool head when thrown into one of the Silver Factory's spicy film stews, to no avail. Pass the Tabasco...

Allen Midgette: Andy called me and said, "Oh, Allen, I'm here with Mary Woronov and Ivy Nicholson and Ultra Violet and we've got a limo and we're going to go stay at Henry McIlhenny's house in Rittenhouse Square and make a movie and I thought maybe you would want to go?" I thought, oh what the hell. So we arrive there, and it is magnificent! Henry has this five-story mansion with antiques, Toulouse Lautrecs on the wall, that French sculptor *(Rodin)*, Degas. I'd seen these things in museums! And I am thinking, "Oh my God." I couldn't understand why a rich person would have Andy and all these weird people come to their house. Henry McIlhenny was a big patron of the arts and the heir to . . . McIllhenny's. Tabasco. Sauce.

Ivy Nicholson: We did many naughty movies, and they would let him! It would be an honor to have Andy Warhol—to say, "Oh, he shot on my grounds." He would do pretty naughty things, but it was art. Really! It was art. He liked shocking people. That is what Salvador Dali was into, too. You can have the best art, but if no one has ever heard of you, how can they buy it? So, Andy knew about making publicity.

Allen Midgette: The next day, Andy says, "We're going to go to this client's penthouse, and they're going to let us shoot there." Well, we arrive at the hotel and Andy gets out, goes to the trunk of the car, and he has a painting that he quickly *staples* to a frame. I could not believe what I was looking at. So, we go up to the penthouse. They had a pool, a sauna, the whole works. Andy says, "Uh, well, why don't we take a sauna?" And I'm thinking, "He's not going in the sauna with that wig on, whatever, the makeup." But I'm a child of the sixties, so to speak; I'm ready to take my clothes off. We come out of the sauna, and now Andy says, "Why don't we shoot something by the pool?" Oh, okay. So now, we're standing by the pool and there's three actresses (Mary, Ivy, Ultra Violet) who are, you know, they're not madly in love with each other, let's face it.

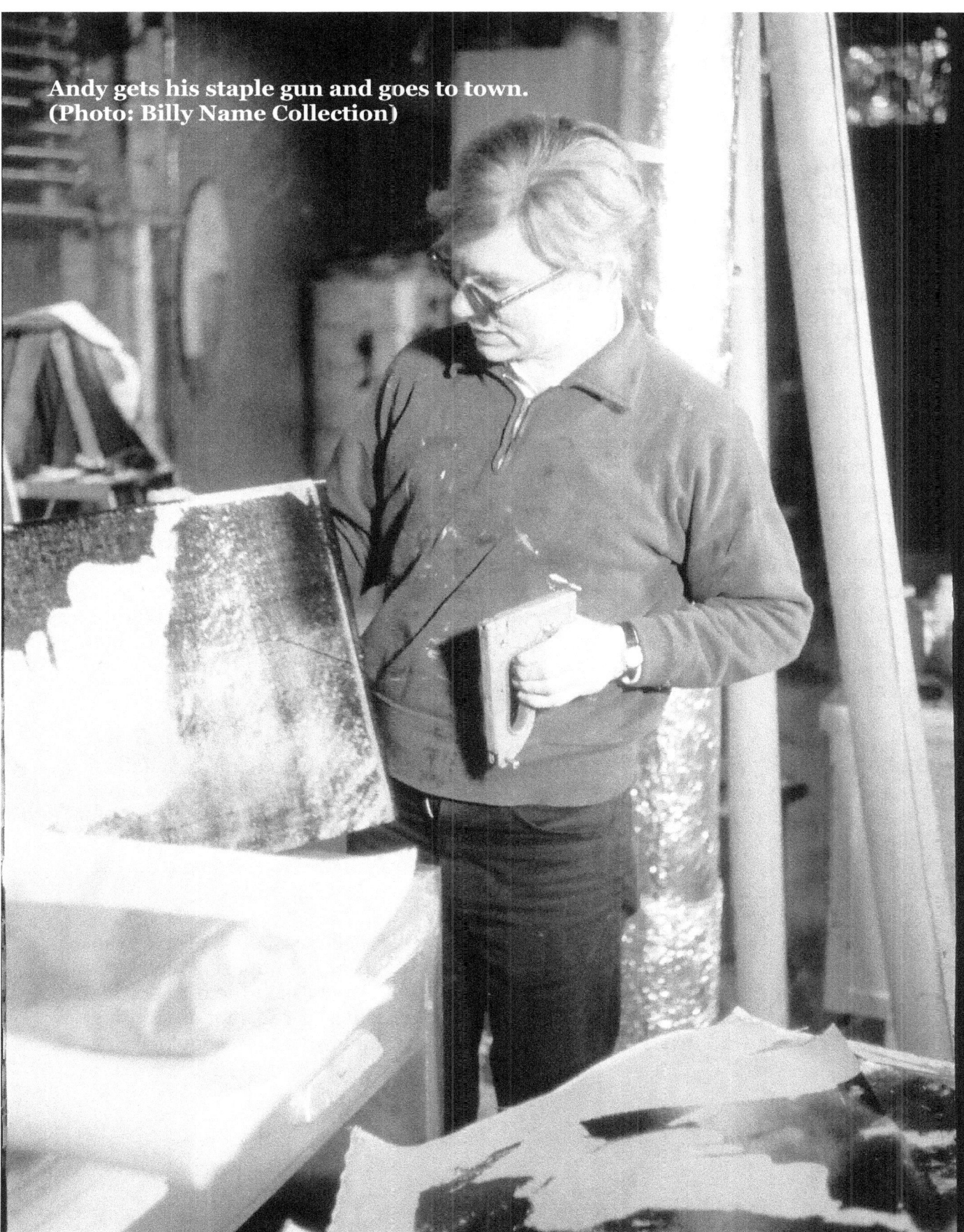

Andy gets his staple gun and goes to town.
(Photo: Billy Name Collection)

Ivy Nicholson: Well, there was some jealousy. We were all such drama queens... And we only got a hundred dollars as salary, but no one noticed that. I mean, to suddenly become a star! You were a star!

Allen Midgette: So, there is Ivy Nicholson, standing in a very rigid position. She suddenly pulls out a photograph and says, "This is my uncle, he was an alcoholic; he died at thirty-seven." All this stuff is coming out and I am thinking, "What is this all about?" So then, that film was over. If you can call these things film, that was the film. Hello?!

Allen had been a serious actor in Italy, working with Bertolucci and Passolini. In 1962 another future Warhol star was also in Italy, strolling through Fellini's 'La Dolce Vita' at fifteen. Nico called Allen "The Italian movie star," which rankled a bit, but Allen was mostly good-natured about the jabs he endured as the token Factory hippie. He and Ondine made an early Warhol film called 'Jail 'on the site where Jonas Mekas' Film Anthology Archives now stands, on Second Street. But back then, it was a prison and courthouse... Allen Midgette's 'Jail' is not to be confused with the Bibbe Hansen film, 'Prison' (1965), another Warhol inspiration. When Warhol met Bibbe, she was a teenager living—more or less—in the downtown loft of her famous father, the 'Happenings' artist Al Hansen, who was not exactly a 'hands-on' parent...

Bibbe Hansen: Andy looked over and he said, "And what do *you* do?" My father beamed proudly and said, "I just sprung her from jail." Andy's eyes grew wide. "Really! Tell me all about it!"... I made two versions of 'Prison'. The first one with Edie and I alone was kind of spare, but it was like a beautiful early Godard black and white. It was a typical classic Factory thing: The picture of one, or the sound for the other didn't come out. So they put the two together to make one.

Jonas Mekas: When they went into sound, Andy needed assistants, people who knew more about cameras and sound, and those assistants began imposing their own styles, views, and contents. I mean, much of the time Andy asked them to do this and that. With the early two films with Mario Montez, when there's a lot of zooming in-zooming out, he did that himself. He was fooling around with that technology.

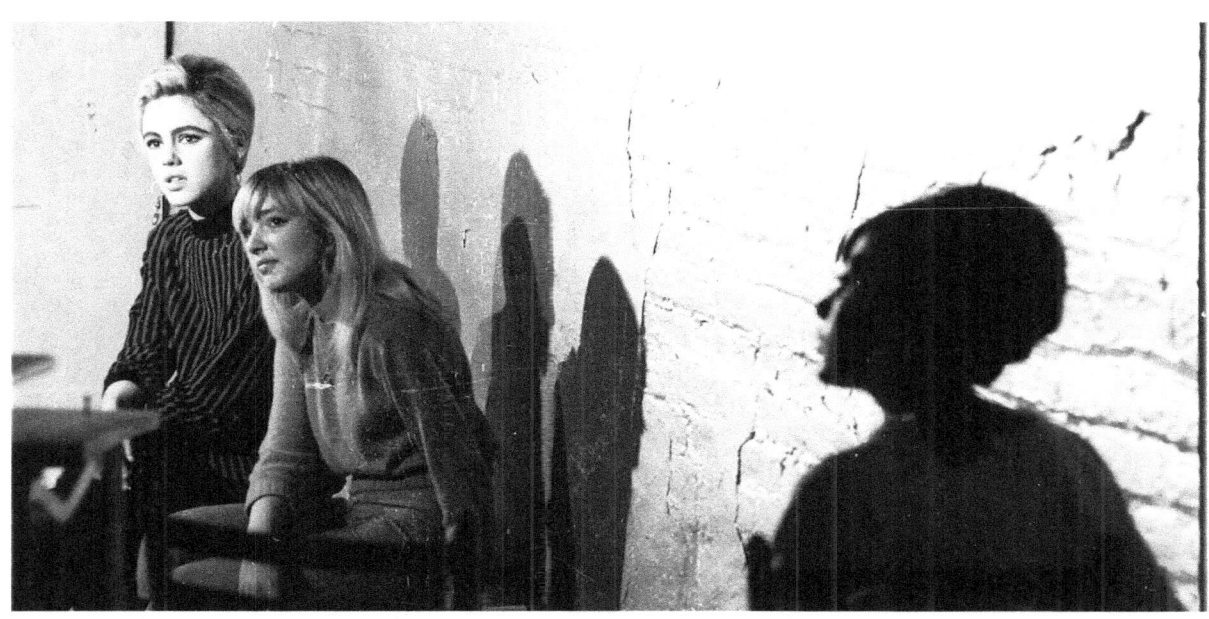

Rising Superstar Edie Sedgwick & neophyte Bibbe Hansen co-starred in both versions of 'Prison', aka 'Girls in Prison'.

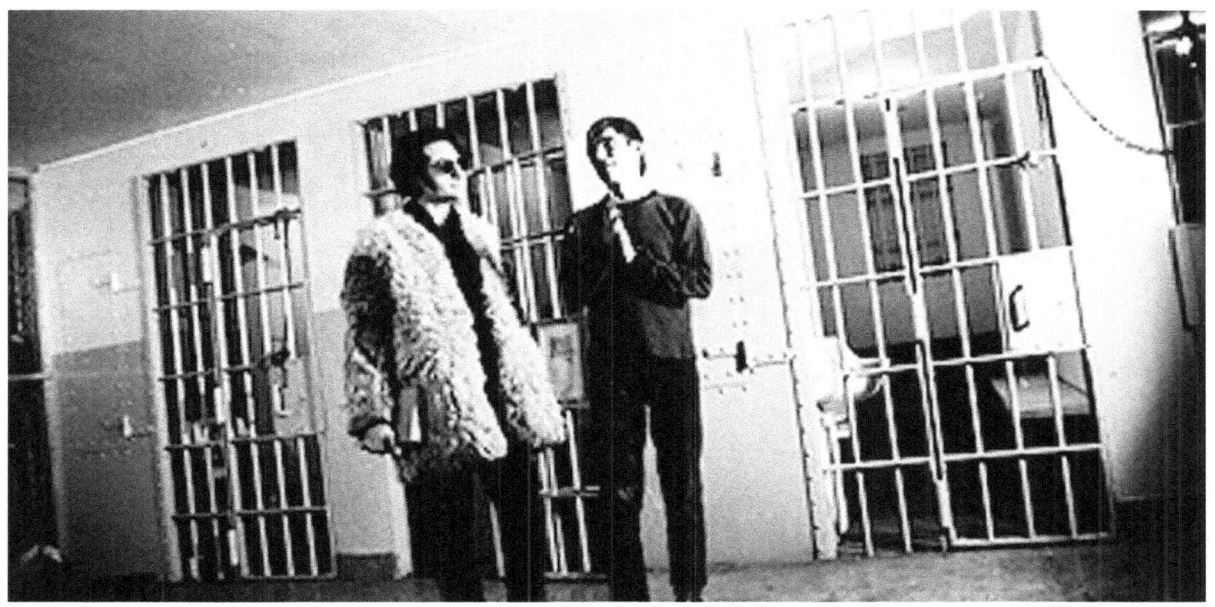

Sheepskin-clad Ondine plays a shyster lawyer trying to help Allen Midgette get out of the film 'Jail' and save his movie career. (Photos: Billy Name)

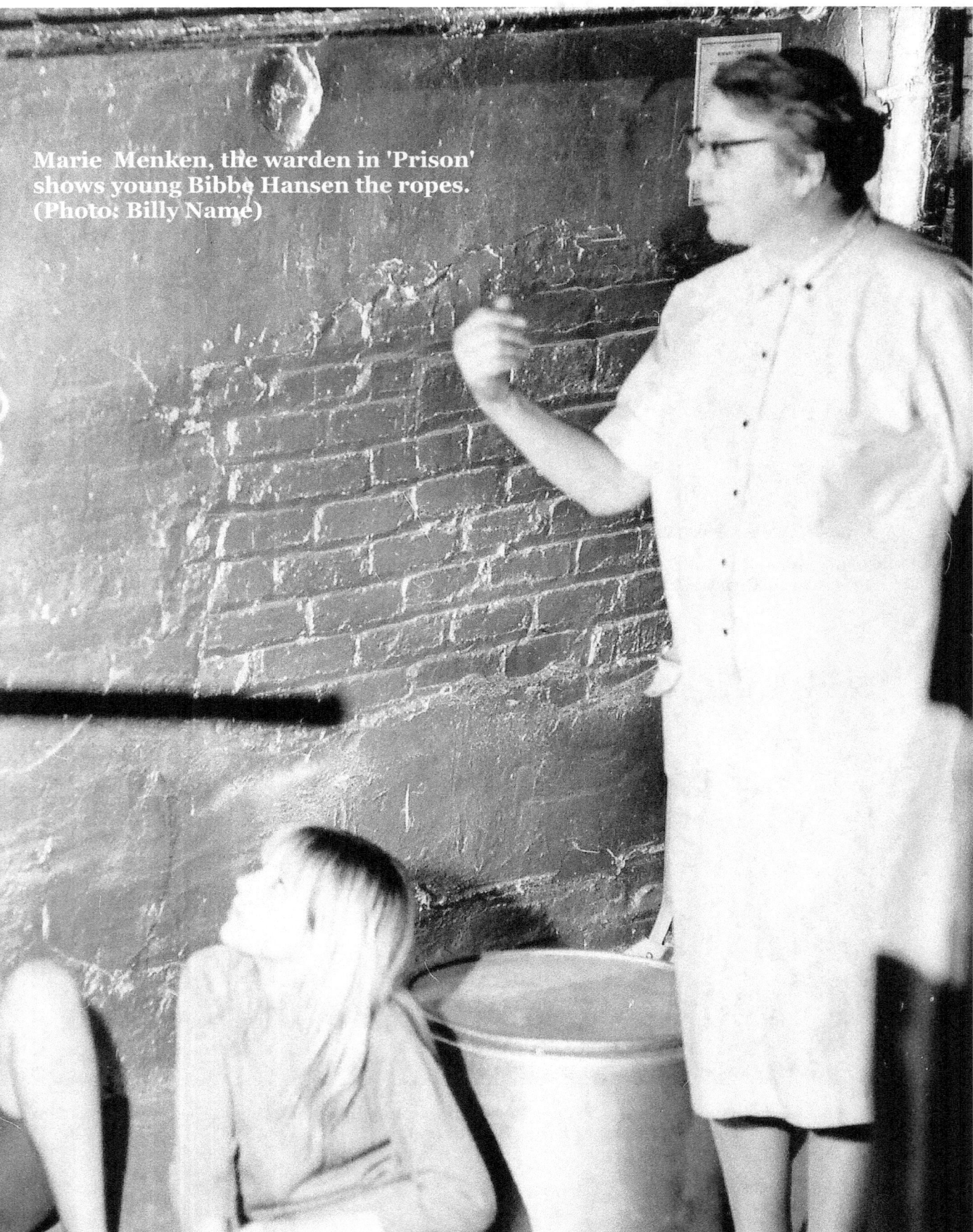

Marie Menken, the warden in 'Prison' shows young Bibbe Hansen the ropes. (Photo: Billy Name)

Billy Name: Great new products were now coming out for filmmakers! You could actually make movies without lights; you just did this brilliant halogen from one side and then it's total dark on the other side so that you have that black and white harlequin face. The bodies are floating in space because the contrast is so intense. So, we were using the new tools and materials simultaneously with having the opportunity to have these crazy, brilliant characters expose themselves in our films.

Warhol's nascent film career offered everyone within shooting range a chance to act out on camera, though the recorded results could often be brutal. Those we interviewed may have had angst aplenty amongst themselves, but virtually all of them agreed: The combustible mix of hustlers, hookers, drug addicts, displaced drunks, and lost souls often led to the very violence that Warhol feared. And these were the *silent* films!

Andy Warhol: The Factory was a place where you could let your problems show, and nobody would hate you for it. And if you worked your problems up into entertaining routines, people would like you even more, for being strong enough to say you were different.

Warhol's early film Factory was not simply a company of misfits and malcontents. He also got a number of sane socialites and heiresses to do things they would never have considered had they not been viscerally connected to the arts. . .

Ultra Violet: Oh yeah, I had the world's most famous tongue. I think some people have measured it from inside to out, and it was about twelve inches. But in all these years it has shrunk a bit. We did do a movie called 'Kiss'. Warhol had seen my tongue and he said, "You must do that film." He must have had a million people in that film, kissing. My tongue would go in and out, and stretch out and go up and right and left, like those cows when they eat. I did some photos kissing (artist) Edward Rucha. . . It's just kiss, kiss, kiss.

Mary Woronov: Yeah, yeah, the tongue. Ultra had the longest tongue in the world, and it was tilted at the end. It was amazing! And everyone was like "Stick out your tongue," so all of a sudden this *thing* went out. . .

Oh, yes, we did find a photo of that phenomenal bovine tongue, and no exaggeration there. So already in our film we had Warhol cows mooing on wallpaper in the Castelli Gallery, vampire bats chittering in 'Batman/Dracula', Factory cats meowing amid the silk-screened flora and fauna, and, naturally, a fruit course, tittering. . .

Mary Woronov: The first film I did with Warhol, they shipped in this lunatic Puerto Rican, Mario Montez. I sat around bored out of my box, and he's tittering away. I don't remember filming, just Mario putting on his make-up for nineteen hours. The next movie was 'Hedy'*, the shoplifting of Hedy Lamarr. Mario is my prey, and I am lethal, being six feet tall, actually. I'm the police and 'she' is the kleptomaniac, and some kind of sexual thing is going on. She looks at me and I bend her fucking arm, and that's it, right? No, Warhol looks up and goes, "Uh, there is still film in the camera." Ronnie gets hysterical, "Arghhh, ughhh!," and flaps around like a fish and finally dies on the floor. The end. Warhol takes the film out of the camera. There is no such thing as a cut. Even I know this is wrong, but I guess that's another way to learn that nothing is wrong.

---

*'Hedy' was one of Warhol's least appreciated films. Its screenwriter Ron Tavel (1937-2009) started his creative life, like Robert Heide, as a downtown playright. Though Gerard did not think much of Warhol's new find, the "skinny, faggy-sounding guy" would play a major role in the Factory, his first collaboration with Warhol being 1964's 'Harlot', starring MarioMontez (born Rene Rivera) made up to look like an exaggerated Jean Harlow. It dealt not with the film star, but the Harlow cult that had sprung up in the sixties. In the film Tavel and Billy Name are heard off-camera waxing poetic on favorite classic female movie stars, while Mario eats many bananas. He died of a stroke in Key West, Florida in 2013, at the ripe old age of 78.

Billy Name: Andy wanted to make stars. Probably the first was Mario Montez, who was also a Jack Smith star. Mario Montez became Andy's first glamour icon. And what kind of film would he make with her? Well, whether it was Mario eating a banana or peeling a banana, she is just being Mario in her dazed glamour heaven, because Mario was a man, but looked like the screen star Maria Montez. It was just glamour, glamour, glamour. At this point he had to film everything! The first year was much more of an open space for those who were participating with Andy, because we were still totally into that avant-garde underground art world thing.

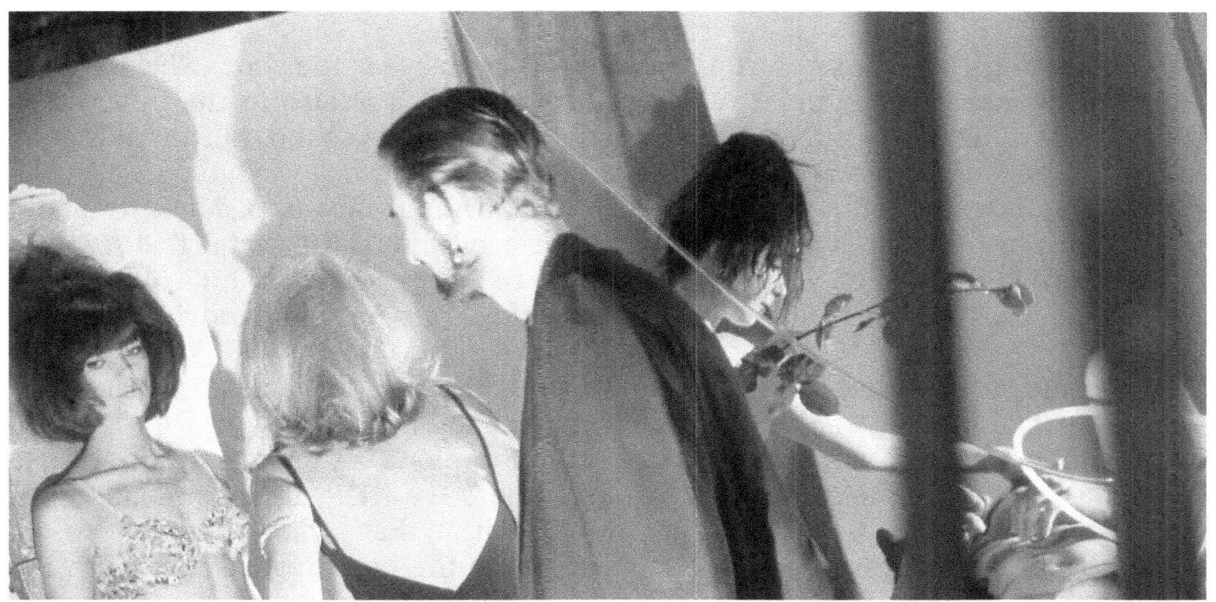
Ivy Nicholson, Jane Holzer, Jack Smith and Beverly Grant siphon blood in 'Batman Dracula'.

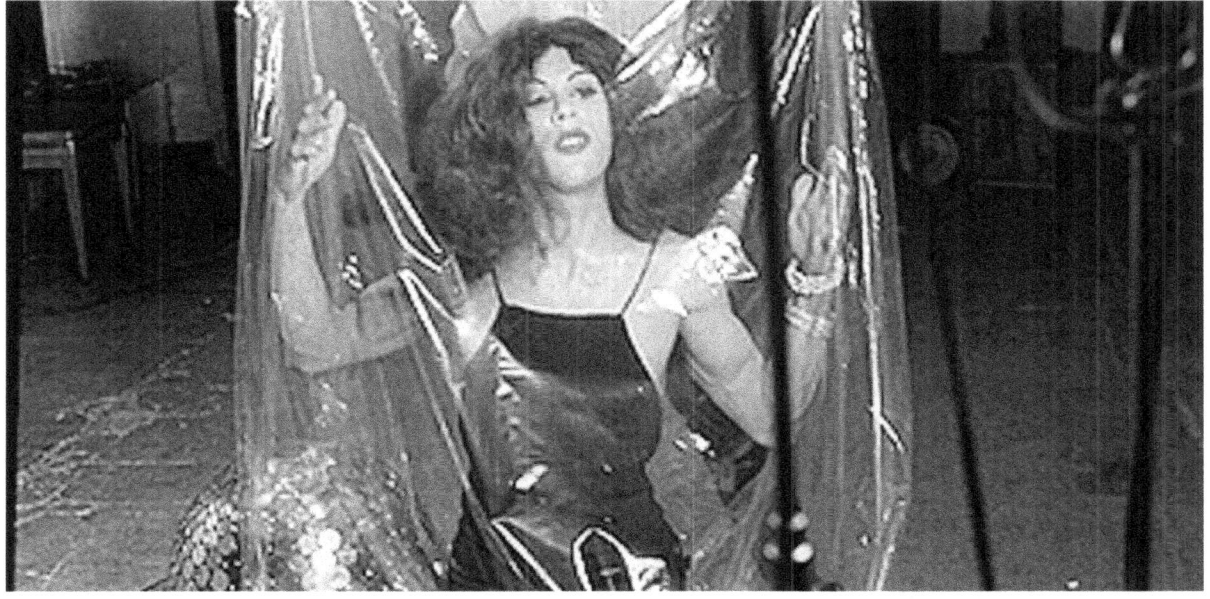
One of a sequential series of dazzling shots (which we animated) of the divine Mario Montez, Warhol's first drag Superstar, wrapped in her dazed glamour heaven.   (Photos: Billy Name)

Gerard Malanga: I was in 'Harlot', and Mario Montez was the star. 'She' played a Jean Harlow character in drag. A boyfriend of Andy's was also in the film, and a girlfriend of a film critic at Newsweek. Andy was shooting sound, but there was no sound. There were voice-overs, two poets talking about what was going on in the picture, but they were off camera, so you are looking at a voice-over movie for about seventy minutes. Towards the end of the second reel, you realise that actual *sound* is being recorded in the film, when Philippe throws a beer can and it lands off-camera. You hear it *crash,* and you suddenly realise that this is a sync-sound movie.

Robert Heide: For the films, there were always the assorted hangers-on, leftover Warholites like myself, who would show up. Nobody really knew, but Andy had a sense of himself as an actor, and he was no dumb blond—Andy was cultured. He loved to go to flea markets with me. We called ourselves 'The dime store kids'. We both came out of the depression era, and think about it, that's what Andy's art was all about. That part of America was disappearing, so the hoarding instinct, with the fiestaware, the cookie jars, that's what the collectibles were about to us—Americana. Pop culture. Mickey Mouse! Andy always said he wanted to be like Walt Disney, who had a factory.

Jonas Mekas: Andy is there in the underground film world, same as George Maciunas, the Fluxus Movement, the Fluxus films. They all have something in common, but there were fifty different filmmakers involved. Same with Andy, before what one could call the 'Hollywood period'. . . What happens when you watch 'Empire'? At first it's slow, nothing. Then, after fifty minutes, you give up and admit to yourself to just be in it, and watch some dust scratches. It becomes a meditation. If you are able to go into that kind of state, and to watch this film, in which supposedly nothing happens, then suddenly, the *white* comes up on the building, the magic moment. If you can be in that kind of state, you won't support war, you won't fight, you are not a soldier, you are not going to kill. You are somewhere else. Yes, of course, one can be that relaxed and go into a kind of Zen experience.

This opinion of a Warhol film differs somewhat with that of another serious well-known underground filmmaker who did not appreciate Warhol's 'Zen experience'. Gregory Markopoulos ('Twice A Man', 'Eniaios') was outraged that the arriviste Warhol was receiving all this attention from Mekas and the press: "I don't know what's going on in this world. Here I spend ten years studying my craft, perfecting my craft, thinking, theorizing about movies and how they're made, and this guy comes along who does absolutely nothing and knows absolutely nothing."

Andy Warhol: Always leave them wanting less.

Victor Bockris: The underground film world had become very active and exciting, lots of parties and sex and drugs, where before it had been the poetry scene. By '64, Andy was going into that world very fast. When he won the Film Culture Magazine Award from Jonas Mekas, the other more established underground film-makers protested, but Andy didn't seem to care . . .

Andy Warhol: You have to do stuff that average people don't understand because those are the only good things.

Victor Bockris: There is a certain Zen Buddhism involved. Andy was an almost impossible man to pin down because as soon as you realized something about him, you had to realize that the opposite was also equally true. On the one hand, he wanted to run a male brothel. On the other hand, he was a kind of Zen guru.

According to biographer Victor Bockris, Andy was really a conceptual artist more than anything, because so many of his things were based upon ideas, especially for the way people should live. His desire to have homosexuality accepted was not so much to flaunt it in the face of people, but to destroy the nuclear family, which he saw as a purely economic construct, not of any value to human beings. This, of course, did not prevent him from creating his own. . .

...SILVER FAMILY

I find that people are fantastic, fantastic, fantastic!
—Andy Warhol

Ivy Nicholson: At the Jonas Mekas Film Culture Award* ceremony, Andy wanted me to eat a banana which I refused. So I got an apple. I was a Countess, after all, married to Regis Du Poleon, but I didn't care if people were titled or wealthy. I had already met kings in my life, multimillionaires. I was one of the most famous models in the world, so I wasn't that impressed—I only had eyes for Andy. And the decor! At the Silver Factory, most of the people were poor, but the decor was incredible! Everyone had their own little magic space. It was like a painting.

---

*In 1964, Jonas Mekas filmed the 'Silver Family' partaking in his Film Culture Awards ceremony. To the horror of the more established underground filmmakers, he had given it to Warhol. The marvelous footage, done in slow motion, worked wonderfully for our Family segment in the film series. A glam Baby Jane Holzer opens the ceremony, followed by Ivy Nicholson's son presenting Warhol with a basket of fruit and vegetables, which he ceremoniously passes around to his devoted followers like Jesus with the loaves and fishes. Gerard Malanga is seen seductively mouthing a cucumber, Ivy aggressively munches an apple, and we all know what happens to a banana in a Warhol movie, even when Jonas Mekas is working the camera. Warhol's fascination with bananas later took on a life of its own when he created that peel-off banana for the fabulous, uber-famous Velvet Underground and Nico album, which we covered, rather exuberantly, in Episode II of the TV series. You may never look at that fruit the same way again...

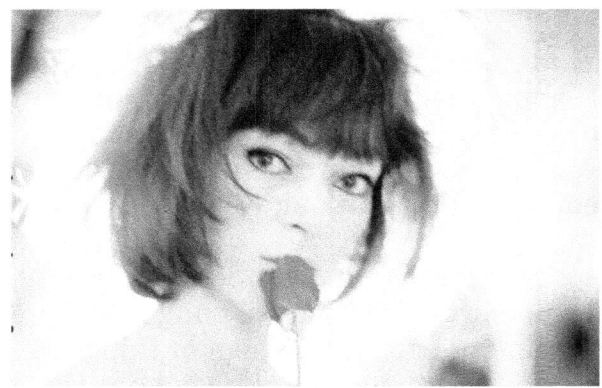

Ivy in a magic space...

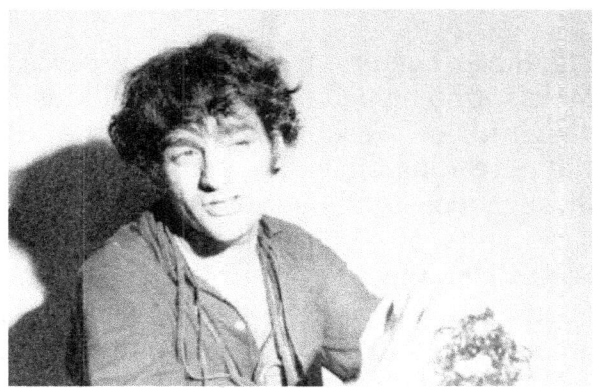

Ondine in a spacy place.

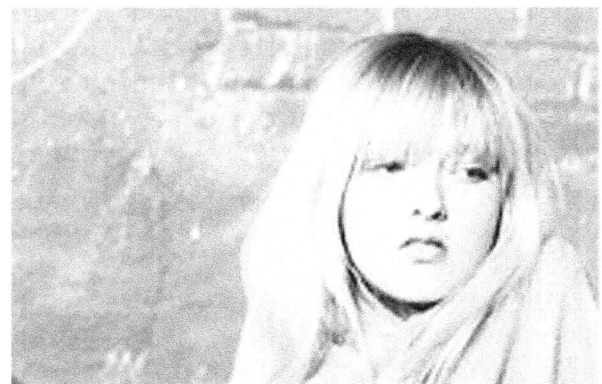

Bibbe in a 'Prison', at the tender age of sixteen, behind silvered Factory walls.

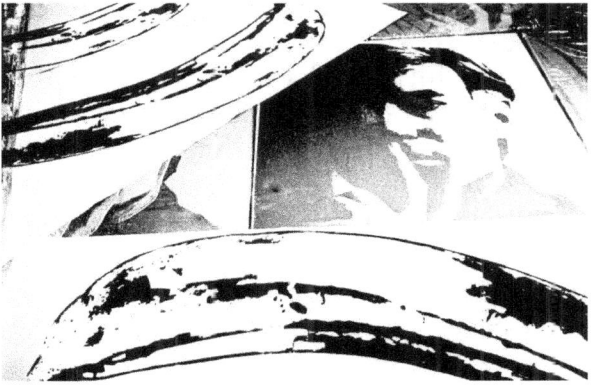

Andy in a self-portrait, in a favorite pose, with a favorite fruit. (All Photos: Billy Name)

The Silver Factory, fruits aside, also became a refuge for barely ripe nubiles. Jonas Mekas, who helped out a lot of lost kids with apprentice jobs, filmed one of the most delightful of Warhol discoveries, the future mother of Beck. (If you have to ask, you're reading the wrong book) There she is, gaily picking flowers while meandering through a pastoral Central Park. For this teenager, reality was quite a bit starker...

Bibbe Hansen: I was on the streets and not living at home. Not being anywhere. Even though it was the sixties we had just come out of the fifties. Young kids were not supposed to be running around the streets and not going to school or things like that. I remember going to dinner with Andy and Gerard and the rest, and one thing led to another. I wound up going back to being a permanent guest, not only the city, but of the state for a couple of years. So, I was out of circulation for awhile.

The angelic-looking Bibbe Hansen let out a delicate peal of laughter. With her long flaxen blonde hair and innocent eyes, it was hard to believe she'd been so often a truant. Despite—well, perhaps because of—her famous artist father (Al Hansen), she was forgotten and went hungry a lot, and got into trouble with the police. After forays on the easily mean streets of Greenwich Village and lower Manhattan, she periodically wound up in Juvenile Detention centers, and Family Court, then on 23rd Street, across from the Chelsea Hotel. Bibbe, serene, arty and streetwise, grew up and gave birth and raised that inventive and brilliant musician who continues to astonish us. As for the adolescent Bibbe's Factory Family, I doubt she had much in common with a big-haired super-socialite like Jane Holzer or a silver-spooned heiress like Ultra Violet, though back then it seemed everyone left home, even Ultra.

Ultra Violet: There were a lot of runaway kids. In a way I was a runaway; I ran away from France, from my family, was sent to a correction home. I was even *exorcised!* I was a rebel, so you still have to find a place where you can fit somehow. It's like a dog without a master; you're lost. The Factory was a place where we could hang out. Edie was certainly a runaway from her family; she rebelled. A lot of loose kids. We were a nucleus there. We can't call it home, let's call it a nucleus, and it's good to be in a nucleus. You have to be part of something. So that Factory was there to swallow up people, to give them something to do.

Jonas Mekas: Andy's Superstars. The first ones came from the underground, from the friends of filmmakers that he met, those who had been in the films of Jack Smith or Ron Rice. But then the second set were the lonely desperate souls that came from different parts of the country, and they somehow ended up at the Factory. Andy>

never said no, never rejected. So, sad and desperate as they were, they felt at home. Andy was like their big father. He never scolded them, never disapproved. They were permitted to improvise, to say whatever they wanted.

Filmmaker Jonas Mekas knew most of the Warhol stars who flamed out early, and seems to have worried about them considerably more than Warhol, especially in their drug-fueled frenzies... While on location in New York in our own filmmaking frenzy, we also encountered, mostly at downtown parties, the steadfast companions who worshipped those fragile fledgling Superstars, who constantly fretted about them, and who never got over them—like Danny Fields, former music manager of The Ramones, who appeared in a number of Warhol films with his adored one-time roommate Edie Sedgwick. He remembered, rather wistfully, how they first met...

Danny Fields: We were Harvard drop-outs living in New York, and one weekend in 1964, they said, "There is this pain-in-the-ass debutante, we can't do anything with her, she has to get out of school, she has shoplifted too much, and blah blah." But Edie was the belle of the ball of the Cambridge that I had left behind, a crowd of fabulous last names and affiliations. They were divine, and Edie was one of them. Now she needed a place to stay, so somehow it was arranged she was going to stay at my loft, my mini-loft in New York... Let's just say it was a disaster. She was very demanding, very much a diva, on the phone day and night, chain-smoking cigarettes, checking her clothes and pulling them off. She was making me crazy, although she was adorable, and she was beautiful and she was wonderful and she was funny. And she was a great *thief*! I had to inspect her every time she walked out the door. Sure enough, there would be a big bottle of Listerine mouthwash. "Why are you taking this? You can afford mouthwash." So, her mother came to find her a suitable apartment on 63rd Street, which they decorated with a huge false rhinoceros and incredible crystal and of course it burned down. That was the first apartment to burn down—this was early '64. We all went to the World's Fair and when we came back, Edie hops off to the Factory where she met Andy, and he fell in love like everyone else did. She signed every check in town. She was the perfect sidekick for him, so Gerard was replaced by her. He couldn't be too smart. He was not always on Andy's side, but Edie was, and Andy was her introduction to New York.

Gerard Malanga: Andy and I were at a party at a film producer's house, Lester Persky, and that is where we met Edie Sedgwick. I really wouldn't factorise Andy being a father to Edie. I would say more of a confidant, more on the level of friend, supporter, companion. They went to a lot of parties together. We did things together.

Gerard may have been the Factory stud, but he apparently never got to first base with androgynous 'poor little rich girl' Edie, since she was in thrall to Harvard grad confidant Chuck Wein. The muscular blue-eyed blond newcomer no doubt woke up the green-eyed monster in Malanga. Wein seemed a bit shady to those who had dealings with him, referring to him as 'Edie's puppet-master'. It was the early sixties, and there was loads of semi-mystical crap flying about, though I expect Warhol was immune to it. . . With the arrival and rapid ascent of the waif-like Edie, Jane Holzer realized her days on Warhol's 'Girl of the Year' throne were numbered, and abdicated with a sense of relief. The crazy meth-heads, drug addicts, and giggling amyl-nitrite poppers would simply carry on with their new fag hag, who clearly adored them.

Louis Waldon: Andy was working in the beginning with people who were insane. They could tell great stories, all these crazy people. But in Ondine and Taylor, Andy had great actors. They had created this movement. No editing, no script, nothing but what you have right there. If you wanted music, Taylor would put a radio on. And Andy went along. He seemed to get everyone to do what he wanted, but people already had their minds made up. Andy just let them do it. And he never said "Fifteen Minutes of Fame." Someone said that one day, and I heard them say it. Andy just adopted everything; he was a collector. He adopted every thing, and every one.

Louis Waldon was not just another good-looking guy who caught Warhol's eye. He had his own eye-twinkling charm, but also real acting chops—and he was straight! Warhol loved bar-hopping with Louis and his macho buddies, just being one of the boys. He feared he would be refused entrance to a regular bar, but Louis could cajole him into it. ("Andy, they're gonna let you in!") Louis and his long, funny, and ultimately poignant history with Warhol deserve its own documentary. . . So does Mary Woronov, and by golly, she's been making one. I just hope it doesn't take quite as long as ours did.

Mary Woronov: The reason why these people all got together? Well, there were people like Billy and Gerard who brought them together, but the reason they stayed together is the same as if you meet someone at a party that you're getting along with, that's on the same wavelength, taking the same drugs. You stay with them. There were things that we liked. I liked transvestites. I liked gay people because they were just nuts! They were rebelling, not like gay people now, kind of fat and happy. They were angry, and so was I! So that's why I stayed there. . . Well, that and drugs.

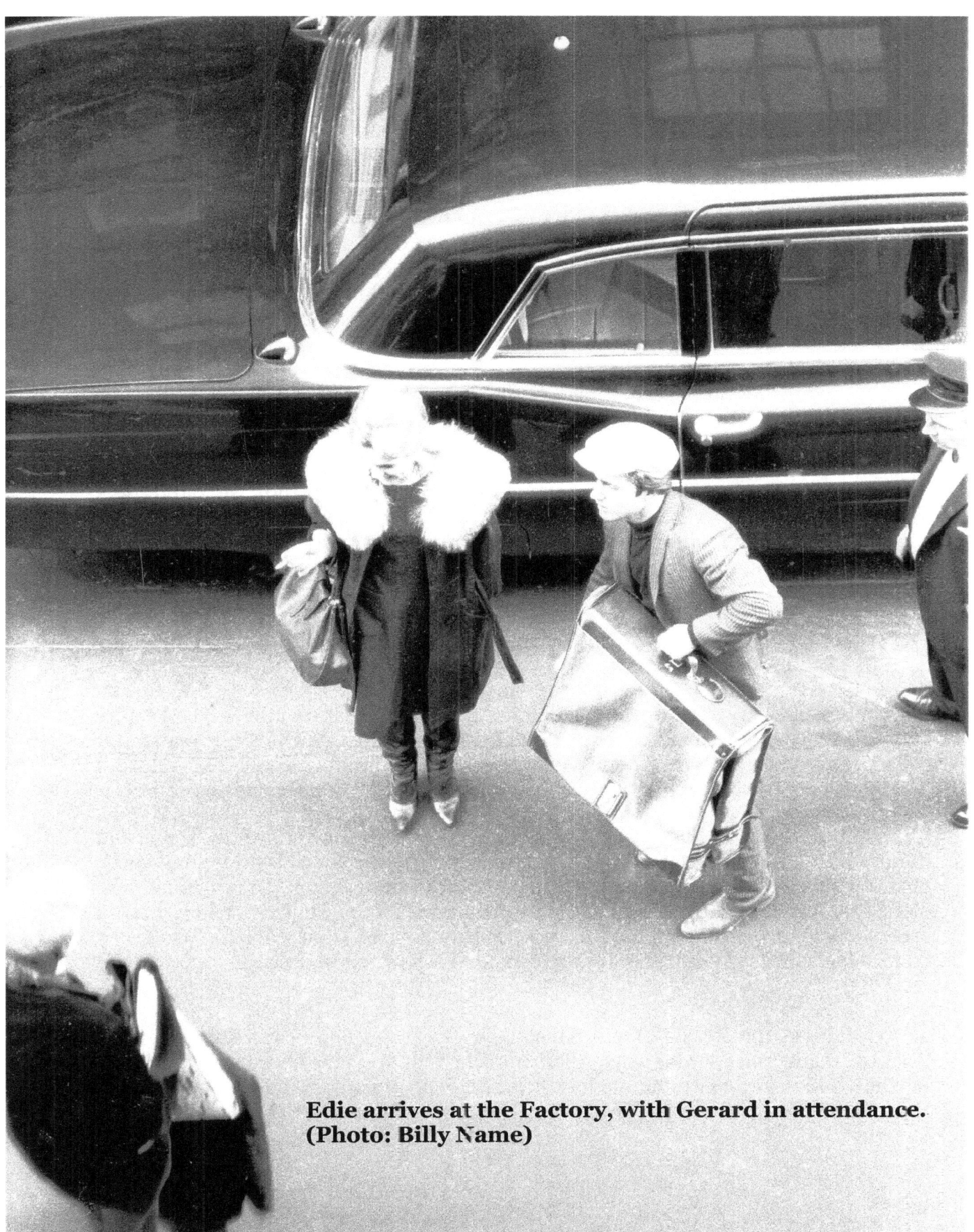

Edie arrives at the Factory, with Gerard in attendance.
(Photo: Billy Name)

Nat Finkelstein: This probably was the first generation of latch key children, from post-World War II wealth. The kids would come home and there would be a fifty-dollar bill pinned to the fridge, and they were on their own. Andy became this great, I wouldn't say father image, but kindergarten. You could do what you wanted and everybody had a great time. And if Andy wanted to get rid of you, all he had to do was make a gesture, and that very bright bitch pack would be sicced on someone and rip them to pieces. Oh, that was a group effort. They were just an extraordinarily bright, vicious grouping of people. Children of the rich. Pampered, spoiled children of the rich. They contributed nothing to society. And they didn't have anything besides Andy, did they? They had Andy, they had speed. And here was this permissive father image who gave them a place to play, who gave them substance.

As with any public figure, especially one as controversial as Warhol, we found there to be a number of different versions of 'The Truth'. Everyone we spoke to had their own fraught Family relationships and singular memories of 'Life with Father'. But, as Warhol would say, "Everybody is right, and everybody is wrong."

Victor Bockris: People say, "Oh, I gave my life to him." And they did, but Andy gave them more, because he was able to inject them with this enormous sense of themselves, and enthusiasm for what he was doing, and what they were doing. You have to understand, and few people do, that Andy was a great romantic. The Factory was really all about romance, in a twisted way—romance for work, romance for collaborative partners. The greatest people in your life are the people that you work with, if you are working creatively and on a daily basis... They become your family.

Allen Midgette: The Factory. It's like a Harold Pinter play, where you're there, and if there were no press people around, you were just on the couch that's falling apart, kind of greasy, not the most inviting thing to want to sit down on. They all have dark glasses on, which is something I had a hard time with, because I was taking LSD in order to *clean* my lenses and see what was really there. So, I was thinking, "God, why do they have those glasses on?" It's night time. They're inside already.

Allen Midgette, the eternal hippie, winsome in buckskins and beads, still resembles Warhol. It got even weirder when Allen mimicked his famous doppelganger, because we filmed him in a bedroom at the Chelsea Hotel, which gradually filled with the aromatic smoke of his homegrown pot... The alarms, naturally, did not go off.

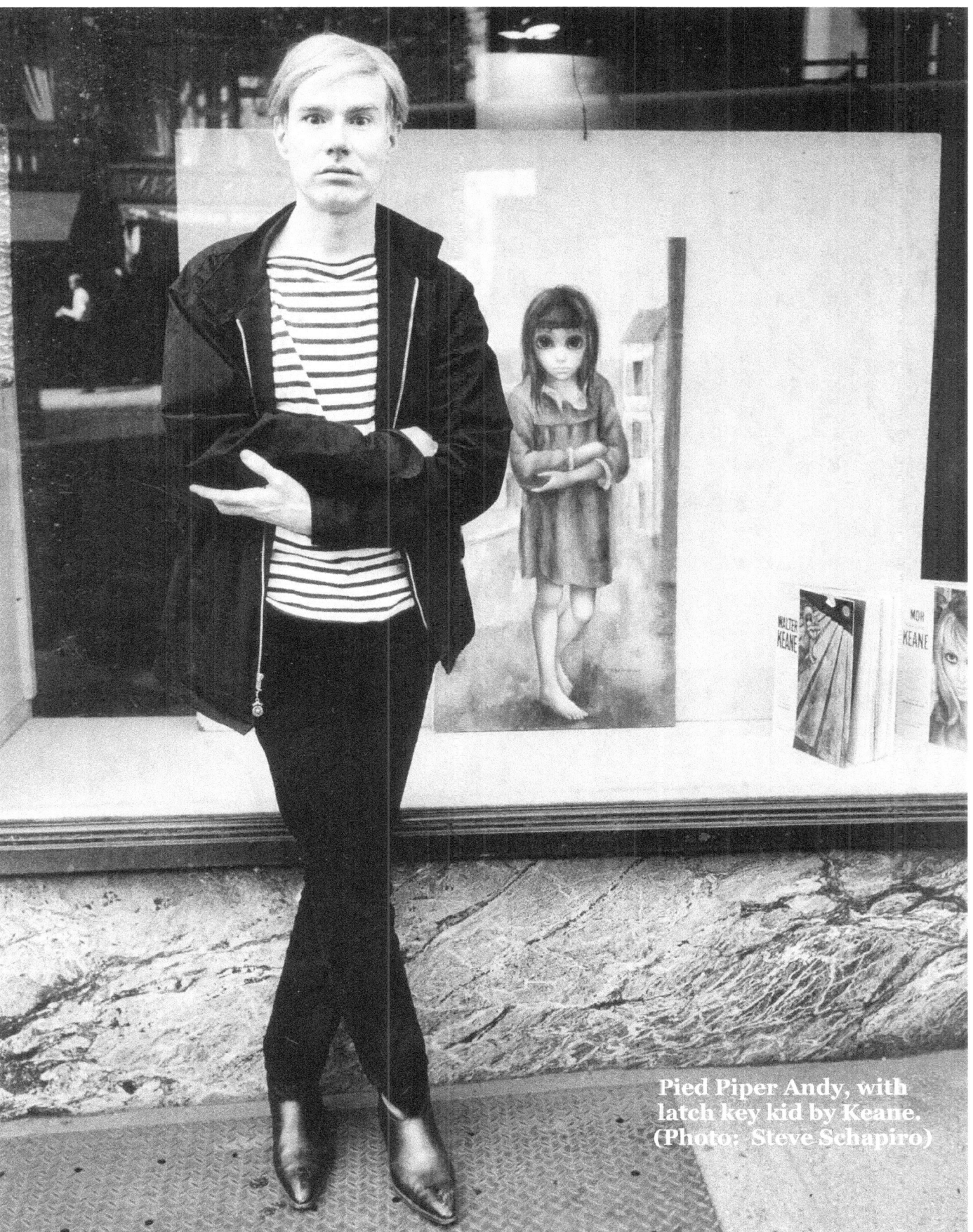

Pied Piper Andy, with latch key kid by Keane. (Photo: Steve Schapiro)

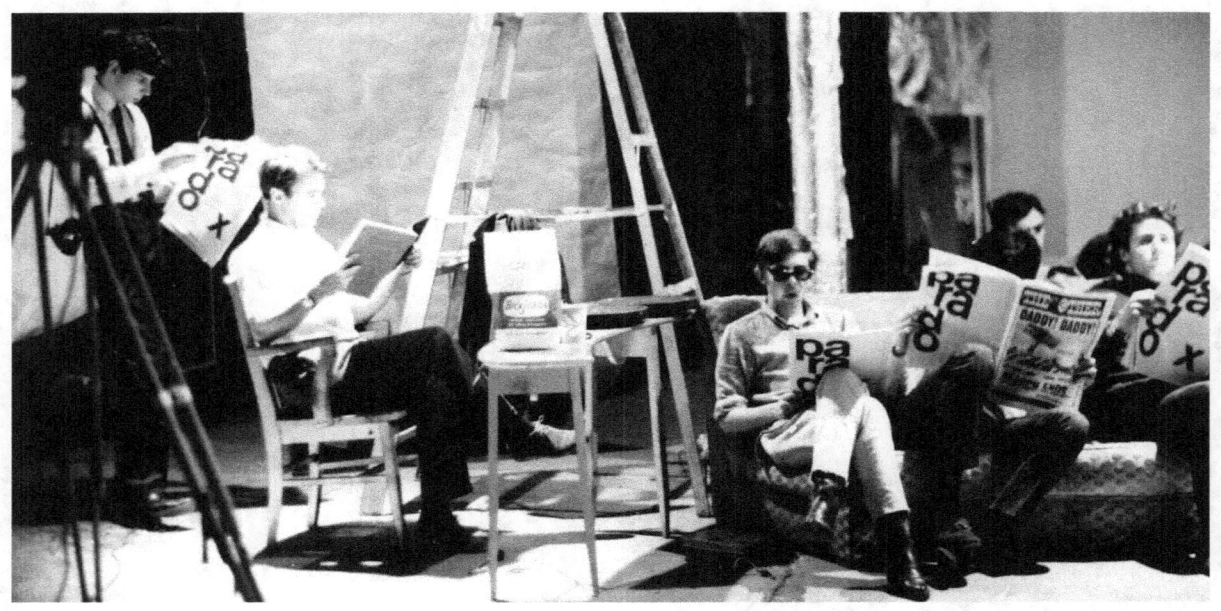
"Like a Pinter play." Factoryites await the next big thing. (Photos: Billy Name)

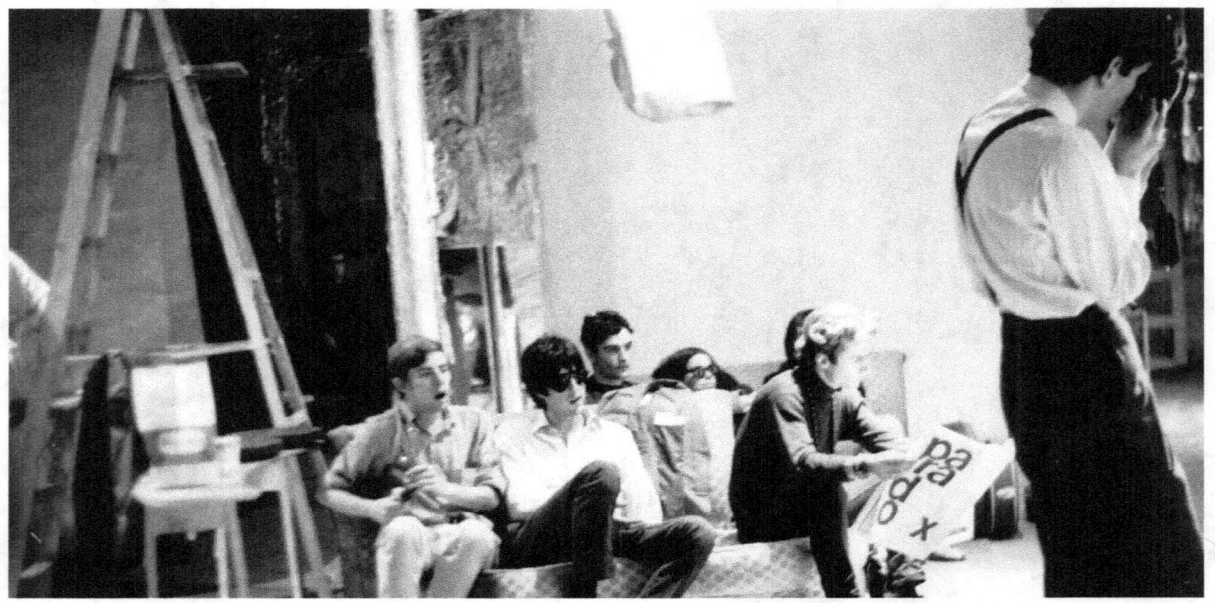
Still waiting for Godot. Standing at right, trying his hand at taking pictures, then sixteen-year old photographer Stephen Shore.

Also at the Chelsea: Slim, dapper, dashingly dressed David Croland was interviewed in the art-congested lobby. Art is actually everywhere, thanks to Stanley Bard, hotel manager extraordinaire, who over the decades graciously accepted paintings and drawings—some truly awful—in lieu of rent from his often financially strapped tenants. David greeted Stanley effusively while we were stealing shots of the artwork. The exceedingly hip publisher of 'LID' Magazine also acknowledged passing semi-famous acquaintances, which included a number of aging Warholites living out their days in shabby splendor at the hotel once synonymous with New York cool. David may seem to be given short shrift here, but he makes up for it later. Clever and straightforward, he is better-looking today than back in '65, when he was 'discovered' and became the boyfriend of Factory star Susan Bottomly (International Velvet). David would figure into many Factory intrigues and later become the surprising (well, maybe to Susan) lover of the ferociously talented Robert Mapplethorpe, who was then living with poet rocker Patti Smith, who—Whoa! That has fuck all to do with the Silver Factory. As Warhol would say, "Who does she think she is?" . . .

David Croland: I was so green, so young. I was quiet in those days. The big stars would come around; we'd get really quiet. I was afraid of them. But Andy had a vibration that was the same for everyone—until they walked out of the room. We'd be sitting in a club, or anywhere, and someone would walk over. It could be a star, a stranger, or one of the groupies, and he would say after they were out of earshot, "Who does she think she is? I mean, who does she think she *is*?" And we'd be like, "I don't know, we're eighteen, we're drunk, we don't give a shit." Andy didn't like small talk; he liked no talk, or Big Talk. "Who does she think she is?" He would say it really slow, and we got it, because it would be a pretentious person. Pretension has to do with lying. It's a soulful thing. He didn't like people who weren't soulful. So that "Who does she think she is?" has to do with just one word: Relax. Throw out. That's two words. Throw out. What was the question?

Sorry David, I forgot it. We offered a cool libation to refresh your recollections, but you languidly waved it away, saying "Drinking doesn't look good on camera." You had a point there. While filming B roll for our series at a Parisian/Egyptian nightclub called 'Andy Waloo', we found ourselves surrounded by wildly skewed 'Warhol' artworks, hookahs, hash, exotic people and erotic cocktails. I got caught in mid-sip of a drink called 'Blow Job' with mouth open and eyes closed, and that was the shot they kept. Throw out. . .

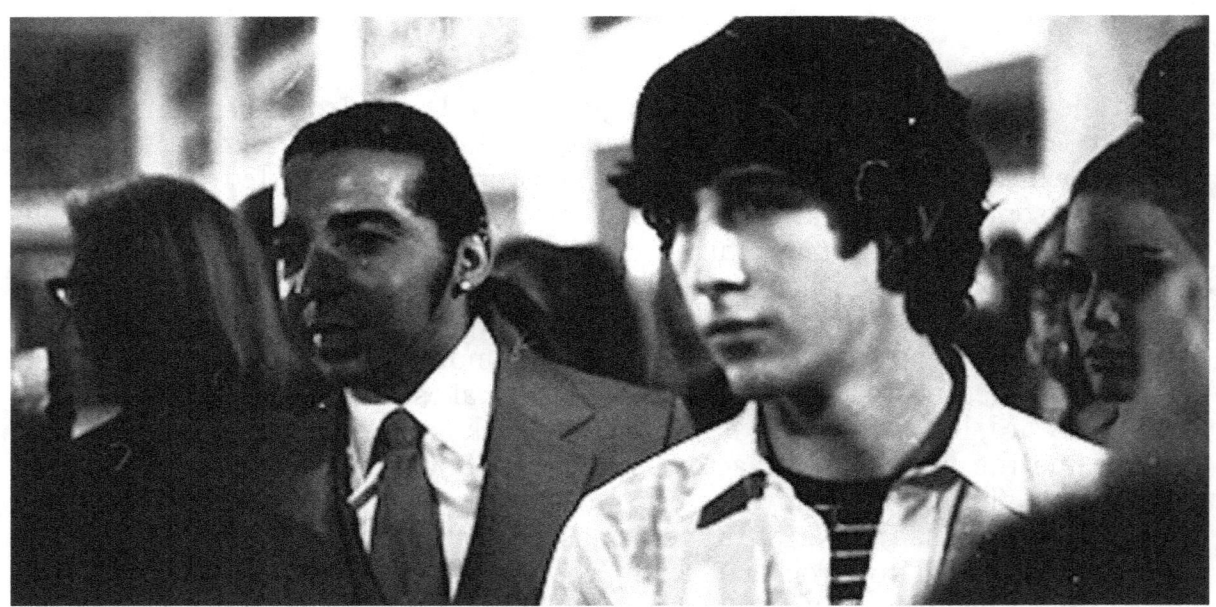

Into the light. . . Young David Croland at a gallery opening, girlfriend Susan Bottomly following behind him on right.

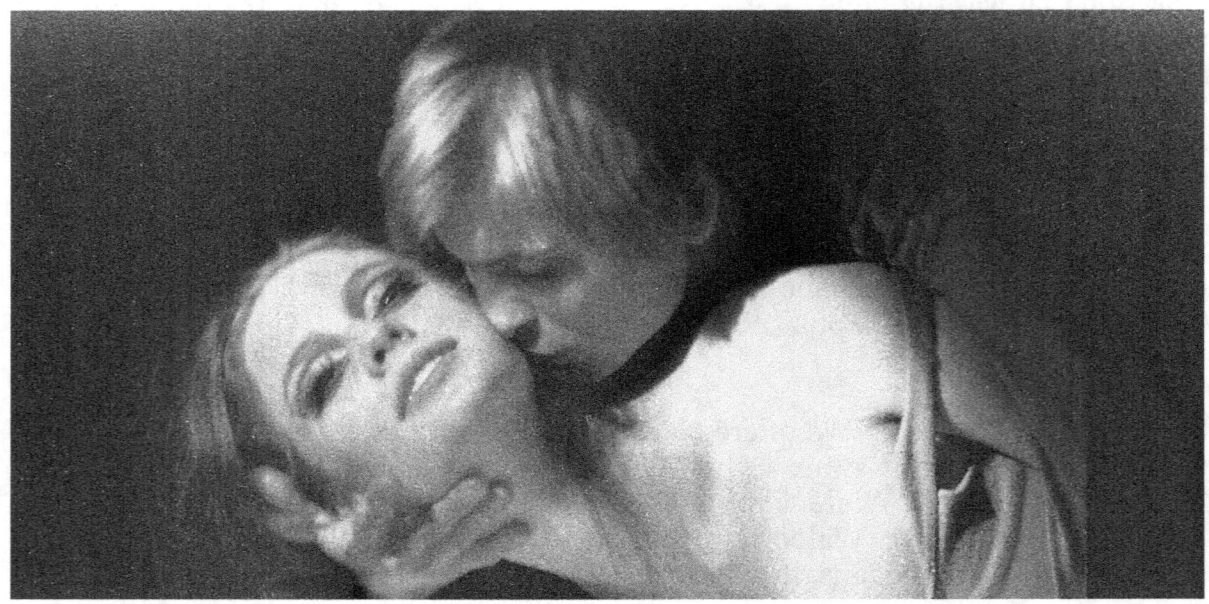

Lights! Action! Susan Bottomly and Allen Midgette cavort for the camera. (Photos: Billy Name)

. . . One former Factoryite who seemed to not mind various stages of *'déshabillage' was playwright Robert Heide. 'The Bed' concerned, well, a huge bed, to which two young stalwarts in their skivvies clung in existential angst, their magic flying carpet "caught in a drug/booze time-warp."* Warhol, of course, filmed it.

Robert Heide: Andy came out of a kind of Polish immigrant background, so he was stingy, fearful and deprived on some level. But it was a family in the same sense that the Living Theatre was, and Andy was a kind of guru in the same sense that theater founders Julian Beck and Judith Molina were. *"We will take care of your life."* However, it could somehow become another dysfunctional family. . . There are many kinds of families, and Andy was good for some people and not others. I think he did try to manipulate people. He tried to make me into . . . well, he said that "Bob likes to give people blow jobs." I never did.

We believe you, Bob. From the footage we saw, you just had one hell of a time. You also mentioned that many of the Factory denizens were into a particularly empty form of Zen Buddhism, a rather vapid and vaguely menacing emptiness, where anything could happen and often did, with Warhol's implicit encouragement. Films like 'Couch', Warhol's (extremely) loose interpretation of Hollywood's casting couch, contained graphic images, not simply of sex between men. Naomi Levine bobbled her enormous breasts in vain for a guy in black leather who seemed more interested in straddling his motorcycle—oh, whoops, that is gay, isn't it? From there it was boys to men, silently bobbing and writhing about as if in an x-rated underground nature documentary. I was about to nod off when without warning a spectacular woman whose name I cannot divulge, at least until the next chapter, is sodomized by Gerard Malanga as she reclines on the rippling muscles of a beautiful black dancer who gives new meaning to the word 'buck'. According to Heide: "Andy would watch, sitting on the floor cross-legged, in a trance." Sounds like Nirvana to me. Or team spirit.

Vincent Fremont: With all the carrying on, at the same time there was a lot of creative energy, people exchanging ideas, writers, artists, movie stars coming in and out. But Andy stayed with his daily crew of people. They were all intelligent. Some think otherwise, but I would disagree. They had extreme sides to them, but they were very intelligent. Andy played the village idiot. By acting blank he could suck in a lot of information. He was one of the great listeners. And he was, in a way, my professional father. I wasn't quite nineteen when I met him, and he taught me, tested me. So you were able to do things that you would not normally have been able to do.

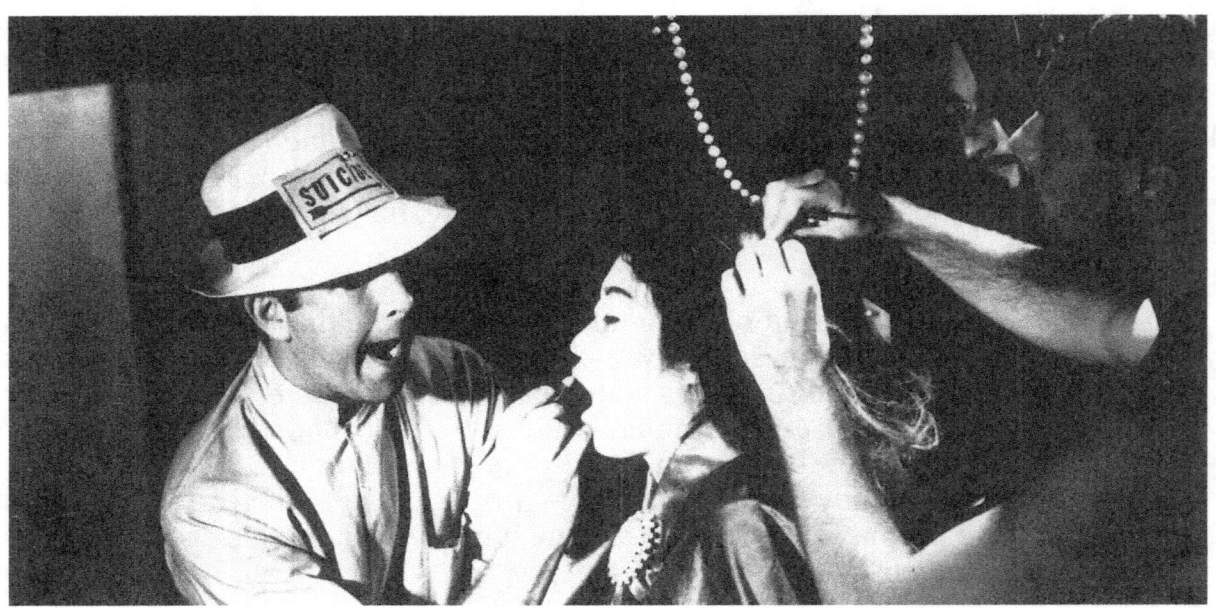
**Robert Heide makes up Dorthy Dean for 'Batman/Dracula' before the bloodshed.
(Photo: Billy Name, from the F catalogue)**

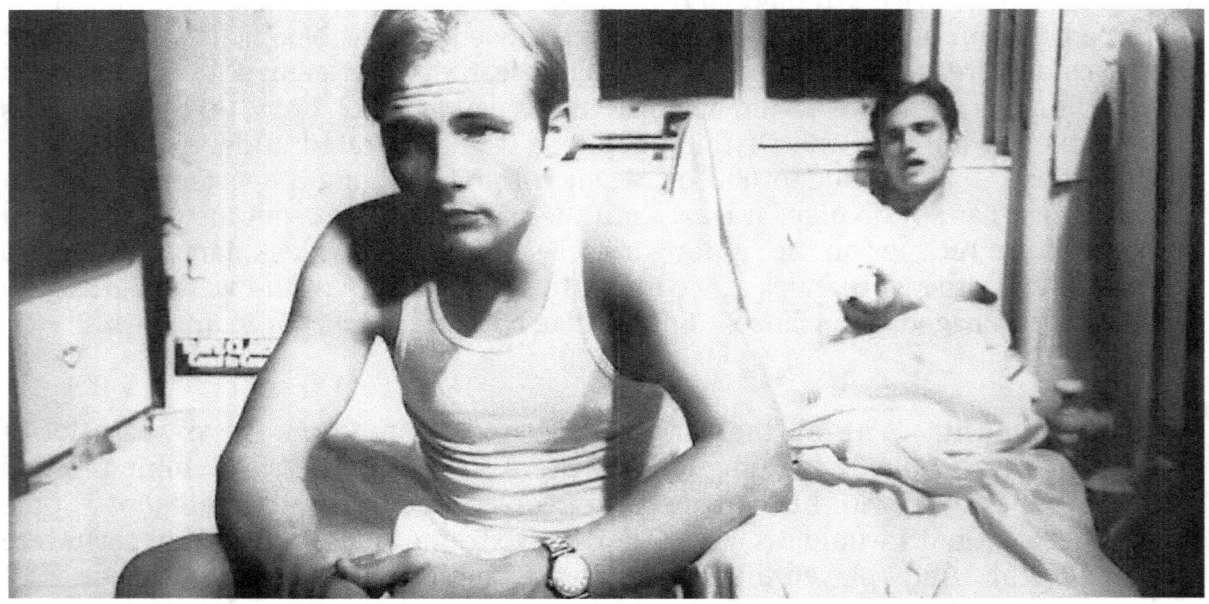
**Heide's existential despair became his play, 'The Bed', filmed for posterity by Warhol.
(Photo: Billy Name)**

According to Factory insider Vincent Fremont, "If Warhol knew that he could trust you, he would give you more responsibility." That philosophy held true for Billy Name, who physically built the Factory, ran it, and worked diligently to "control the chaos." In a cruel Shakespearean twist, Gerard Malanga, the talented poet who became Warhol's trusted assistant, would one day be seen to betray that trust. But as Shakespeare has oft shown us, there are many sides to a story, and, frankly, I'd be more inclined to follow Gerard into that dark, creaking, sometime foreboding Factory elevator...

Gerard Malanga: First, you'd take this old-fashioned freight elevator to the fourth floor, open this big door, and enter this silver palace, the 'Tin Foil Palace'. Then you would have to try find Andy in the midst of all that. Andy behaved like a boy. Whether out of calculation or sincerity, Andy was always the boy, and he created an aura around himself where people would just readily do anything for him. Andy was never a threatening person. He always made us feel important, and therefore we would just want to do whatever he said. We all pretty much got along with each other. We never really took ourselves seriously. I am busy doing my thing, writing poetry, making movies. I never thought, "Oh, I'm going to be in a movie." It was an adventure. I mean, it certainly wasn't an office situation. We even had a pay phone at the Factory. We had to make a phone call, we had to put a dime in the phone.

Victor Bockris: Right. Well, aside from the artistic communal aspects, I think the idea for the Factory started in Andy's mind when he had St. Vitus Dance at the age of six. His mother moved his bed down into the dining room so he would be in the center of the house. He was making collages out of magazines, and she would give him a Hershey bar every time he did good work. I think the idea of the Factory came from that, and the idea of the triangular power structure that would be its engine came from the way his mother created a struggle between the three brothers for her attention. That was basic to his understanding of how you get three people under your control... There was another inspiration for the Factory: Warhol often spoke to Gerard Malanga about his fantasy of running a male brothel, where he'd have rows of beds like in a dormitory, and he'd be the headmaster and charge you to go to bed number seven and so forth. Well, he was attracting young gay men to come hang out and act out their sexual fantasies in his films.

Andy Warhol: People's fantasies are what gives them problems. If you didn't have fantasies you wouldn't have problems, because you'd just take whatever there was.

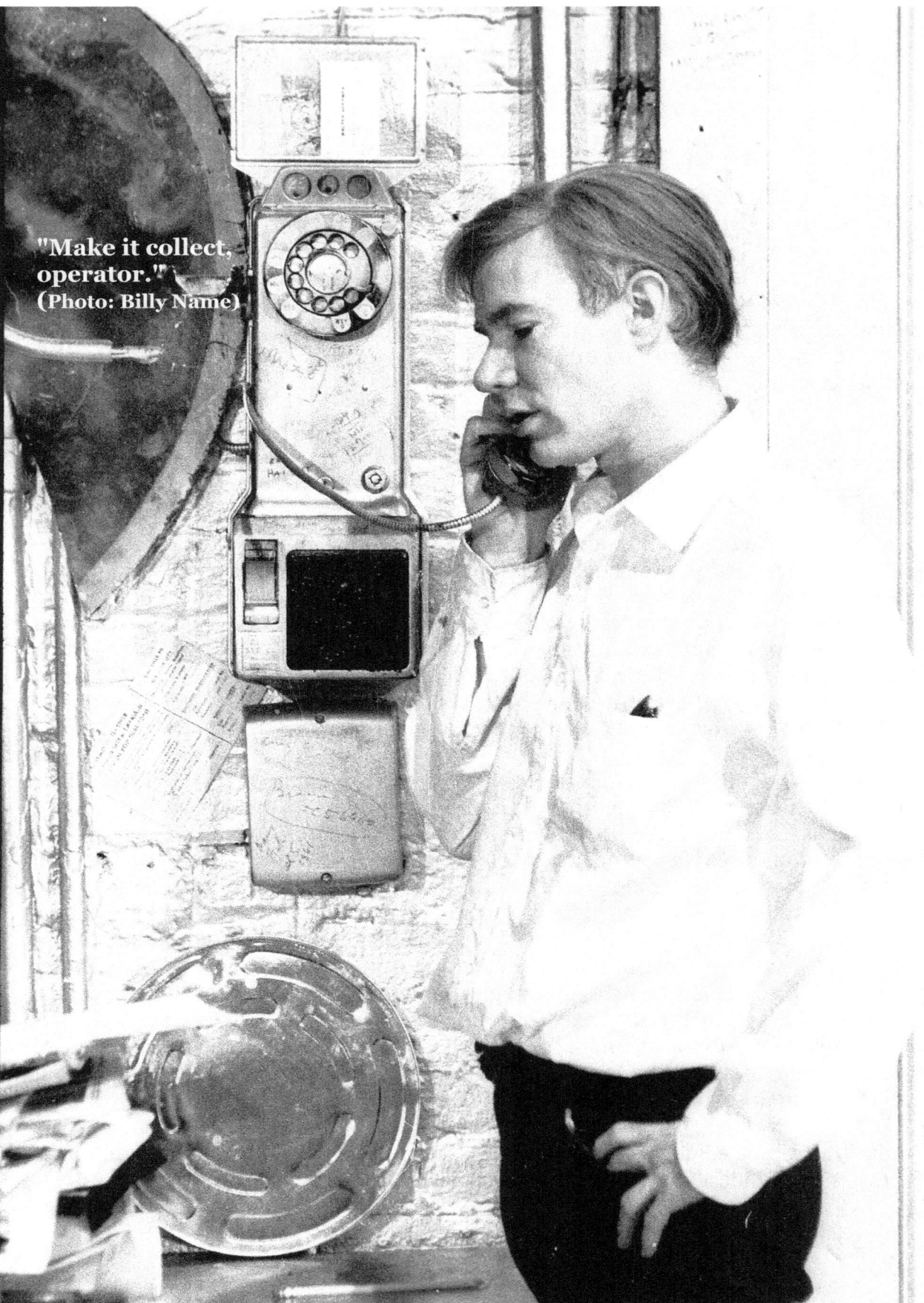

"Make it collect, operator."
(Photo: Billy Name)

Warhol's own erotic fantasies were probably preferable to the reality. His traumatic childhood bout with St. Vitus Dance instilled in him a horror of being touched, and it left him with a blotchy skin condition that would plague him for the rest of his life. Ivy Nicholson, Ultra Violet, Gerard Malanga and Billy Name all spoke of Warhol's aversion to pysical contact, which would certainly account for his fascination with voyeurism. . . After our initial interviews, we met up with Billy and Gerard once again for an impromtu discussion of their time in the Silver Factory. Gerard had last seen Billy in 1970, during Billy's homeless period. Now, forty years later, the two Factory survivors sat together at the Mansfield Hotel, named after author Katherine Mansfield ('Ship of Fools'), sharing drinks and memories. They'd brought along photographs, book collections and museum catalogues of their work to share with us, and some surprising off-the-cuff revelations that we scattered throughout the documentary, such as the story of Billy's show in Tokyo, Japan, and the difference one little typo can make. . .

Billy Name: I did three hundred prints from negatives in three nights so that I would have consistent printing quality for a single exhibit. It was to be called 'Andy Warhol's Factory, Factory Photos by Billy Name'. But it came out as 'Andy Warhol's Factory Photos, Factory *Photo* by Billy Name' with a big F in a circle. I always called it the 'Fuck Catalogue'.

Gerard Malanga: Okay, I'm gonna make the big point here. First of all, Billy and myself started out at the same time at the Factory. Because of the creative environment, we were allowed to do what we wanted to do. Andy encouraged us in that way. Billy started out in photography, and later I started in film, and we're still very active in what we do. We kind of complement each other in the tradition that we've engaged ourselves in, which is the meaning of photography.

Billy Name: Very true. Well, we were both youngsters in the master artist's studio, and then we mastered our own fields. We'd sprung from the same cultural eon or period where all that wonderful stuff was going on in Manhattan, the early sixties. The Factory is not a singular phenomenon that came from nowhere; it was still the inner art world, so you would just work with the people you interacted with because they were all fabulous, all a part of the underground night life in New York City. But it's lower than underground. It's subterranean ground. These were people who were seriously, aesthetically attuned artists. But, so, what's that term? Non-functional. Dysfunctional!

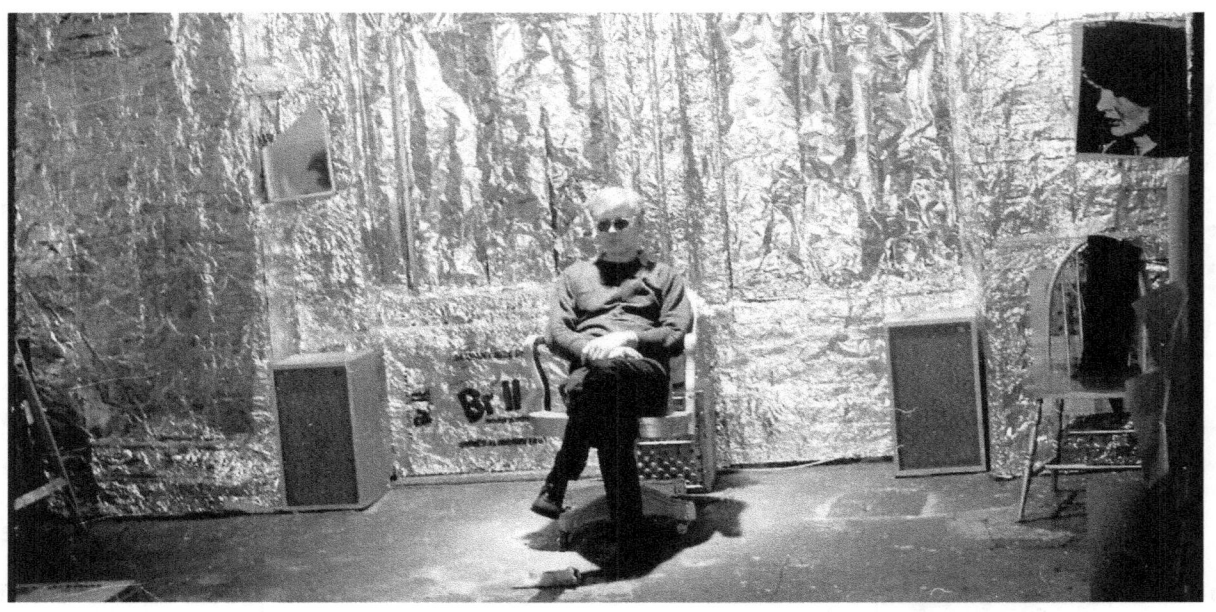

Andy enjoys a rare moment of meditative quiet in an empty Factory. (Photos: Billy Name)

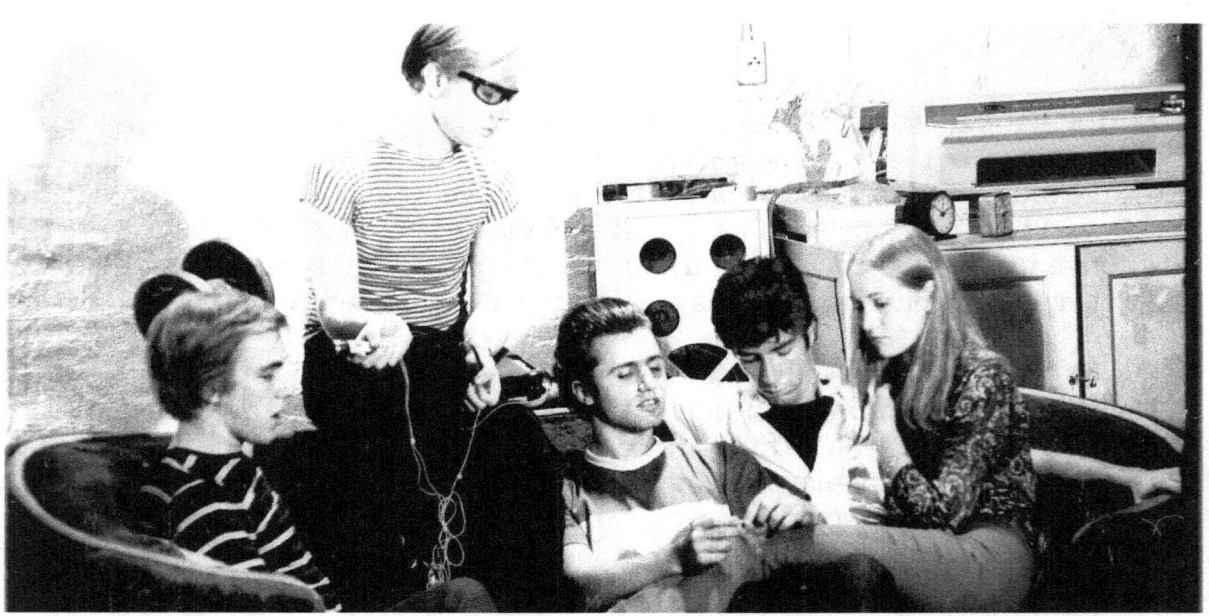

Andy also enjoys the company of his young Factory family, Chuck Wein, Gerard, Roger Trudeau and Genevieve Charbon. Note Andy's little tape recorder.

At the end of this premier episode of our 'Factory People' TV series, we did indeed give an action-packed preview of the upcoming dysfuntional attractions, so necessary to ensure fidelity from fickle viewers . . . See Edie Sedgwick run off with Bob Dylan! See Nico run of with Jim Morrison! Watch Warhol run off with the boffo box office receipts of 'Chelsea Girls'!! Oh, we were shameless. But television viewers in the ought decade have a few hundred other choices, and good luck with the multitude enjoying their assorted attention deficit disorders, which seemed not to exist in the sixties unless drug-induced. . . "But hey," you say, "let's change the subject already." True, this has been thus far mostly about Warhol's Factory People, and their sexual fantasies and search for fame. "But what about the art? Isn't that what he's famous for?" Oh, right. The Art. And just when he's getting ready to quit. By now, it is fairy obvious that the core of Warhol's Factory family justifiably felt themselves to be participating in a cutting-edge artistic experience. Many of those who came later were simply along for the ride, or their own private agenda. No matter, all would be welcomed into the silver-foiled lair, kept on the hook with vague promises. Warhol's signature mix of aloofness and approachability became his trademark, ignoring or putting on the press and the art establishment, at the same time seeking their favor.

Andy Warhol: Just ordinary people like my paintings. It took intelligent people years to appreciate the Abstract-Expressionist school, and I suppose it's hard for intellectuals to think of me as art. I've never been touched by a painting. I don't want to think. . . It's nothing in the end anyway. It doesn't matter what anyone does.

I sense Warhol would not mind that in our series the time frames overlap with merry abandon. It didn't bother me, or most of our European viewers, because *'Les Années Soixante'* were just that—The Sixties. . . While basking in the Parisian accolades of his '65 visit, Warhol announced his 'retirement' from painting. In Episode II we went into more detail, because, in retrospect, it may have been a ploy to command higher prices. If so, it worked like a charm—now everyone wanted a piece of the 'High Priest of Pop Art'. This did not go down at all well for the macho artists behind Abstract Expressionism. Alpha males like Pollack, Gorky, Newman and Rothko, in breaking with the Cubist/Surrealism past, had been creating startling works that had little to do with technique, or for that matter, skill. For them emotions were everything. So while they drowned their hubris and sorrows and commiserated at the Cedar Bar, the art movement that had made stars of them all was declared obsolete, seemingly overnight. It had to hurt.

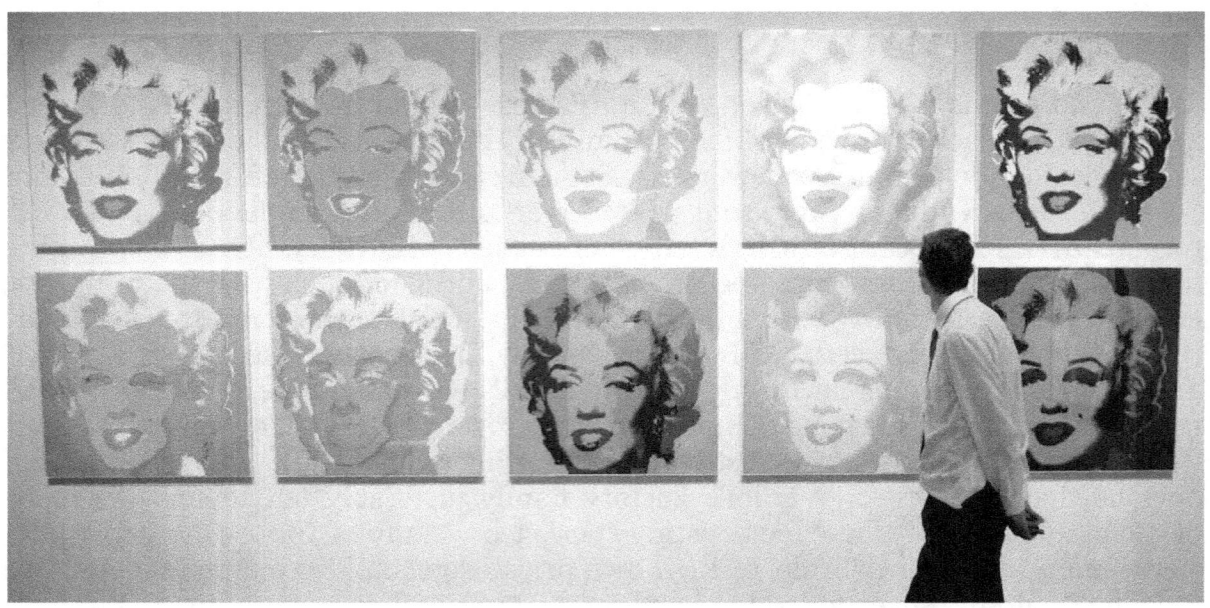

"The semaphoric image of those lips, those eyes, that hair seems fated to be the most lasting artistic icon of the past hundred years" --Peter Schjeldah, The New Yorker. (Photo: Corbis)

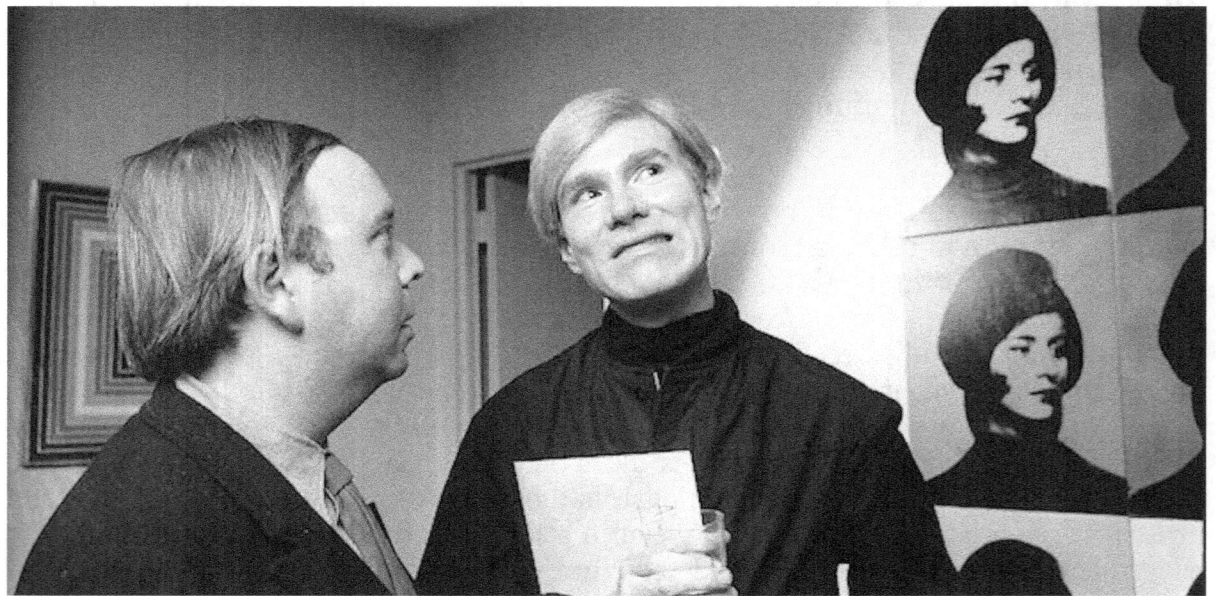

Art maven Henry Geldzahler and artist Andy enjoy a night of art. (Photo: Steve Schapiro)

Andy Warhol: I'm not the 'High Priest of Pop Art', that is, popular art. I'm just one of the workers in it. There's five Pop artists who are all doing the same kind of work, but in different directions. I'm one... I don't regard myself as a leader of Pop art or a better painter than the others.

Oops, sorry—I promised not to pretend art expertise. Those certainly more qualified and better-informed have a less lopsided view of Abstract Expressionism, and how Warhol and his fellow Pop artists upended everything... As art critic for The New Yorker Peter Schjeldahl, in his riveting essay 'Barbarians At The Gate' (May 15, 2000) put it: "In effect, these Marilyns reproduce reproductions of reproductions, encapsulating several declensions from the suffering of one Norma Jean Mortenson." ... Vincent Fremont, the Founding Director of the Andy Warhol Foundation for the Visual Arts, also garnered a thing or two from his mentor and long-time friend.

Vincent Fremont: When the Pop movement started, there were all these artists living in Manhattan that didn't know each other, yet were all on the same wave length. It was extraordinary that they didn't compete with each other. It was very unusual to have a group of artists actually support each other in a way, and work in tandem without stepping on each other's feet. Andy sees Lichtenstein's cartoon paintings and says he's doing them better, and stops doing it.

Billy Name: Oh, there was a lot of resentment when people like Robert Rauchenberg, Jasper Johns, Claes Oldenberg, Roy Lichtenstein, and Andy Warhol completely threw away what the Abstract Expressionists had established as art. It wasn't intentional. It was just these were the kids and they have the ball now and it's their playground.

Ultra Violet: What's extraordinary about art, I remember when Abstract came on the scene, I thought we were going to do Abstract Art forever. We had had enough of Figuratism. Lo and behold it lasted ten, twenty years, then Pop art comes in...

Andy Warhol: Don't think about making art. Just get it done. Let everyone else decide whether it's good or bad, whether they love it or hate it. While they're deciding, make even more art.

Henry Geldzahler, Warhol's lifelong friend (and sometime foe), was also aware of Warhol's self-imposed emotional detachment. They spoke almost daily, according to biographer Victor Bockris. One time, at two-thirty in the morning. Warhol called, frantic. "Henry! We have to talk!" Geldzahler, wondering what was so important it couldn't wait, was met by a trembling Warhol at the Brasserie: "We have to talk, Henry—*say* something!"

Henry Geldzahler, to Warhol
Do you know what a painting is going to look like before you do it?

Warhol
Uh, yes.

Geldzahler
Does it end up looking like you expect?

Warhol
Uh, no.

Geldzahler
Are you surprised?

Warhol
No.

With the unwavering support of Henry Geldzahler, Warhol was soon to become quite famous, which did little to lessen the venality of his critics. Perhaps to simply protect himself, he became even more obtuse in his dealings with the public, which made for entertaining (if one-sided) interviews. In upcoming Book II, where the middle might sag and go pear-shaped, it skids along on a Warholian banana peel—just too damn much was happening at the same time, like everybody was on speed or something. You think? Those were heady precinct-shattering days, and in the course of our interviews it becomes clear why, when Warhol was at the top, he shockingly "quit art" to concentrate on making his script-less direction-less, pointless movies. . .

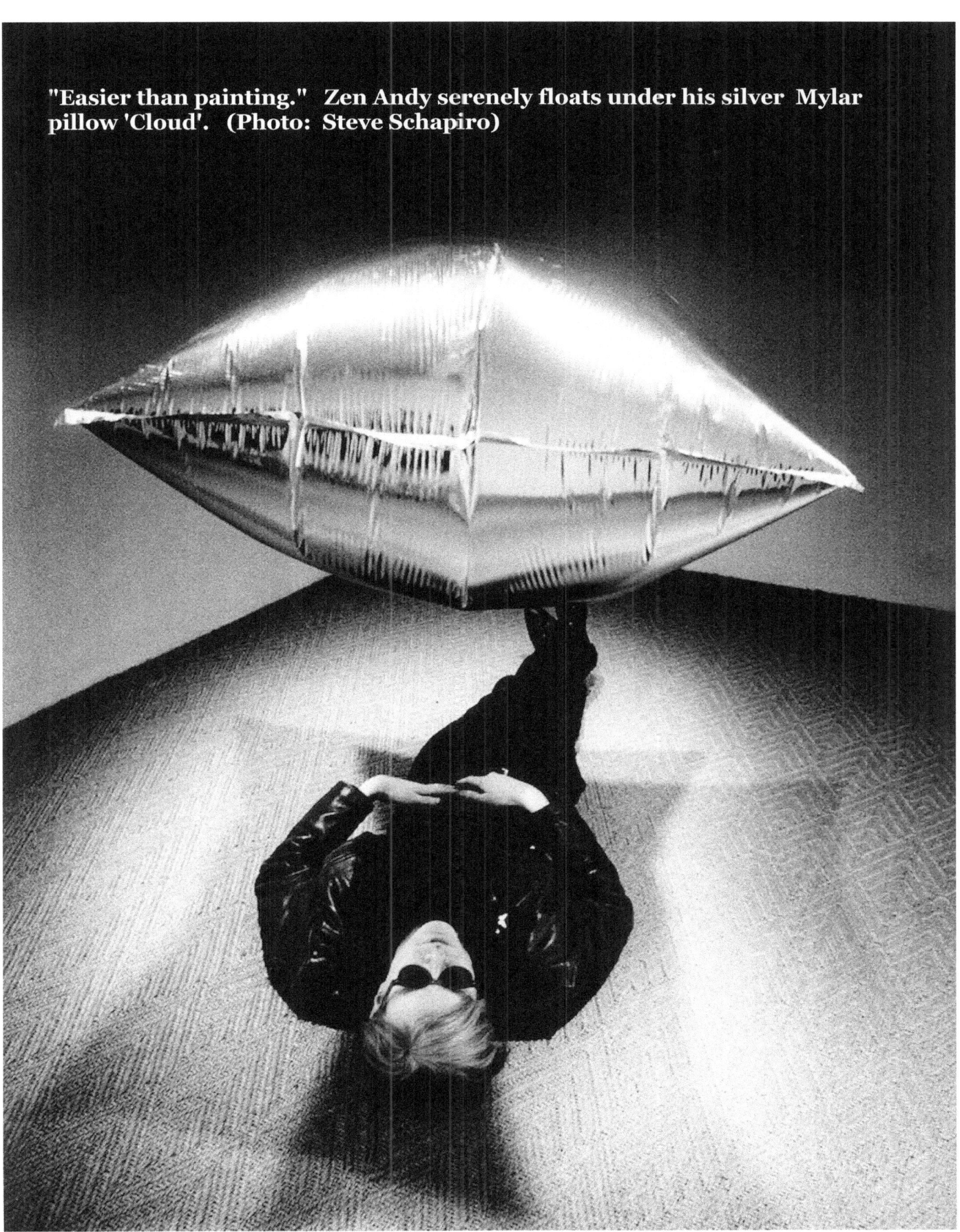

"Easier than painting." Zen Andy serenely floats under his silver Mylar pillow 'Cloud'. (Photo: Steve Schapiro)

www.ingramcontent.com/pod-product-compliance
Lightning Source LLC
Chambersburg PA
CBHW080255180526
45167CB00006B/2540